Mining Royalties

Mining Royalties

A Global Study of Their Impact on Investors, Government, and Civil Society

James Otto
Craig Andrews
Fred Cawood
Michael Doggett
Pietro Guj
Frank Stermole
John Stermole
John Tilton

 THE WORLD BANK

©2006 The International Bank for Reconstruction and Development / The World Bank
1818 H Street NW
Washington DC 20433
Telephone: 202-473-1000
Internet: www.worldbank.org
E-mail: feedback@worldbank.org

2 3 4 5 09 08 07

This volume is a product of the staff of the International Bank for Reconstruction and Development / The World Bank. The findings, interpretations, and conclusions expressed in this volume do not necessarily reflect the views of the Executive Directors of The World Bank or the governments they represent.

The World Bank does not guarantee the accuracy of the data included in this work. The boundaries, colors, denominations, and other information shown on any map in this work do not imply any judgement on the part of The World Bank concerning the legal status of any territory or the endorsement or acceptance of such boundaries.

Rights and Permissions
The material in this publication is copyrighted. Copying and/or transmitting portions or all of this work without permission may be a violation of applicable law. The International Bank for Reconstruction and Development / The World Bank encourages dissemination of its work and will normally grant permission to reproduce portions of the work promptly.

For permission to photocopy or reprint any part of this work, please send a request with complete information to the Copyright Clearance Center Inc., 222 Rosewood Drive, Danvers, MA 01923, USA; telephone: 978-750-8400; fax: 978-750-4470; Internet: www.copyright.com.

All other queries on rights and licenses, including subsidiary rights, should be addressed to the Office of the Publisher, The World Bank, 1818 H Street NW, Washington, DC 20433, USA; fax: 202-522-2422; e-mail: pubrights@worldbank.org.

ISBN-10: 0-8213-6502-9
ISBN-13: 978-0-8213-6502-1
eISBN: 0-8213-6503-7
DOI: 10.1596/978-0-8213-6502-1

Cover photo: Copper mine, Salt Lake City, Utah, United States; Digital Vision/Getty Images.
Cover design: Naylor Design.

This book was made possible through generous funding by:
bhpbilliton

Library of Congress Cataloging-in-Publication Data

Mining royalties : a global study of their impact on investors, government, and civil society / James Otto . . . [et al.].
  p. cm. -- (Directions in development)
  ISBN-13: 978-0-8213-6502-1
  ISBN-10: 0-8213-6502-9
  1. Mineral industries--Finance. 2. Mines and mineral resources--Taxation.
  3. Mining leases. I. Otto, James. II. Series: Directions in development
  (Washington, D.C.)

HD9506.A2M5454 2006
338.2'3--dc22
                                                              2006041849

Contents

Figures

Tables

Foreword

Of the issues currently debated in the international mining industry, none is as pertinent and possibly challenging as mining taxation. At this moment of high commodity prices, in early 2006, many mining companies—juniors and majors, local and international—are stepping up their exploration activities into countries where there is little experience with mining legislation or taxation. Governments face the need to devise and implement appropriate and modern tax regimes. Even in countries with experience in minerals exploitation, public perceptions of company windfall profits often provoke calls for renegotiation of contracts or revisions in taxation legislation. In matters of mining taxation, governments rarely believe that companies pay too much tax; companies rarely believe that they pay too little tax; and citizens rarely believe that they actually see tangible benefits from the taxes that are paid.

Behind these rather simplistic perceptions, however, there is the very complex topic of how mining taxes are devised, assessed, paid, and accounted for. One of the main forms of government income from mineral exploitation is the royalty, most commonly characterized as the payment due to the sovereign owner in exchange for the right to extract the mineral substance. To the best of our knowledge, this book is the only comprehensive treatment of both the theoretical underpinnings and practical application of royalties and their relation to the overall taxation regime. It is a topic of great interest to the countries where the World Bank is working with governments to try to encourage new investment in mining while simultaneously ensuring that adequate and fair taxation is practiced.

This book provides a general discussion of the concepts behind mining taxation, a "nuts and bolts" guide to royalties, examples of royalty calculations and the ways in which these interact with other forms of taxation, as well as financial effects on investments under varying conditions. The book discusses implications for investors and governments of various tax regimes and provides specific country case examples. Finally, the book includes a chapter that addresses transparency, governance, and management of revenue streams—an increasingly important topic in the international community.

A product of eminent experts in the field of mining taxation, this work could not have been completed without the generous support of BHP Billiton. The World Bank is pleased to support the publication of the book and considers it a comprehensive and practical explanation of royalties, which will be an extremely useful tool for governments, companies, and civil society to better understand the concepts and application of mining taxation. We hope that this book will enable all stakeholders and interested parties to engage in constructive and informed deliberations regarding mining royalties.

Rashad-Rudolf Kaldany
Director
Oil, Gas, Mining and Chemicals Department
The World Bank Group

Preface

Background

Mineral sector regulatory and fiscal systems have been undergoing major reforms across the globe. It has been estimated that during the past 20 years over 110 nations have either replaced their mining law or made major amendments to it.[1] Along with this effort to modernize their mining acts, nations often review their approach to fiscal impositions. In an era of globalization, competition to attract exploration and mining investment has intensified. Nations have increasingly concerned themselves with comparing their approaches to mineral sector regulation and taxation to systems in other nations. The trend has been for nations with relatively high tax to reduce tax levels and, conversely, for nations with low tax levels to increase theirs. This has resulted in an increasingly level playing field (see Otto 2002). Part of this introspective effort has been to look at various forms and levels of taxes, including royalty.

Over the past 20 years, many mineral-exporting countries have reduced their general income tax rates and have exempted mining operations, and many other industrial activities, from other taxes such as import duty, export duty, and value-added tax, or they have zero rated them (assessed the tax but set the rate at zero). Withholding taxes on interest and remitted dividends and profits have also been reduced. Royalty has come under particular scrutiny as other types of taxes have been scaled back or eliminated. In part, this scrutiny can be attributed to efforts to maintain or provide competitiveness, but in some nations royalty is increasingly looked at in terms of its applicability to fiscal decentralization objectives. Reform efforts have been uneven, but the overall trend has been a reduction in many taxes applied to mining.

Many nations impose royalty tax, but some nations—as diverse as Chile, Greenland, Mexico, Sweden, and Zimbabwe—do not.[2] In most nations that impose royalty tax, policy makers are interested in determining whether the level of royalty and its computational method are competitive and efficient. In nations that do not impose royalty, there are occasionally calls for creating one.

Purpose of the Study

In this age of reform and globalization, government policy makers and private sector investors need to have access to the types of information that will aid in informed decision making. Taxation is a complex matter, and well-meant but ill-conceived schemes can significantly affect any industry. Mining is particularly sensitive to tax-imposed effects because of its cost structure and vulnerability to substantial market-driven demand and price swings. The purpose of this study is to provide a comprehensive, objective, and neutral analysis of royalty taxation that can be used by governments, industry, and civil society in deliberations concerning the merits and demerits of royalties and their various forms.

Although this study is directed mainly at royalties levied by governments, the methods and principles can also be applied to royalties between private parties. Such private party royalties are common, particularly when minerals in the ground are privately owned or when an interest in mining rights is transferred or made accessible to another party.

Scope and Organization

This study is organized into six chapters. Chapter 1 introduces the study and summarizes its general recommendations. In Chapter 2, mining taxation is discussed in general terms to provide the broad basis that is essential to understanding the nature of the mineral sector and the various tax approaches that are available and are applied to it. The chapter introduces public policy issues, establishes the unique characteristics of the mining industry compared with other types of industries, explains the concept of economic rent, and lists the tool kit of tax types. It also identifies major trends and discusses the importance of looking at the complete fiscal system when examining any one part of it.

In Chapter 3, the analysis shifts from general tax issues to topics specific to royalty taxes. The chapter explains the rationale for imposing or not imposing a royalty tax and introduces and examines the various methods of collecting royalties, from the points of view of both governments and taxpayers. Challenges encountered in administering various forms of royalty are examined, and examples from selected nations illustrate a variety of approaches to royalty taxation, with extracts from relevant laws. Finally, the chapter explains the wide array of royalty methods chosen and used by nations and private parties.

Chapter 4 links the royalty methods identified in Chapter 3 to their effects on mine economics. A variety of royalty methods are applied in a cash-flow analysis of three model mines. Conditions are varied in each of the models to illustrate the impact of royalties on project economics. A quantitative model is also presented that illustrates the impact of selected royalties on mine life and reserves. A summary of the microeconomic implications of selected royalty approaches concludes the chapter.

With the microeconomic basis laid, Chapter 5 moves back to the bigger picture and tackles issues such as the impact of royalty taxes on the investment climate and on civil society, market implications of royalty taxes, distribution, and implications for governments.

Chapter 6 both summarizes the major findings of the study and suggests a number of best-practice approaches. It discusses how governments and companies account for and disclose the taxes and payments generated by the mining sector. This issue is increasingly the focus of international attention as a result of serious questions being raised regarding the economic and social contributions of the industry in many developing countries. The chapter explains the case for transparency, outlines the general principles of disclosure and reporting, and discusses the key challenges to disclosure. It also outlines the Extractive Industries Transparency Initiative, one approach to revenue reporting that is gaining adherents among developing countries and mining companies operating within them.

A number of appendixes have been included on a companion CD. Appendix A1 contains brief summaries and selected statutes relating to royalties in a broad cross-section of nations around the world. Appendix A2 contains sample spreadsheets of the results of mine models that were analyzed earlier in the study. Finally, Appendixes A3 and A4 provide examples of administrative and distributional approaches to collecting royalties.

Neutrality of Authors

In approaching the subject of royalties, the authors have strived to maintain a neutral, informative approach and do not advocate for or against royalty taxes. Whether a royalty is good or bad will depend on the unique circumstances of the royalty beneficiary (whether a public or private entity), the situation of the mine being assessed, and the observer's point of view. The information and analysis contained in the study are intended to provide concerned parties with an understanding of the implications of applying or not applying various forms of royalties to a mine or mines.

References

Hetherington, Russell. 2000. "Exploration and Mining Titles in Africa: An Introductory Review." Hetherington Exploration and Mining Title Services, Willoughby, NSW.

Otto, James. 1996. "The Changing Regulatory Framework for Mining Ventures." *Journal of Energy and Natural Resources Law* 14 (3): 251–61.

———. 2002. "Creating a Positive Investment Climate." Proceedings of the World Mine Ministries Forum, Toronto, March 13–15.

Notes

1. In 1996, Otto compiled a list of 110 nations that had implemented new or revised mining codes or initiated drafting efforts between 1985 and 1996. Today the number would be even greater (Otto 1996). Hetherington (2000) noted that, since 1990, the vast majority of African nations have introduced a new mining act. In his 2000 Africa region count, he reported that since 1990, 30 nations have passed a new act, 12 are currently reviewing their act, and only 13 acts predate 1990.

2. As this study goes to press, Chilean lawmakers are considering a draft royalty bill, and the president of Zimbabwe has announced his intention to seek royalties.

Acknowledgments

The authors of this study would like to thank BHP Billiton for funding the work underlying the study and the World Bank for publishing it. Additional thanks go to Drs. Shefa Chen and Gaomai Trench, Senior Geologists, of the Geological Survey of Western Australia, for assistance in translating the Chinese legislation; and to Daniella Correa, Graduate Research Assistant for University of Denver Sturm College of Law, for her assistance in translating South American statutes. Graeme Hancock and Shadrach Himata, Director and Assistant Director, respectively, of the Papua New Guinea Department of Mining, are acknowledged for providing relevant material for Papua New Guinea. Discussions with Karl Harries were useful in understanding the role of royalties between private parties. Michael Gunning, at Saskatchewan Industry and Resources, provided explanations of the royalty structures for uranium and coal in that province. Finally, special thanks go to Kathy Kelly for her assistance in the technical editing of the manuscript, and the World Bank's Allison Berg (Oil, Gas, and Mining Policy Division) and Aziz Gokdemir (Office of the Publisher) for their help in producing the book.

Acronyms and Abbreviations

APT	additional profits tax
ASM	artisanal and small-scale
ATCF	after-tax cash flow
BEE	black economic empowerment (Africa)
COW	contract of work
EBITDA	earnings before interest, taxes, depreciation, and amortization
EITI	Extractive Industries Transparency Initiative
ENAMI	Empresa Nacional de Mineria
ETR	effective tax rate
FOB	free on board
GAAP	generally accepted accounting principles
GDP	gross domestic product
IAS	International Accounting Standards
ICMM	International Council for Metals and Mining
IMF	International Monetary Fund
IPO	initial public offering
IRR	internal rate of return
LME	London Metals Exchange
MDF	minerals development fund

MDGs	Millennium Development Goals
MPRDA	Mineral and Petroleum Resources Development Act
NGO	nongovernmental organization
NPI	net profit interest
NPR	net profit royalty
NPV	net present value
NSR	net smelter return
OECD	Organisation for Economic Co-operation and Development
OPEC	Organization for Petroleum Exporting Countries
PPI	producer price index
PSA	production sharing agreement
RSBC	Revised Statutes of British Columbia
TBVC	Transkei, Bophuthatswana, and Ciskei
VAT	value-added tax

CHAPTER 1

Introduction

Across the globe, no type of tax on mining causes as much controversy as royalty tax. It is a tax that is unique to the natural resources sector and one that has manifested itself in a wide variety of forms, sometimes based on measures of profitability but more commonly based on the quantity of material produced or its value. Many nations have reformed or are now reforming the ways in which they regulate and tax the mining sector, and as part of that effort, royalty concepts are being reexamined. That examination may be emotive, as when politicians strive to defend and uphold principles that relate to the nation's permanent sovereignty over the national mineral endowment, or when companies strive to maintain reasonable profits for their shareholders. The purpose of this study is to provide a comprehensive, objective, and neutral analysis of royalty taxes that can be used by governments and industry in deliberations concerning the merits and demerits of royalties and their various forms.

This study was conducted under the leadership of Professor James Otto, who has worked for more than two decades with governments in the design of their mineral taxation systems. Joining him was an impressive team, drawn from many of the world's leading mining universities, including Fred Cawood, Senior Lecturer and Associate Professor at the School of Mining Engineering, University of the Witwatersrand (South

Africa); Michael Doggett, Director and Associate Professor, Mineral Exploration Master's Program, Queens University (Canada); Pietro Guj, Associate Professor, Mineral Economics, Western Australia School of Mines, and formerly both Deputy Director-General of the Western Australian Department of Minerals and Energy and Director of the Geological Survey of Western Australia; Professors Frank and John Stermole, from the Colorado School of Mines Division of Economics and Business and the University of Denver (U.S.); and John Tilton, Professor at the Mining Centre, Pontificia Universidad Católica de Chile, and formerly the head of the Division of Economics and Business at the Colorado School of Mines (where he maintains a dual appointment). Craig Andrews, Lead Mining Specialist in the World Bank's Oil, Gas, and Mining Policy Division, provides a chapter on transparency in the management of revenue streams. Members of the team brought together a knowledge base that encompassed geology, mining engineering, mineral economics, project analysis and evaluation, law, and government administration.

This study was organized into six chapters that addressed, in turn, the rationale and need for a comprehensive, neutral analysis of royalty taxes; the nature of the mineral sector and the various tax approaches that are available and are applied to the sector, including the specific types of royalty taxes, examples of the taxes, and their issues; the effect of royalties on mine economics and on production decisions pertaining to reserves, cutoff grade, and mine life; the impact of royalty taxes on the investment climate, civil society, and markets; governance and management of revenue streams by recipient governments, including enhanced transparency; and a summary with recommendations. The appendixes on the companion CD contain a wealth of information, including extracts pertaining to royalty tax from the laws in approximately 40 jurisdictions.

The major conclusions of the study are that the geological, economic, social, and political circumstances of each nation are unique, and an approach to royalty taxes that is optimal for one nation may be impractical for another. The answer to the central question of whether royalties are inherently good or bad depends on the circumstances of the parties involved, project economics, and one's point of view. The issue of transparency in the management of revenue streams is increasingly a focus of international attention. Though it is not possible to hold out one approach to royalty taxation as ideally suited to all nations, or to all mines within one country, it is possible to offer recommendations that can be applied in most situations. These include the following:

1. When designing a tax system, policy makers should be aware of the cumulative effects taxes can have on mine economics and on potential levels of future investment. When determining which taxes and levels of taxes to apply to the mining sector, policy makers should not only consider ways to achieve individual tax objectives, but also take into account the cumulative effects of all taxes. Such awareness must recognize the importance of each tax type in achieving specific objectives. The overall tax system should be equitable to both the nation and the investor and be globally competitive.

2. Nations should carefully weigh the immediate fiscal rewards to be gained from high levels of tax, including royalty, against the long-term benefits to be gained from a sustainable mining industry that will contribute to long-term development, infrastructure, and economic diversification.

3. Mining companies should play a role. Governments will be able to arrive at better-reasoned decisions if they are provided with quantitative assessments by companies on the effects of royalty taxes on issues such as potential overall investment, closure of marginal mines, and the implications of those closures on the national mineral reserve base.

4. A nation with a strong desire to attract investors should consider either forgoing a royalty tax and relying on the general tax system or recognizing investors' strong preference to be taxed on their ability to pay. A nation seeking to differentiate itself from the nations it competes with for mineral sector investment may find that a royalty tax based on income or profits is an investment incentive. Although profit-based royalty schemes are inherently more difficult to implement than other royalty schemes, governments that can effectively administer an income tax are better able to manage a profit- or income-based royalty tax.

5. Governments that impose royalty taxes should do the following:
   - Consult with industry to assess the effects that changes to the royalty system will have on the mining industry.
   - Implement a system or systems that are transparent and provide a sufficient level of detail in the relevant law and regulations that make it clear how the tax basis is to be determined for all minerals.
   - Select a royalty method or methods that are suitable for efficient and effective administration within the capacity of the tax-collecting authority.

- Give a high priority to strengthening both financial reporting and the institutional capacity of administrative agencies responsible for levying and collecting mineral sector taxes. The government would thus be able to consider the complete range of royalty options rather than be limited to the simplest methods.
- Carefully consider all royalty options based on ability to pay (profit-based systems).
- Avoid excessively high unit- or value-based royalty rates that will significantly affect production parameters such as cutoff grade and mine life.
- Provide a means whereby mines experiencing financial duress may apply for a deferral or waiver of royalty, provided that clearly predefined criteria are met.
- Allow royalty payments to be deducted from income subject to income tax or allow royalty to be credited against income tax.
- Impose alternative measures on artisanal and small-scale operators in cases in which the general royalty scheme would not be enforceable.

6. Policy makers and companies should consider the following means whereby affected communities can share directly in the benefits of the mines:

- Recognizing that such benefits may be made available through a variety of means that may or may not include taxation.
- Balancing the overall mineral taxation system, including the royalty tax, in such a way that provides an incentive for companies to invest in sustainable development initiatives at the community and regional levels.
- Requiring mining companies to pay a share of royalty (or other mining taxes) directly to communities without the funds moving through the central tax authority, or alternatively, setting up a system in which the designated community share is paid centrally but is distributed in a transparent and timely manner.

7. Policy makers and companies should bear joint responsibility for treating royalty payments in a transparent manner that promotes public accountability. Overall, the aim should be for revenues generated by the mining sector to contribute to economic growth and social development. Particularly in developing countries, a lack of accountability and transparency in such revenues often exacerbates poor governance and contributes to corruption, conflict, and poverty.

To that end, the Extractive Industries Transparency Initiative (EITI), which is gaining international support, is a process by which countries and companies voluntarily agree to systematically record and disclose the revenues paid by extractive industry companies and received by governments.

8. From a macroeconomic governance perspective, the optimization goal should be to maximize the net present value of the social benefits flowing from the mineral sector over the long term, including government tax receipts. This approach implies a balance, because if taxation is too high, investment and the tax base will decrease as investors shift their focus to other alternatives, and if taxation is too low, the nation will lose revenue useful to serve the public welfare.

CHAPTER 2

Taxation of the Mineral Sector

Mining normally creates wealth or economic surpluses. This potential provides the incentive for private companies to explore for, develop, and then exploit mineral deposits. Although companies generally are driven by the pursuit of profits, the goals and objectives of the sovereign governments that control the terms and conditions under which private interests have access to mineral deposits are quite different. Their actions and policies, including the taxes they impose on the mineral sector, are designed to promote various social goals—economic development, for example—as determined through the prevailing political processes.

This chapter looks at mineral taxation as a whole. In particular, it addresses a number of topics and issues that will be important as the focus narrows to mineral royalties.

Mineral Taxation in General

General Policy Issues

All governments, in the process of determining the structure and nature of the taxes they impose on mining and on the mineral sector in general, encounter the following public policy issues.

Optimal level of taxation on mining   The more the government taxes the mineral sector, the greater the share of wealth created by mining that flows to the government. This means, of course, that less of the wealth is flowing to the companies. Therefore, rising tax rates undermine companies' incentive to carry out exploration, to develop new mines, and even, if the increases are sufficiently large, to remain in production at existing operations. Thus, one critical issue for public policy is determining the optimum level of mineral taxation.[1] Clearly, a tax rate that takes all of the wealth is too high, because it kills the goose that lays the golden egg. On the other hand, a tax rate of zero is likely to be too low, leaving the state with only the nontax benefits that flow from mining and mineral production. Somewhere between these two extremes is an optimal level of taxation that maximizes the net present value (NPV) of the tax revenues or, more appropriately, the NPV of all social benefits the country receives from its mineral sector (see Figure 2.1).

Unfortunately, in practice it is not easy to determine the optimal level of taxation, which would require knowledge of how a firm's behavior is altered in the present and, more importantly, in the future by changing levels of taxation. In addition, estimating future tax revenues requires knowledge of the flow of future profits the domestic mineral sector is likely to generate, which depends on trends in metal prices and on production costs.

Figure 2.1. Government Tax Revenues as a Function of the Tax Rate

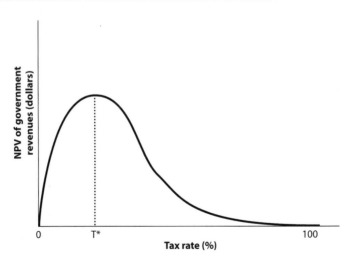

Source: Author J. Tilton.

Note: T* is the optimal tax rate.

However, two things are known about the optimum level of taxation. First, the government can take its share of the wealth created by mining, either in the form of taxes or in the form of nonpecuniary benefits. The latter are government-imposed requirements on mining companies (or voluntary contributions) that raise production costs. For example, the government may require or pressure mining companies to build and maintain roads in remote regions that are used by the general public as well as for mining. It may force or otherwise encourage companies to provide schools, hospitals, and other social services in areas surrounding a mine. It may insist that companies use local suppliers or domestic workers, or that downstream processing be done domestically. The more such requirements increase production costs, the smaller the benefits the government can reap in the form of tax revenues, and hence the lower the optimal level of taxation.

It is also clear that raising the level of taxation shifts toward the present the flow of benefits a country receives from its mineral sector over time. This is because a tax increase will almost always raise tax revenues over the first few years following its implementation. Over the longer run, however, the higher tax level is likely to discourage exploration and mine development, and so reduces tax revenues below what they would have been. As a result, raising the level of mineral taxation, such as imposing a new or higher royalty, almost always looks successful from the point of view of the government in the short run. It can take several years or longer for the negative effects on tax revenues to become apparent. Even then, the negative effects are hard to assess because they require comparing actual tax revenues with what revenues would have been in the absence of the tax increase.

Optimal mix of taxes   Many different types of taxes can be, and are, imposed on the mineral sector. Each, including the various forms of royalty, has its own set of advantages and disadvantages with respect to economic efficiency, the division of risks between the state and companies, ease of administration, and other considerations.

Economists, for example, often fault royalties that impose a tax on each tonne of metal mined (or the market value of each tonne of metal produced) on the grounds that such taxes introduce inefficiencies in production decisions. For the firm, such a royalty is an additional cost of production. Low-grade ore, just economic enough to exploit without a royalty, may no longer be profitably extracted after a royalty is introduced.

In that regard, a tax on corporate income or profits is more efficient, because such a tax does not alter the optimal output of companies striving to maximize profits, and marginal ore will remain profitable to exploit. It would be wrong, however, to assume, as some have done, that corporate profit taxes and royalties based on profits have no distorting effects on firms' behavior. Such taxes do reduce firms' anticipated net present value and internal rate of return on both existing operations and potential new projects. As a result, high taxes on corporate profits and profit-based royalties encourage companies to close marginal operations sooner than would otherwise be the case and tend to reduce the economic attractiveness of new projects. However, their effect will be less than that of high levels of taxes that are not based on profitability.

The mix of taxes also influences the distribution of risks between the state and mining companies. Mining is a particularly risky activity. This is partly because of the long gestation period associated with the development of most new mines and the difficulty of anticipating prior to development all the potential technical, geological, economic, and political problems. In addition, most mineral commodity markets are highly volatile over the business cycle, with wide price fluctuations. When the world economy is booming, prices can be two to three times higher than during periods of slow or declining growth. As a result, profits vary greatly for individual mining companies over time. They also vary greatly at any point in time among mining companies. Some mines turn out to be bonanzas; others never return a profit, even during the years of high prices.

A corporate profits tax and royalties based on profitability tend to distribute the risk of mining evenly between the state and companies. When before-tax profits are down by 20 percent, both tax revenues flowing to the government and after-tax profits realized by companies are down by more or less the same amount. A unit- or value-based royalty shifts more of the risk to companies. Even when prices are depressed and companies are in the red, the government continues to receive a certain amount for each tonne of metal produced and sold. Conversely, a progressive income tax or "additional" profits tax tends to shift more of the risk to the government, because it merely imposes a tax on profits that rises with profits or, alternatively, with the internal rate of return or net present value realized by a mine.

Normally, companies are in a better position to assume risks and are less risk averse than governments. In such cases, the state may want to impose a mix of taxes that shifts more of the risks to companies; however, such a strategy has a cost. To compensate companies for assuming more risk, the government must be willing to allow firms to capture a large share of the expected profits, which means lower expected government revenues.

The mix of taxes also affects the flow of government revenues over time. An import duty, for example, on trucks, drills, ball mills, and other imported capital goods produces tax revenues during the development stage of a project. Revenues come from a unit- or value-based royalty at the time of production, from a corporate profits tax or profit-based royalty once the project is profitable, and from an additional profits tax only after the designated profit hurdle has been met. Moreover, with a corporate profits tax, provisions allowing the accelerated depreciation of capital equipment can postpone the flow of tax revenues for years.

Another important consideration in determining the mix of taxes is the difficulty of tax administration and the possibilities for evasion. Some taxes, including many types of royalties, are easy to administer and difficult to evade. Government officials simply need to know a company's total sales or production to determine its tax liability. This not only reduces administrative costs, it reduces the incentives firms have to devote resources to tax reduction efforts. Perhaps more importantly, it reduces the opportunities for corruption. These advantages are less in evidence with the corporate profits tax and profit-based royalties. Assessing the appropriateness of costs, such as management fees paid to parent companies and other nonmarket transactions, is difficult, and companies that invest time and resources in efforts to reduce and avoid taxes may receive good returns.

Specificity or uniformity   Another policy issue concerns the specificity of the tax code. For tax purposes, many countries consider the mining and the mineral sector special. This is in part because, for some countries, this sector plays a dominant role in the economy, accounting for a large share of all government revenues and foreign exchange earnings. In such instances, it is not unusual for the government to negotiate specific agreements covering a variety of issues, including taxation for individual large-scale, or "mega," projects. In addition, there is the widespread perception that the mineral sector is different, and so should be taxed differently, because it exploits a nonrenewable resource. In some instances that resource involves unusually rich and, hence, extremely profitable mineral deposits. This justification for tax specificity is also considered later in this section in the discussion of economic rent and user costs.

Other countries—Chile in recent years, for example—have taxed mining companies the same as all other companies. There are several benefits with this approach. It eliminates the ability of particular industries to obtain favorable tax legislation and so reduces the incentives for companies to lobby and plead for special favors. Uniformity also reduces the complexity of the tax codes, and makes them easier to administer. It eliminates or decreases the likelihood of one industry being singled out for special tax increases. This is particularly important for mining companies, and may be beneficial to the host country as well, as we show next.

Tax regime stability and the challenges raised by the obsolescing bargain and populism   Companies that are deciding whether to invest in a mineral project are largely influenced by the expected return after taxes and by risks. An important component of any assessment of risk is the perceived stability of the existing tax regime. Companies that plan to invest hundreds of millions of dollars or even billions of dollars in a new mine and mineral complex are very wary of possible changes in the tax burden after their investment is made and no longer mobile.

From the perspective of governments, the perception of tax regime stability is also important. Given the risk-return trade-off for firms, the greater the perception of stability, the lower the expected return investing firms require and, hence, the greater the share of wealth from mining the government can collect in the form of taxes or other benefits.

Unfortunately for both companies and governments, however, tax regime stability is hard to guarantee. One reason is the difficulty of binding future governments to the current promises and agreements. At some point, maybe 5 or 10 years after the decision to proceed, a new government may well be in power. Another reason is the shift in bargaining power that occurs over the life of a mineral project. This shift was described years ago by Raymond Vernon as the obsolescing bargain (1974). Before a mineral project is developed, considerable uncertainty surrounds its future profitability for various reasons. As a result, companies are often reluctant to proceed without promises of favorable tax treatment. The host government, often keen for numerous reasons to see the project developed, tends to be accommodating. Once the project is completed, the invested capital is sunk and cannot be withdrawn from the country. Moreover the uncertainty regarding profitability dissipates. Some projects turn out to be unprofitable, whereas others are quite profitable.

In any case, unhappiness with the agreed-upon tax regime may arise whether a project is successful or unsuccessful. Unprofitable projects consume the country's nonrenewable resources but tend to return little or nothing to the state in the form of taxes. Moreover, the public may be suspicious that the lack of profitability reflects either company incompetence or, in the case of international companies, the export of profits abroad to avoid taxes. Profitable projects, on the other hand, do pay taxes, but they are consuming what are obviously valuable domestic resources, and often the public believes that too much of the wealth being generated is going to the companies, particularly in the case of highly successful projects.

These concerns may be accentuated by populism, in the case of the mineral sector, in which many multinational companies are likely to be operating. The public in general, often unaware of the possible negative implications in the long run, is quite likely to support higher taxes on the mineral sector, particularly taxes on large foreign companies. Politicians can easily frame the debate in terms of those who support the interests of the country and its citizens versus those who are more concerned about the interests of foreign companies and their wealthy shareholders. However, if the level of taxation is already at or above the optimal level, further increases are not only bad for mining companies, they are bad for the country. Moreover, changes in the tax regime undermine the investment community's perception of stability, raising the perceived risk of investment in the country. A higher perception of risk and uncertainty means that more of the expected wealth creation from any project must go to the company, as compensation for the higher risk, and less to the state. In short, changing the tax regime will likely reduce the optimum level of taxation as well.

Since changes in the tax regime can increase perceptions of risk and reduce the optimal level of taxation, how should countries respond when the perception of risk is falling over time? Indonesia, over several decades, offered mining companies different generations of contracts. The first generation was the most favorable from the viewpoint of foreign mining. The government was willing to provide companies with extra compensation for investing after a period of political and social unrest. When these investments proved attractive, and hence reduced the perceived risk of investing in the country, the government offered the next generation of investors slightly less attractive terms. This process continued through several generations. Once an agreement was reached, it was not changed, so companies knew before they invested what the tax regime would be. Most importantly, they knew that once they were in production, the likelihood of changes was slight.

Governments and companies may also enhance the stability of the tax regime by minimizing to the extent possible the likelihood that the government and the public will be unhappy once the project is in operation. This might be done by collecting the government's expected share of the wealth through a mix of taxes. A modest royalty on output would ensure that the state received something for its exploited resources even when the operation was unprofitable. Similarly, imposing some sort of additional or progressive profits tax when projects are highly successful would help protect the government from public accusations that it left too much money on the table to the detriment of the public interest. In the end, however, all parties have to realize that private companies need to be adequately compensated for the risks they take when projects are successful, and for the losses they suffer on unsuccessful projects.

Distribution and use of tax revenues   Though much of the public debate over mineral taxes focuses on the appropriate division of wealth between companies and the state, as well as on other issues discussed above in this section, much more important is how the tax revenues are distributed and ultimately used. For a decade or so, economists, policy analysts, and others have been debating the positive and negative impacts of mineral production and exports for economic growth and development, particularly in developing countries. One of the conclusions emerging from what is called the resource curse debate is that mineral production can both foster and hinder economic growth, with the outcome being largely determined by how governments use the taxes and other funds they receive from the mineral sector.[2]

Given the volatility of mineral prices and profits over the business cycle, one issue in the debate concerns the usefulness of a commodity stabilization fund. When mineral taxes are high, thanks to a boom in the mineral sector, the government deposits some of its mineral taxes into such funds. Revenues are then withdrawn when mineral prices and taxes are low. Such arrangements exist, or have existed, in Chile, Namibia, Nauru, Norway, Papua New Guinea, and other mineral-producing countries; they have worked well in some countries and not as well in others. An associated issue is what to do with the money while it is in the fund. Investing profits abroad, rather than domestically, helps insulate the domestic economy from the adverse microeconomic effects that a mineral boom can cause, thereby reducing the prospect of what is commonly called the Dutch disease from occurring.

The government must also decide how to distribute mineral tax revenues. Historically, they have been largely retained by the central government with little going to provinces and the regions where mining occurs. In recent years, however, more of the revenues have been allocated to the provinces and mining districts in response to their increasing requests.

Why the Mineral Sector Is Unique

The concept that governments often give the mining sector special treatment was mentioned in the previous section and is expanded in this section. Nations tax economic activities to generate revenues for the public good and to guide taxpayer behavior. In achieving either objective, a government needs to decide whether the mining sector will be taxed the same or differently than other economic activities. Deviation from the general application of taxes is termed *discrimination*. Discrimination can be by sector, such as subjecting all mines to a tax not imposed on other types of activities; by subsector, such as giving a special incentive to sand and gravel mines that produce less than a million tonnes per year; or by project, such as allowing an individual mine to operate under a negotiated tax agreement. The extent to which mines are taxed specially will depend on the government's desire to provide tax uniformity or to take into account special attributes. Otto (2004) sums up the policy dilemma as follows:

> Tax systems that discriminate between sectors by offering non-uniform treatment are by their nature complicated and place a greater burden on regulatory agencies. In addition, if one sector, such as mining, is granted special treatment other sectors will also seek accommodation based on their "unique" characteristics.[3] Most economists argue that tax discrimination by type of economic activity leads to distortions in the economy. By providing incentives (or disincentives) to one sector, investment may be lost (or gained) in another sector. However, at the present time, most countries tax their mining industry differently than they do other sectors. This sector discrimination is usually justified based on two principles—uniqueness and ownership. (8)

Justification for special tax treatment   The mining industry has long argued that the industry is different from many other economic activities and should therefore receive special treatment. The following attributes illustrate the ways mining enterprises differ from at least some other types of projects:

• A lengthy period of exploration takes place during which there is no revenue.
• The amount of capital required during the development and construction phase is relatively greater than in most other businesses.
• Once the mine is built, the capital is captive and not transportable.
• Equipment tends to be specialized and is available only from a few manufacturers worldwide, so it must be imported.
• Mines can have long lives and will be subject to regime changes and policy instability.
• Revenues are cyclical because commodity prices move up and down more so than is experienced by most other businesses.
• The scale of operations can be very small or very large.
• Large costs will be incurred at the time the project closes (reclamation is required).
• Substantial costs unrelated to production may be incurred, such as investment in community infrastructure or programs.

Today, most nations, even those that profess a general policy of striving for broad tax uniformity, provide at least some special accommodation to tax-paying mines. Table 2.1 lists examples of selected factors that are unique to the mining sector and the tax policy response.

Ownership as a rationale for imposing royalty tax   Another way in which a mine differs from other businesses is that it exploits a nonrenewable resource that, in most cases, the taxpayer does not own. In the majority of nations, minerals are owned by the state, by the people generally, or by the crown or ruler. In other instances, mainly European civil law nations, the owner of the land where the minerals occur owns the minerals. The owner of minerals, like the owner of any other form of real property, has an interest in receiving payment for the taking of the property interest. Such a payment, in effect an ownership transfer tax, is often used as the justification for a royalty. Thus, industries that exploit resources such as timber, petroleum, and minerals often enjoy the types of special tax incentives described in Table 2.1, but in some cases, they also must pay an additional tax, a discriminatory tax, to ensure that the mineral owner

Table 2.1. Unique Attributes of the Mineral Industry and the Tax Policy Response

Reason for special treatment	Tax policy responses
A lengthy and costly exploration program will precede the start-up of a mine. During this exploration period there will be no present income against which to offset these costs.	• Offset preproduction (preincome) exploration expenses against future income (loss carry-forward, amortization).
Mine development is exceptionally capital intensive, and an operation will initially need to import large quantities of diverse equipment and expertise from specialized suppliers.	• Provide various means to accelerate recovery of capital costs once production commences. • Allow service costs to be carried forward and amortized after production commences. • Reduce rate or exempt from import duties. • Reduce rate, exempt, refund, or offset for value-added tax (VAT) on imported equipment and services.
Mined product is destined for export markets.	• Reduce rates or exempt from export duties. • Exempt from VAT or zero rate exports.
Different minerals have very different labor, cost, price, value added, environmental, and social attributes.	• Vary royalty rate for different groups of minerals.
The scale of operations may be small or large.	• Vary royalty rate by size of production. • Exempt small-scale operations from some types of taxes.
Mines produce raw materials that are prone to substantial price changes on a periodic basis related to the business cycle.	• Waive certain types of taxes, usually royalties, from time to time for projects experiencing severe short-term financial duress. • Allow losses to be carried forward.
After mining ceases and there is no income, a mine will incur significant costs relating to closure and reclamation of the site.	• Require a set-aside of funds for closure and reclamation in advance of closure and provide some sort of deduction for this set-aside against current income tax liability.
Many mining projects will have a long life span and companies fear that once their captive investment is in place, government will change the tax law, negatively affecting their returns.	• Stabilize some or all of the relevant taxes for at least part of the mine life. • Stabilize taxes by statute or in the form of an agreement.
Where the level of investment is particularly large (a megaproject), investment may be possible only under a severely modified tax system.	• Enter into a negotiated agreement with the company and include special tax provisions that supplant the general tax law in whole or in part.
A company may enjoy special tax treatment for one operation but may have ongoing exploration that may lead to other operations.	• Apply ring-fencing principles (accounts from the mine may not be mixed with accounts for activities outside the mine).

Source: Otto 2004.

receives at least some compensation for the transferred property right. Some nations forgo such a tax, perhaps recognizing that compensation for the ownership loss may take forms other than fiscal revenues, such as employment, infrastructure, and so forth.

In times of protracted low commodity prices, the public may become antagonistic to mines that exploit nonrenewable public resources and do not pay income-based taxes. Otto (2004) noted the following:

> It is politically difficult to maintain a royalty-free minerals sector fiscal system. The reason is simple. In times when prices are low or costs are high a mine may not generate profits and there will be little or no payment to the state. Likewise, if substantial investment tax incentives are provided, no profit or income based taxes will be paid (at least early in the mine's life). Although minerals belonging to the state or to the people will be extracted and sold, and in many cases exported, there will be little or no benefit to the national treasury. This is rarely politically sustainable.[4] (10)

On the one hand, public pressure may be brought on mines that are perceived to be enriching themselves with no public benefit, but if the operations are viewed by the public as essential or important to the public good, such as where they are a major employer, the public may be receptive to forgoing a royalty. For example, should an operation be forced to close during an economic downturn, the cost to society of the mine closing may be greater than the benefit provided by a royalty. Many nations for this reason allow for royalty to be deferred in certain circumstances. One of the most difficult messages to convey to the public is that, although forgoing a royalty may result in reduced tax revenues in unprofitable years, imposing a royalty may in fact reduce the overall tax revenues if mines leave resources in the ground. Minerals left in the ground when investors choose to invest elsewhere because of royalty tax make no direct contribution to the public good.

Use of taxation to shape taxpayer behavior   The mining sector is also unique in that the business may result in major impacts on local communities and the environment. The tax response to such impacts can take the form of incentives that encourage a company to invest in affected communities. These could be deductions against income tax for approved investments in community infrastructure, or penalties to encourage companies to avoid or minimize an activity, such as a fee-per-unit volume of material placed in tailings.

Use of profit-based taxes, including royalty, that recognize project uniqueness   An advantage of taxes that are based on profitability, including some profit-based royalties, is that they inherently recognize that no two projects are the same and that project economics will differ widely. In other words, because they are based on profitability, that is, the ability to pay, profit-based taxes can apply a uniform system that automatically discriminates for every project. Such profit-based taxes preclude the necessity of attempting to gauge a tax rate or base that addresses the average project. For example, when setting a unit-based royalty rate per tonne of ore, what may be quite reasonable for a low-cost mine may be prohibitive for a high-cost mine. In contrast, a 5 percent royalty based on a measure of profitability would automatically adjust the amount payable based on high or low profits.

Ricardian Rent, Hotelling Rent, Scarcity Rent, and User Costs

Mining differs from many other industries in several important respects (see Tilton 2003). First, the basic raw materials that mining is exploiting—mineral resources in the ground—are often owned by the state. For that reason, many contend, the state should receive compensation for this vital input (beyond the normal taxes paid by other industries), which it contributes to the mining process.

Second, mineral resources are nonrenewable on any time scale of relevance to the human race. As a result, an opportunity cost is incurred in consuming mineral resources today, since once exploited they are no longer available for use in the future. This means that future production will have to rely on poorer quality resources and, consequently, more expensive resources, or use alternative materials.

Third, although many mines fail to earn a competitive rate of return on their capital or are, at best, just marginally profitable, a few are true bonanzas. Inevitably, the latter tend to attract the attention of the public and raise questions about how the riches, which after all are based on a country's geologic legacy, should be equitably divided among the company, the government, and other stakeholders.

All of these issues are closely associated with what economists and others call economic rents; thus, mineral taxation inevitably raises the issue of economic rents and the related equity question of rightful ownership. Few topics in the field of mineral taxation generate more debate and confusion.

The pages that follow discuss the nature of economic rents in general, and then examine the two types of economic rents most closely associated with mining and mineral commodities. The first is known as Ricardian rent, the second as Hotelling rent, scarcity rent, or user costs. Finally, several types of royalties are examined from the perspective of economic rent.

The nature of economic rents   An economic rent is a payment or monetary return to the owner of a factor of production or to a firm (which controls a bundle of factors of production) that does not alter its economic behavior. For example, a successful folk singer earning half a million dollars a year may have a next best economic opportunity of teaching folk singing at a salary of $50,000. If he is willing to remain a folk singer as long as his salary is at least $50,000, he is earning $450,000 yearly in economic rents. This is the amount of his salary that government could tax away without altering his behavior in terms of the services he is willing to provide to the market. Firms similarly earn rents when the prices they receive for the goods and services they produce exceed what is necessary to attract them into an industry or, if they are already in an industry, what is necessary to keep them from reducing their output or closing down entirely.

The well-known economist Joseph E. Stiglitz (1996) describes economic rent in his textbook *Principles of Micro-Economics* in the following way:

> Economic rent is the difference between the price that is actually paid and the price that would have to be paid in order for the good or service to be produced . . . Anyone who is in the position to receive economic rents is fortunate indeed, because these "rents" are unrelated to effort . . .
>
> Firms earn economic rent to the extent that they are more efficient than other firms . . . Consider a market in which all firms except one have the same average cost curve, and the market price corresponds to the minimum average cost of these firms. The remaining firm is super-efficient, so its average costs are far below those of the other firms. The company would have been willing to produce at a lower price, at its minimum average cost. What it receives in excess of what is required to induce it to enter the market are rents—returns on the firm's superior capabilities . . . (298–99)

John Cordes (1995), in "An Introduction to the Taxation of Mineral Rents," describes economic rent in a somewhat different, though consistent, manner:

> Economic rent can be defined as the difference between existing market price for a commodity or input factor and its opportunity cost. Opportunity

cost is the reservation price or minimum amount owners of the goods or service would be willing to accept . . .

Thus, economic rent is a surplus—a financial return not required to motivate desired economic behaviour. Its existence implies predominantly distributional rather than resource allocation consequences. From a public policy viewpoint all rents could be taxed without altering current decisions on production and consumption. Resource owners would still earn acceptable or needed returns on their investment so output would remain the same. Consumption levels would not change because under competitive conditions producers cannot shift the tax burden to raising prices. As a result, economic rent could be redefined as the magnitude of returns which could be taxed away without causing the pattern of resource use to be altered. (26)

It is important not to confuse rents with wages, interest, or profits, which are compensation for the services of labor, capital, and entrepreneurship. Taxing these payments reduces the incentives for the owners of these resources to provide their services to the market, and so distorts the behavior and performance of the economy.

Ricardian rents David Ricardo, a British economist, was one of the first to explore economic rents. Writing in the early 19th century, he noted that agricultural land could be separated according to its fertility. Land in the most fertile class can produce a given quantity of food (a bushel of corn, for example) at lower cost than land in the second most fertile class. Similarly, land in the second most fertile class has costs below those of land in the third class, and so on.

Figure 2.2 illustrates such a situation. The amount of land in the most fertile class—class A, in this example—has the capacity to produce an amount of food, such as corn, equal to $0Q_a$, and its costs per unit of output (per bushel of corn, for example) are $0C_a$. The production capacity of the second most fertile class—class B—is Q_aQ_b and its costs are $0C_b$. In a similar way, the capacity and costs of land in classes C, D, and so on can be assessed.

When a population is small, and when the need for agricultural land is sufficiently modest that the most fertile class of land can produce all the food that is needed, there is a surplus of the best land. Because the price for a bushel of corn is determined by production costs, the market price is P1, and no land owner is receiving economic rent. As the population grows, the demand for food and agricultural land expands. Once all of

Figure 2.2. Ricardian Rent Varies with Land Fertility

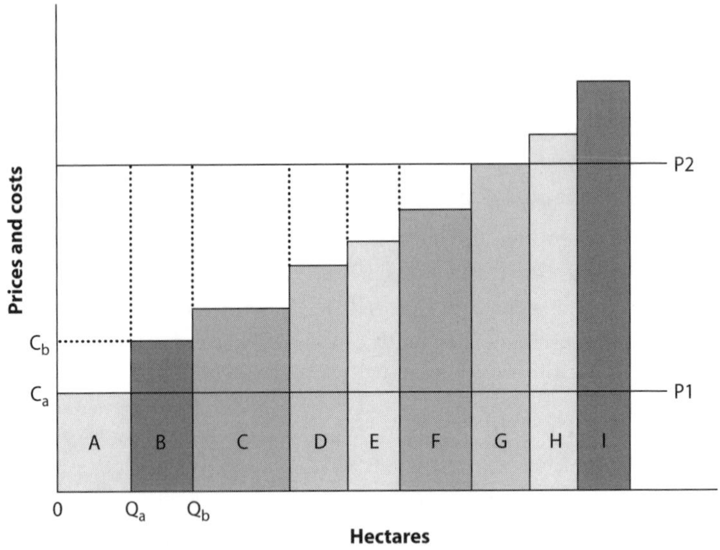

Note: Each of the columns A through I represents land of different quality or fertility. The height of each column reflects the costs of producing a given quantity of food, such as a bushel of corn. For example, for the most fertile land, the land in column A, the costs of production are $0C_a$. For land in column B, the costs of production are $0C_b$. The amount of food that each class of land can produce is given by the width of its column. So the most fertile land, column A, can produce the quantity $0Q_a$ of food, and the land in column B the quantity Q_aQ_b. P1 is the market price of food when demand can be completely satisfied by the most fertile land in column A. P2 is the market price when demand requires food production from land in columns A through G.

A similar figure can reflect the rent in mining. In this case, the columns reflect individual mines of declining quality that produce copper or another metal. The horizontal axis measures mine capacity rather than hectares, and the vertical axis reflects production costs and prices for copper or another metal rather than for food.

the best land (class A) is under cultivation, farmers have to start planting the next best land (class B). As the population continues to expand, ever poorer and hence more costly tracts of land will be brought into production. For that to happen, prices must rise to cover the costs of production on the poorest class of land needed. If the supply needed by the population grows to include land within class G, for example, the market price for a bushel of corn will rise to P2 (see Figure 2.2).

At price P2, the owners of land in classes A through F, which are all more fertile than the land in class G, are enjoying economic rents, or what are also called *Ricardian rents*. The owners of the best land (class A) are willing to cultivate their land as long as the price is P1 or higher. At P2, on each unit of output, they are realizing a rent equal to the difference between P2 and P1. The total rent earned by this group of landowners (class A) is that difference times its capacity, which is reflected by the rectangular column that extends from the top of its production costs to the price line P2. The rent earned by the landowners in classes B through F is similarly given by the rectangular column above their production costs and below price P2. As the figure shows, the economic rent per unit of output is greatest for landowners in class A with the most fertile land, and declines as fertility drops. The owners of land in class G, the marginal land in use, receive no economic rent.

Mineral deposits, like tracts of agricultural land, have different levels of quality. A few copper mines, for example, have high-grade ore and valuable by-products. They are located near the surface and are within easy reach of ocean transportation. For these and other reasons, some mines have very low production costs. Other copper deposits are not quite so fortunate but are still profitable to exploit. So, just as Ricardo ranked agricultural land by its fertility, mines can be ranked by production costs. In Figure 2.2, for example, column A could reflect the production costs (OC_a) and capacity of the lowest-cost mine, column B the costs and capacity of the next-lowest-cost mine, and so on. If the production of mines A through G is required to satisfy demand, the market equilibrium price for copper will be P2. Mines A through F will be earning rent, whereas mine G will just be covering its production costs.

Economic rents of the type just discussed are widely considered an appropriate target for taxation for two reasons. First, most taxes distort the economy and diminish its efficiency. An income tax on wages, for example, shifts the supply curve of labor downward. As a result, society consumes less output and more leisure than in the absence of such a tax. Taxing economic rent, however, does not affect the availability of labor, capital, and other factors of production, and so is free of such distortions. Second, taxing economic rents seems to many to be fair or equitable. Economic rents are gifts or payments for which recipients contribute nothing. Why, for example, should the landowners in Ricardo's world benefit from population growth while others do not? Indeed, the rest of society ends up worse off because of rising food prices.

As a result, it is perhaps not surprising that the economic rents associated with rich mineral deposits are frequently used to justify special taxes on mining. Why, the argument normally goes, should the benefits created by the country's geologic legacy not flow to all its citizens, rather than to the owners of mining companies, many of whom may be foreigners? Though this argument has considerable popular appeal, close scrutiny raises two reservations.

1. Economic rents are not confined to the mineral sector but exist wherever there is a fixed factor of production. Ricardo focused on agricultural land, but economic rents are also found with forests, fisheries (cultivated and natural), vineyards, and hunting lands. As cities grow, landowners in the center realize economic rents as their property values soar.

Indeed, public policy itself often creates economic rents. When a city builds a subway, apartments within easy walking distance of a station enjoy a rise in value. When land is rezoned, allowing homes to be built or the land to be used in a way previously prohibited, its value typically increases. The construction of recreational centers or the formal protection of open space benefits nearby homeowners.

As a result, taxation designed to capture economic rent cannot logically be applied solely to mining. Economic rents are found throughout the economy, and the equity argument for taxing economic rents may be strongest where public policy creates the rents.

2. A reasonable case can be made that economic rents in the mining sector, though substantial in the short run, actually do not exist in the very long run. To see why, one has to appreciate how the magnitude of economic rent varies with time.

In the short run, mines have an incentive to operate as long as they are recovering their out-of-pocket or variable costs. Those costs, approximated by what is known within the mining industry as *cash costs*, typically include labor, materials, energy, and other expenses that cease when production stops. However, they exclude the capital and other fixed costs that a company incurs over the short run, whether or not it is operating. Therefore, when the market price is below its average production costs but above its average variable costs, a mine, though losing money, is losing less than it would if it shut down. By continuing to operate, it is recovering at least some of its fixed costs. Given this incentive to remain in production as long as the market price is at or above average variable costs, mines receive short-run economic rents that reflect the difference between price and those average variable costs.

In the long run, of course, mines have to recover their full costs of production, which include their invested capital and a competitive rate of return on that capital. If they fail to do so they will cease production, rather than invest the new capital needed to remain in business. So the long-run economic rent being earned by a mine is the difference between the market price and its average total costs, an amount significantly smaller than its short-run economic rent.

Figure 2.3 illustrates this situation by examining the economic rent being earned by a particular mine (mine B, in this instance). It assumes that the mine's cash or variable costs are given by OC_b. As long as the market price remains above OC_b, this mine has an incentive to continue mining in the short run. When the market price is P2, the mine is earning an economic rent equal to the difference between P2 and OC_b on each unit of output. As shown in Figure 2.3, this total rent can be divided into three components: quasi-rent, other rent, and pure rent.

The first, *quasi-rent*, reflects the mine's return on its capital and other fixed costs. This rent exists only in the short run. In the long run, a mine not recovering its fixed costs will shut down.

The second, *other rent*, arises from several sources. Of particular importance is the cyclical volatility of metal prices. When the economy is booming, prices tend to rise sharply, increasing the economic rents earned by all mines. Over the business cycle, however, these positive rents are offset by the negative rents realized when the economy is weak and metal prices are depressed. So, as was the case with quasi-rent, other rent exists in the short run but not in the long run.[5]

The third, *pure rent*, is really the Ricardian rent. It arises because the quality of the mineral deposit that a mine is exploiting is superior to that

Figure 2.3. Sources of Rent for Mine B

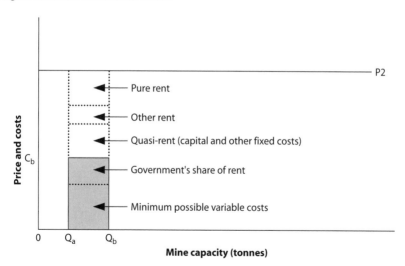

Source: Author J. Tilton.

Note: P2 is the market price for the metal produced by mine B; OC_b is the mine's production costs; and Q_aQ_b is the mine's production capacity.

of the marginal mine or the highest cost mine in operation (mine G in Figure 2.2). Mine quality depends on the grade of the ore, the nature of its mineralization, the depth of the deposit, access to ocean shipping, and numerous other factors affecting production costs.

Those who advocate taxing economic rent usually have in mind the pure rents associated with mining. They reflect the benefits created by the country's geologic legacy, and unlike quasi-rent, persist in the long run. No operating mine should close down even in the long run because the government taxes away the pure rent.

This argument, while true, overlooks an important consideration. Creating pure rent in the mineral sector requires not just the mining of valuable mineral deposits, but also either their discovery through exploration or their creation by innovation and new technology from previously known but uneconomic deposits. Prior to discovery and the development of profitable production technologies, mineral resources cannot be exploited. It is the quest to create and capture pure rent that provides the incentives for exploration. Geologists scouring the hills for new ore bodies are not looking for marginal deposits; they are searching for bonanzas with all the associated pure rent. Similarly, the search for new technologies that convert uneconomic mineral deposits into valuable ore is driven by the hope of capturing the pure rent such successful innovations create.

Thus, taxing away the pure rent will affect economic behavior, and so distort the economy in the very long run. A country that taxes the pure rent associated with mining has to be prepared to subsidize new exploration or conduct exploration itself. Otherwise, it is destined to watch its mining sector decline over time as its known mines are depleted and not replaced.

One of the dangers for public policy is that the decline may take some years. The large economic rent associated with mining in the short run (the quasi-rent, other rent, and pure rent) means that higher tax rates on mining almost inevitably raise government revenues at first. The negative effects on mine output, and in turn revenues, may take years to become apparent; likewise, they take many years to reverse. Fortunately, there is an earlier indicator that mining taxes are too onerous. A decline in exploration expenditures relative to other countries often provides the first indication that a country is losing its competitiveness in attracting investment into its mineral sector.

Hotelling rent, scarcity rent, and user costs   In 1931, Harold Hotelling, an American economist, published a seminal article titled "The Econom-

ics of Exhaustible Resources." The article pointed out that firms exploiting a nonrenewable resource behave differently than other firms. As all
good introductory textbooks on microeconomic theory show, firms that
are competitive and maximize profits have an incentive to expand their
output until their marginal cost (the cost of producing the next unit of
output) just equals the market price. If they cease production before this
point, they can increase profits by producing more. If they go beyond
this point, the cost of producing the last output exceeds the price they
receive, and so they can increase profits by producing less.

Hotelling noted that firms incur an opportunity cost in addition to
their production costs in the process of producing mineral commodities.
This is because increasing output by one more unit today, rather than
leaving the required mineral resources in the ground, reduces the mineral resources available in the future. More specifically, the opportunity
cost identified by Hotelling is the net present value (NPV) of the future
profits that are lost because mineral resources are reduced by an additional unit of output today. As a result, profit-maximizing, competitive
firms producing mineral commodities will only expand their output up
to the point at which the market price equals the production costs of the
last unit plus its opportunity cost. Thus, mine G, the marginal producer
shown in Figure 2.2, will remain in production only if the market price is
sufficiently above its variable or cash costs to cover this opportunity cost,
as shown in Figure 2.4. Otherwise, the firm's profitability (measured by
the NPV of its current plus future profits) is enhanced by ceasing production today and saving its mineral resources for the future.

This opportunity cost identified by Hotelling is commonly referred to
as Hotelling rent, scarcity rent, or user costs. Though the three terms are
used interchangeably, this study uses the term user costs because, if the
market price does not cover this cost plus the current costs of production, the mine will have an incentive to shut down and keep its mineral
resources in the ground for the future. Thus, user costs (or Hotelling rent
or scarcity rent) reflect real costs, albeit costs incurred in the future, and
not really economic rent at all. As a result, their confiscation will alter
economic behavior and allocation of resources.

Several aspects of user costs need to be highlighted. First, user costs
are the NPV of the future profits forgone by using marginal mineral resources (that is, the ore of mine G) to produce an additional unit of output today rather than saving these resources in the ground for the future.
When intramarginal mineral resources are consumed (that is, the ores of

Figure 2.4. User Costs in the Mining Industry

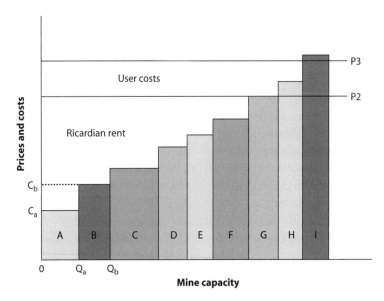

Source: Author J. Tilton.

Note: Each of the columns A through I represents mines of different quality. The height of each column reflects the costs of producing a given quantity of metal, such as copper. For example, the mine shown in column A has production costs of $0C_a$, and the mine in column B has production costs of $0C_b$. The amount of output that each mine can produce is given by the width of its column. So the lowest-cost mine (column A) can produce $0Q_a$ pounds of copper, and the second-lowest-cost mine (column B) can produce Q_aQ_b pounds. P1 is the market price of copper when demand can be completely satisfied by mine A. P2 is the market price when demand requires production from mines A through G. P3 is the market price of copper when demand requires production from mines A through G and user costs exist. User costs, which may arise in the production of nonrenewable resources such as metals, reflect the NPV of the profits lost in the future from producing one more unit of output during the present period (see text for more on user costs).

mines A through F), the NPV of the lost future profits reflects both user costs and pure Ricardian rent.

Second, under given conditions, user costs can be shown to reflect the current market value of marginal resources in the ground and the expected costs of discovering new marginal resources. As a result, user costs reflect the value of mineral resources arising from the fact that they are nonrenewable.

Third, although rich mineral deposits are quite valuable in the sense that if sold they would fetch a high price, the available empirical evidence suggests that this value comes from the associated Ricardian rents, not user costs. Indeed, empirical studies attempting to measure user costs find, for the most part, that they are negligible or zero, not only for the metals, but for oil and other energy sources as well (see Tilton 2003; Adelman 1990). This finding is consistent with the behavior of mine managers. Instances are rare if not nonexistent of mine managers deliberately cutting back output when price is greater than production costs in the belief that the increase in future profits, discounted back to the present, more than compensates for the loss in current profits. Indeed, few mine managers are even familiar with the concept of user costs. However, mine managers may not consider user costs simply because the exploitation of reserves over time is optimized by the decision regarding mine capacity. Once capacity is set, it determines the optimal output (see Cairns 1998).

Why user costs should be negligible or zero is not entirely clear. It may simply be that finding new marginal mines—porphyry copper deposits with 0.5 percent copper, for example—is easy and thus cheap. Although finding rich deposits is difficult and expensive, the value of such deposits largely or entirely reflects their associated Ricardian rent. Uncertainty also may contribute to negligible user costs. The NPV of the expected future profits created by cutting current production will be heavily discounted when technological change and other developments have the potential to render uneconomic in the future mineral deposits whose costs today are below the prevailing market price.

What does all of this imply for mineral taxation? The widespread justification for taxing the mineral sector, based on economic rent, and, moreover, for taxing firms in this sector more than in other sectors, seems questionable. The value of mineral resources arising from their nonrenewable nature appears to be negligible. Moreover, since user costs are not rents but rather true costs, attempts to capture those costs will distort economic behavior and performance. Although sizable economic rents do arise in mining as a result of differences in the quality of deposits, the presence of sunk costs, and other considerations, those rents largely disappear in the long run and completely disappear in the very long run.

This situation might suggest to some that the government should impose little or no taxation on the mineral sector; however, that conclusion follows only if the ultimate purpose of mineral taxation is the capture of economic rent (and specifically the capture of those economic rents that persevere over the very long run). As noted at the beginning of this section, governments, like companies, have goals and objectives. Although private companies presumably are largely driven by the pursuit of profit, governments strive to promote the welfare of society, through economic development and other means. Thus, the ultimate objective of mineral taxation is not the capture of economic rents, but the promotion of the social welfare, however that concept is defined by the prevailing political process. The optimal tax rate (see Figure 2.1) for this purpose is not closely tied to the capture of economic rent. It could generate more or less tax revenue than a taxation policy designed to capture any economic rent that persists over the long run.

Some types of royalties are better suited to the collection of economic rent than others. Royalties based on mineral volume or weight are least appropriate, because they are wholly insensitive to measurements of rent. Value-based royalties are only slightly better—they will move up and down with price but are not tied to the cost side of the project's economics. Profit-based royalties are better yet because they take into account receipts and costs, although they too do not account for a return on capital. Pure economic rent–based taxes have been proposed for the mining sector but have not found favor with either governments or industry. The closest approaches have been efforts in countries such as the Philippines and Papua New Guinea (now repealed) to levy an additional profits tax based on a calculation that seeks to determine (1) whether a profit threshold has been reached and (2) all amounts that exceed a defined internal rate of return to which a tax rate is then applied. The sliding-scale royalty based on a ratio of costs and profits in Ghana, which is described in detail in Chapter 3, also appropriates some economic rent but neglects return on capital. Taxes based on economic rent principles can be applied to any business but almost never are. The one exception is petroleum, for which, from time to time, particularly in times of very high prices, governments may devise and apply some form of additional tax based on the firm's rate of return.

Identification of Tax Types and Their Classification

Governments have many options to choose from when designing fiscal systems, and various types and forms of taxation methods can be used. The methods applied to the mining sector usually fall into one of two main categories of tax: *in rem* or *in personam*.

In rem taxes are charges assessed against the mineral deposit or against the inputs and actions needed to exploit it. These charges can be divided into two groups: taxes that affect the variable costs of the project (such as unit-based royalties, ad valorem–based royalties, sales taxes, and excise taxes) and taxes that affect the fixed costs of the project (such as certain types of property taxes, import duties, registration fees, land rents, value-added tax, some types of stamp duties, and withholding taxes on loan interest and services). *In rem* taxes rarely take into account the concept of profitability.

In contrast, *in personam* taxes are charges against some definition of net revenues, that is, revenues less qualifying costs. Examples include income tax, progressive or additional profits tax, withholding tax on remitted dividends, royalty based on some measure of profit, and royalty based on some measure of income. Table 2.2 indicates the main types of taxes that governments have applied to the mining sector and whether they are based on some measure of net revenue.

Generally, *in rem* types of taxes have a greater likelihood of causing distortions in decision making pertaining to cutoff ore grades, mine life, and reserves than *in personam* types of taxes. When designing a tax system, policy makers should be aware of the cumulative effects that taxes can have on mine economics and potential levels of future investment. Such awareness must recognize the importance of each tax type in achieving specific objectives and the implications of their cumulative effects.

Purposes of Tax Types and Their Integration into a System
The previous section identified a variety of tax types and their potential to cause production distortions. Although any one type of tax taken alone may have a small or large impact, the combined effect of a number of taxes can be appreciable. Table 2.3 identifies some of the objectives behind tax types and indicates their prevalence.

All the tax types classified in the table as *in rem* are not based on a measure of profit, and if that taxable activity takes place, they are certain to be paid. Several such tax types, for example, land fees and unit-based royalties, provide a more or less stable base of annual revenue. One of the challenges to government is to obtain a level of annual tax revenues sufficient to cover base governmental operating expenses. Nations that are mineral export dependent can be particularly vulnerable to commodity price fluctuations and may place a heavier emphasis on *in rem* taxes than nations with more diversified economies. Such nations also have other tools available to accommodate revenue cycles, such as the special revenue stabilization funds created by some jurisdictions, among them Alaska, Nauru, Norway, and the Russian Federation, where some revenues in high-yield years are set aside for possible use in low-yield years.

Table 2.2. Taxes Sometimes Levied on the Mining Industry, and Their Basis

Tax type	Basis
In rem taxes (unit or value based)	
Unit-based royalty	Set charge per unit
Ad valorem–based royalty	% of mineral's value (definition of value may vary)
Sales and excise tax	% of value of sales
Property or capital tax	% of value of property or capital
Import duty	% of value of imports (usually)
Export duty	% of value of exports
Withholding on remitted loan interest	% of loan interest value
Withholding on imported services	% of value of services
Value-added tax	% of the value of the good or service
Registration fees	Set charge per registration event
Rent or usage fees	Set charge per unit area
Stamp tax	Set charge per transaction or % of value of the transaction
In personam taxes (net revenue based)	
Income tax	% of income
Capital gains tax	% of profit on disposal of capital assets
Additional profits tax	% of additional profits
Excess profits tax	% of excess profits
Net profits royalty or net value royalty	% of mineral's value less allowable costs
Withholding on remitted profits or dividends	% of remitted value

Source: Author J. Otto.

Mineral sector investors will be concerned about the overall level of taxation, that is, the effective tax rate, and the extent to which *in rem* taxes not based on profitability are a part of that tax burden. *In rem*–type taxes raise the level of perceived risk because companies will be concerned that they may have significant calls for tax in years when the mine is already suffering losses from market or poor operating conditions. When determining which taxes and levels of taxes to apply to the mining sector, policy makers should not only consider ways to achieve individual tax objectives, but also take into account the cumulative effects of all taxes, in particular *in rem* taxes.[6]

Not all taxes work independently of one another. In almost all nations, the income tax system allows for the deduction of royalties in computing taxable income. Thus, while the application of a unit-based or ad valorem–based royalty may have production-distorting effects in early

Table 2.3. Policy Objectives of Tax Types and Their Prevalence

Tax type	Objective	Prevalence
In rem taxes		
Unit-based royalty	To provide stable and certain revenues (stable because commodity price fluctuations have no impact); an ownership transfer payment	Commonly used, particularly for industrial and bulk
Ad valorem–based royalty	To provide at least some revenue; an ownership transfer payment	Commonly used
Sales and excise tax	To provide revenue based on the volume of economic activity; a tax on inputs	VAT has replaced sales tax in many nations; excise tax may be reserved for special items, such as fuel
Property tax	To provide stable revenue based on the value of the physical plant; often goes to the local level of government	Commonly used
Import duty	To provide revenue; to give national producers an advantage; historically, to fund port development and the customs office	Most countries exempt or zero rate mining equipment
Export duty	To provide revenue; an incentive to service local demand	Eliminated on minerals by almost all countries
Withholding on remitted loan interest	To provide revenue; to encourage greater equity; to encourage local financing	Commonly used
Withholding on imported services	To provide revenue; to encourage the use of local services	Commonly used
Value-added tax	To provide revenue; to capture a portion of value added	If product is exported, most nations negate the effect on inputs and outputs through exemption or refunds
Registration fees	To provide operating revenues to administrative offices	Commonly used
Rent or usage fees	To provide stable revenue, often to local government for land use	Commonly used

(continued)

Table 2.3 *(continued)*

Tax type	Objective	Prevalence
In rem taxes		
Stamp tax	To provide revenue on trans-actional value	Commonly used in developing nations with civil law systems
In personam taxes		
Income tax	To provide revenue based on ability to pay	Universally used
Capital gains tax	To capture profits on disposal of capital assets	Common in developed nations, not applied in many developing nations
Additional profits tax	To capture a part of exceptionally high profits	Very rare
Excess profits tax	To capture a part of exceptionally high profits	Very rare
Net "profits" royalty or net value royalty	To provide revenue based on ability to pay	Mainly used in nations with well-developed tax administration
Withholding on remitted profits or dividends	To provide revenue based on ability to pay; to encourage retention of capital within the country	Commonly used

Source: Author J. Otto.

years when no income tax is payable, the impact will be lessened as the deductions are realized. For example, in a country that imposes a 30 percent income tax rate and a 2 percent royalty, in years when no income tax is payable the royalty rate will be 2 percent, but in years when the deduction is fully realized, the net royalty effect will be effectively 2 (2×0.3) or 1.4 percent. Most nations allow for the carry-forward of losses from one year to another, and deductible royalty payments in early years will thus further reduce income tax liability later in the project. A reasonable, low royalty rate in systems that allow indefinite loss carry-forward may have less effect on long-term recovery of minerals (reserves) than is popularly believed. However, although the impact of a low royalty on reserves mined over the long term may be minimal for many mines (excepting marginal mines with a bulk of their ore near the cutoff grade), the threat posed by the necessity to pay substantial *in rem* taxes during years when the mine is operating at a loss poses a significant threat to all mines that do not have cash reserves to bridge the loss-generating period.

In a succession of efforts led by James Otto, a copper mine financial model was built, and the tax systems in over 20 nations were applied to it (see Table 2.4). Among other results, measures of the effective tax rate in each nation were calculated based on all major taxes and fees paid to government, including royalties. Such models can be useful for understanding the impact that the introduction of a new tax or a change in a rate or base can have on international competitiveness. Such models are particularly useful for looking at the impact of a mix of taxes and incentives. It is interesting to note that the absence of a royalty does not guarantee a low overall effective tax rate—Mexico and Greenland do not impose royalty taxes yet have relatively high effective tax rates. Likewise, Western Australia, which imposes royalty, has a lower total effective tax rate than Chile, which does not. However, the investor's rate of return is higher in Chile than in Western Australia, largely owing to the payment of royalty in the early years of the project. To obtain any target level of taxation or revenue, governments have a wide variety of options to choose from. Most nations may have little or no flexibility with regard to some types of tax rates, for example, the income tax rate or the withholding tax rate, but the basis may be open to adjustment (for example, depreciation on mining capital equipment may be accelerated, allowing large deductions in the early years of a project). An exception to rate inflexibility is often royalty. Because it is unique to the mining sector, it is perhaps politically easier to modify from time to time than taxes that apply to all sectors.

Evolution of Mineral Taxation

Different nations have different expectations, needs, and administrative capabilities with regard to the taxing of their mineral sectors. What constitutes an ideal tax system for one nation may be suboptimal for another. In addition, informed governments will be concerned about investor preferences, recognizing that investors can discriminate about which tax jurisdictions to invest in. The evolution of a nation's mineral taxation system will be influenced by a number of factors.

Regardless of national circumstances, there has been a global trend to reduce the applicability and level of *in rem* taxes applied to the mineral sector. For example, 25 years ago many nations applied import duties to mining equipment and levied export duties, at least on ores and concentrates. Today, most nations have eliminated or greatly reduced import

Table 2.4. Comparative Economic Measures for a Model Copper Mine in Selected Jurisdictions

Country	Foreign investor's internal rate of return (%)	Total effective tax rate (%)
Lowest taxing quartile		
Sweden	15.7	28.6
Western Australia	12.7	36.4
Chile	15.0	36.6
Zimbabwe	13.5	39.8
Argentina	13.9	40.0
China	12.7	41.7
Second lowest taxing quartile		
Papua New Guinea (2002)	13.3	42.7
Bolivia	11.4	43.1
South Africa	13.5	45.0
Philippines	13.5	45.3
Indonesia (7th, COW)	12.5	46.1
Kazakhstan	12.9	46.1
Second highest taxing quartile		
Peru (2003)	11.7	46.5
Tanzania	12.4	47.8
Poland	11.0	49.6
Arizona (U.S.)	12.6	49.9
Mexico	11.3	49.9
Greenland	13.0	50.2
Highest taxing quartile		
Indonesia (non-COW)	11.2	52.2
Ghana	11.9	54.4
Mongolia (2003)	10.6	55.0
Uzbekistan	9.3	62.9
Côte d'Ivoire	8.9	62.4
Ontario (Canada)	10.1	63.8

Source: Otto 2004.
Note: COW = contract of work. Values in the table for all jurisdictions except Mongolia (2004), Papua New Guinea (2002), Peru (2003), and Indonesia (2003) are extracted from Otto, Cordes, and Batarseh (2000). Taxation systems change frequently and the table should be used with caution.

duties, and almost all nations have zero rated or exempted all minerals from export duties. As value-added tax systems have been introduced, almost all nations have negated the impact of this tax on exporting mines through exemption, zero-rating, or refund schemes.

In nations with royalty taxes the trend has been to reduce the rates at which they are assessed, until today, with the exception of diamonds and certain other precious stones, ad valorem rates usually do not exceed 3 or 4 percent. In addition to adjustments in the royalty rates, many nations with ad valorem royalties now allow an adjustment in the value basis for certain non-production-related expenses such as transportation, handling, and insurance. Many use a net smelter return (NSR) approach for appropriate minerals. Some jurisdictions have moved away from unit- and value-based royalties to royalties based on profits.

In preceding sections of this study it was noted that some nations do not, or did not until recently, impose royalty taxes. However, in nations without royalty tax, there is from time to time pressure to impose them. For example, just prior to 2000, Western Australia moved to impose a royalty on gold production. In 2000, the mineral-producing nations of Chile, Greenland, Mexico, Peru, South Africa, Sweden, and the United States did not impose royalty.[7] As of the date of this study, Peru has imposed a royalty and South Africa will do so in the near future. In Chile, a bill has been introduced to create royalties, and in the United States, calls for federal-level royalties have intensified. Greenland is considering a royalty on precious metals and diamonds. In most nations where minerals are the property of the state or of the people collectively some sort of royalty is imposed.

What is not clear is whether there is a trend in the form royalty taxes take. At present, the ad valorem form is most popular, except for industrial minerals, for which unit-based royalties prevail. However, some nations with competent tax administration structures have been moving toward profit- or income-based mining tax systems. Almost all Canadian provinces have replaced traditional forms of royalty with mining taxes based on adjusted income. Likewise, Nevada, in the United States, and the Northern Territory in Australia use profit- or income-based royalty systems. These jurisdictions enjoy a relatively high level of mineral sector investment and also benefit from significant mineral sector fiscal revenues. The question then might be posed as to what conditions indicate that a nation is ripe to move from unit- and ad valorem–based royalties to a profit- or income-based royalty system. The answer to that question will be unique for every nation, but in all cases, some factors indicate whether such a shift may occur. Examples of these factors include the following:

- Economic diversification. If a government's economy and tax base are well diversified, it has less reason to impose a discriminatory tax on mining and less of a need to rely on taxes that are certain and stable from year to year. Some would argue that, overall, a government's long-term fiscal take from the sector may be greater with a profit-based system than with a system that does not take profitability into account.
- General level of tax compliance. Unit and ad valorem-type taxes are less vulnerable to evasion than are tax systems based on net income or profits. If the general income tax system is working well, governments may have less need to rely on more evasion-resistant tax methods.
- Administrative capability of the tax authority. Profit- and income-based royalty schemes are inherently more difficult to implement than unit- and value-based royalty schemes, and governments that have capable, well-funded, and competently staffed tax administration systems are better positioned to manage a profit- or income-based tax.
- Well-developed and well-understood general income tax system. A royalty tax that is based on income or profit may be able to define certain deductible costs using guidelines and procedures developed for general income tax purposes (for example, depreciation rules).
- Experience gained with similar schemes in other sectors. Governments that have experience with income- or profit-based taxes and their accounting in other resource sectors may be more willing to use it in mining (for example, production-sharing agreements that define accounting rules).
- Nations that have a strong desire to attract investors. Mining investors prefer to be taxed on their ability to pay, and a nation seeking to differentiate itself from other nations that it competes with for mineral sector investment may use an income- or profit-based royalty system as an investment incentive.

Today, nations use a wide variety of methods to assess royalty. Appendix A1 presents extracts from royalty statutes from around the world. What is remarkable about an examination of those statutes is their lack of uniformity. Even in nations that levy the same sort of royalty, the calculation basis varies from country to country. Furthermore, in countries where mining royalties are partly or wholly vested in the states or provinces (such as Argentina, Australia, Canada, and the United States), the determination of royalties shows little or no consistency across jurisdictions. There is no indication that there is an evolving convergence at this time.

References

Adelman, Morris A. 1990. "Mineral Depletion with Special Reference to Depletion." *Review of Economics and Statistics* 72 (1): 1–10.

Cairns, Robert D. 1998. "Are Mineral Deposits Valuable? A Reconciliation of Theory and Practice." *Resources Policy* 24 (1): 19–24.

Cordes, John A. 1995. "An Introduction to the Taxation of Mineral Rents." In *The Taxation of Mineral Enterprises*, ed. James Otto, 26. London: Graham & Trotman.

Davis, Graham A., and John E. Tilton. 2005. "The Resource Curse." *Natural Resources Forum* 29 (3): 233–42.

Hotelling, H. 1931. "The Economics of Exhaustible Resources." *Journal of Political Economy* 392: 137–75.

Otto, James. 2004. "International Comparative Tax Regimes," 50 *Rocky Mountain Mineral Law Institute* 17: 1–45.

Otto, James, John Cordes, and Maria L. Batarseh. 2000. *Global Mining Taxation Comparative Study*. Golden, CO: Institute for Global Resources Policy and Management, Colorado School of Mines.

Stevens, Paul. 2003. "Resource Impact: Curse or Blessing? A Literature Survey." *Journal of Energy Literature* 9 (1): 3–42.

Stiglitz, Joseph E. 1996. *Principles of Micro-Economics*, 2nd ed., 298–99. New York: W.W. Norton.

Tilton, John E. 1977. *The Future of Nonfuel Minerals*. Washington, DC: Brookings.

Tilton, John E. 2003. *On Borrowed Time? Assessing the Threat of Mineral Depletion*. Washington, DC: Resources for the Future.

Tilton, John E. 2004. "Determining the Optimal Tax on Mining." *Natural Resources Forum* 28 (2): 147–48.

Vernon, Raymond. 1974. *Sovereignty at Bay*. New York: Basic Books.

Notes

1. For more on the optimal level of taxation, see Tilton (2004).

2. For a review of this literature, see Stevens (2003) and Davis and Tilton (2005).

3. One can contrast the tax systems of Greenland and the United States. In Greenland, there is very little sectoral tax discrimination and the administrative

apparatus is simple and small. However, in the United States it can be argued that the tax system is more or less based on sectoral discrimination that requires a complex administrative system. Pressures on politicians within systems that discriminate can be intense as each sector positions itself for special treatment.

4. See Otto (2004). Most mineral-producing nations impose a royalty. Those that do not impose royalties periodically come under pressure to do so. For example, in the United States there is a continuing call for imposing a royalty on minerals transferred to the private sector under the 1872 mining law's system of staking claims. In early 2004, the governments of Chile, New South Wales (Australia), and South Africa were considering doing so. Peru, which did not previously impose royalty tax, passed royalty legislation that went into effect in 2004.

5. *Other rent* also encompasses monopoly rent, rent due to ability, and rent due to public policy. Like the rent due to cyclical fluctuations in market price, rent due to public policy eventually alters firm behavior and is confiscated by the government. See Tilton (1977).

6. The methodology to undertake a numerical analysis of effective tax rate is described and illustrated for over 20 nations in Otto, Cordes, and Batarseh (2000).

7. The United States' situation is complex. Some minerals, such as coal, may be assessed a royalty by the federal government, but most hard-rock minerals are not assessed. State governments may assess a severance tax, that is, a royalty, on some types of minerals occurring in some types of land.

CHAPTER 3

Mineral Royalty Instruments

The previous chapter examined mineral taxation in general and identified key taxation topics and issues. This chapter turns specifically to royalties. It begins with a discussion of the rationale for having or not having a royalty and then identifies the prevalent types of royalties. Information on royalties in selected nations includes extracts from their laws to illustrate particular approaches. Tables organized by region summarize and compare the royalty approach in over 30 mineral-producing nations. For example, some nations allow royalty obligations to be reduced, deferred, or waived during hard times. Finally, royalty arrangements between private parties are examined and contrasted with government-imposed royalties. In this chapter, the reader should remember that royalties are only part of the overall tax system and that shortfalls or advantages of different royalty types may be balanced or magnified by other tax types.

Purpose of Mineral Royalties

Although the structure and rates of mineral royalties vary widely internationally, most are collected for the same reason, that is, payment to the owner of the mineral resource in return for the removal of the minerals from the land. The royalty, as the instrument for compensation, is payment in return for the permission that, first, gives the mining company access to the minerals and second, gives the company the right to develop the resource for its own benefit (Cawood 2004). In contrast, in some civil law nations, the legal basis for a royalty paid to the state is a payment for a continued right to mine, with no actual or implied mineral ownership by the state. (See also "Ownership as a rationale for imposing royalty tax," in Chapter 2, for a discussion on the royalty entitlement to the owner of the minerals.)

The evolution of royalty instruments has become more complex over time as the legal description of mineral rights ownership developed alongside the separate tenure for mineral developers under mineral law. The owner of the mineral rights is defined in property law, which varies from country to country. An owner could be a community as a group of people, whose communal ownership stems from ancient customary law; an individual, as is the case in countries where there are traces of civil law; or a government exercising sovereignty over the mineral resources within its territory in terms of international law. The impact of having national sovereignty over natural resources must not be underestimated (see Barberis 1998). As states started to take control of mineral resources, they introduced mineral royalties, which over time were incorporated into the general fiscal regime.

An alternative perspective is the view that a mineral royalty is symbolic of the "willingness to pay for risk reduction" (Otto and Cordes 2002). The concept of risk to both owner and mineral developer is important to consider because the structure and rate of the royalty instrument represent the trade-off between the risks the investor is prepared to accept and those of the owner. More recently, the concept of national sovereignty over natural resources, alongside a growing understanding of sustainable development in the mineral sector, is causing mineral royalties to be viewed as instruments of socioeconomic change. This has prompted some states to introduce mineral development funds, channel a portion of the royalties to lower levels of government, or enforce higher royalty payments for holders of mineral development rights when value is added in foreign economies. In general, the collection of mineral royalties provides governments with a relatively flexible fiscal policy tool. Royalty payments are more amenable to simple, targeted distribution to lower levels of government or affected stakeholders than are general revenues collected under income tax provisions.

Types of Royalties and Assessment Methods

Should a government decide to impose a royalty, it can approach the assessment in a variety of ways. The approach taken will affect both investors and government. This section examines specific approaches and types of royalties and gives examples of how selected types of generic royalties are calculated. Not all parties view royalty types in the same way, and the merits and demerits of various royalty approaches are discussed from the points of view of both investors and governments. Some royalties are relatively easy to assess and monitor, and others are more difficult. This section discusses the administrative implications of selected royalty types and notes which government entity is appropriate to administer various royalty types.

General Approaches to Assessing Royalties: Specificity or Uniformity?

A key policy decision when designing a royalty tax system is to determine the extent to which the system will discriminate between different mineral types. Will a uniform system be applied to all minerals or will each mineral be treated uniquely?

Historically, many governments used a royalty system whereby each type of mineral produced was subject to a unique assessment method. The relevant provision in the mining act, the schedule to the act, or the regulation was lengthy, given that a wide variety of methods were described. The usefulness of using a unique assessment method for each mineral type is that it can be tailored to the marketing, physical properties, and relative profitability of that mineral. However, such systems can be difficult to apply to products that contain multiple minerals, such as a concentrate containing a number of metals. In addition, a detailed assessment method—for example, one that assumes a particular metal content in all lead concentrates nationwide—may quickly become outdated as new technologies are introduced or as a variety of deposit types start to be exploited. Some statutes set royalty rates tied to a fixed price specified in the law; unfortunately, this method inevitably fails or requires amendment when the market price changes, making the statutorily fixed price obsolete as a result of inflation. Some nations that use a government-established reference price publish a royalty schedule or regulation periodically. If administrative resources are sufficient, this can be an effective way to keep government-set reference prices up-to-date.

Increasingly, assessment methods that are tailored for each individual type of mineral are found either in nations with many mines and a mature and capable tax authority (such as Australia and the United States) or in negotiated state agreement acts that cover individual mines. One of the clear advantages of royalty systems that are based on profitability or income is that they can be applied to any type and scale of mineral operation without the need to differentiate between the types of minerals being produced. Because they are based simply on revenues and costs, calculation procedures can be similar for all mine types and sizes.

The following example, from a now-repealed mining law provision, illustrates an approach that both assumes a metal content and is based on a statutory reference price structure. Such systems are inherently unstable because of the inevitable technological and commodity price changes.

Example of a system in which the royalty method is unique to each mineral type (statutorily defined grades and prices)

78(1) For the purpose of computing a royalty —

(a) gold shall be deemed to be 800 in 1,000 fine gold;

(b) tin ore shall be deemed to contain not less than 72.5 per cent of metallic tin;

(c) columbite shall be deemed to contain not less than 65 units of combined Cb_2O_5 and Ta_2O_5 per ton[ne];

(d) wolfram shall be deemed to contain 65 per cent W_2O_5;

(e) lead ore shall be deemed to contain 78 per cent of lead;

(f) zinc ore shall be deemed to contain 55 per cent of zinc;

(g) mixed ores containing tin ore, columbite, tantalite, or wolfram shall be deemed to be wholly of whichever mineral attracts the greatest royalty.

    The exporter of such mixed ore shall, on furnishing satisfactory proof of the actual composition of such ore, be entitled to a refund of the difference between the royalty paid on such ore and that which would have been payable if the actual composition had been known at the time that the said ore was exported.

(h) mixed ores containing lead and zinc shall be deemed to be lead ores.

Fourth Schedule

1. On the tin ores where the price of metallic tin is that shown in the first column below then the royalty per ton[ne] of metallic tin contained in the ore shall be computed at the rates shown in the second column.

Up to N 2,200.00	11 per cent of the value;
Up to N 2,400.00	12 per cent of the value;
Up to N 2,600.00	13 per cent of the value;
Up to N 2,800.00	14 per cent of the value;
Up to N 3,000.00	15 per cent of the value;
Up to N 3,200.00	16 per cent of the value;

2. On lead ores or metallic lead containing on an average less than four ounces of silver per ton[ne], two per cent on the value. If containing not less than four ounces of silver per ton[ne] an additional three per cent on the value of the silver;

3. (a) On Tungsten ore when the value per unit:
Does not exceed thirty-five shillings, the royalty will be one per cent on the value;
Exceeds thirty-five shillings, the royalty will be one per cent on the value plus one-tenth per cent for every shilling or fraction of a shilling by which the value exceeds thirty-five shillings, but so that no royalty shall be payable at a higher rate than five per cent on the value.[1]

Although many nations have moved away from an approach in which every mineral type has its own unique royalty, this approach is still used in some jurisdictions (usually jurisdictions with many mines and a mature and well-funded tax administration). Informed jurisdictions using this approach now avoid setting mineral content assumptions and specified monetary values. The example below (a partial table) is from Western Australia. Although this is an improvement over the preceding example, the set fees in column 2 will require redefining every few years.

Example of a system that assigns a unique royalty method to each mineral type but avoids inflation and metal content types of problems

Column 1	Column 2	Column 3	
Mineral	Amount per tonne according to quantity produced or obtained (A$)	Percentage of the royalty value	The rate as specified hereunder (A$)
Aggregate	30 cents		
Agricultural limestone, incl. lime-sands and shellsands	30 cents		
Attapulgite		5	
Bauxite		7 1/2	
Building stone	50 cents		
Chromite		5	
Clays	30 cents		
Coal (including lignite) not exported			$1 per tonne, to be adjusted each year at 30 June in accordance with the percentage increase in the average ex-mine value of Collie coal for the year ending on that date when compared with the corresponding value of Collie coal for the year ending on 30 June 1981.
Exported		7 1/2	
Cobalt			The rate is (a) if sold as a concentrate, 5% of the royalty value; (b) if sold in metallic form, 21/2% of the royalty value; or (c) if sold as a nickel by-product (d) (i) in the period beginning on 1 July 2000 and ending on 30 June 2005 　(I) 21/2% of the royalty value; or 　(II) if an election is made under regulation 86AB(2), the rate calculated in accordance with the formula set out in subparagraph (ii); (ii) after 30 June 2005, the rate calculated in accordance with the following formula.

(continued)

Column 1	Column 2	Column 3	
Mineral	Amount per tonne according to quantity produced or obtained (A$)	Percentage of the royalty value	The rate as specified hereunder (A$)
Cobalt (continued)			$P \times \dfrac{U}{100} \times \dfrac{2.5}{100} = \$R \text{ per tonne}$ Where P = the gross cobalt metal price per tonne f.o.b. in Australian currency or its computed equivalent used for the purpose of calculating the actual sale price of cobalt metal in the nickel by-product (under usual conditions of sale, without special discounts); U = the number of units per hundred of cobalt metal in the nickel by-product sold; R = the royalty.
Construction limestone	30 cents		
Copper			The rate is (a) if sold as a concentrate, 5% of the royalty value; (b) if sold in metallic form, 21/2% of the royalty value; or (c) if sold as a nickel by-product after 30 June 2005, the rate calculated in accordance with the following formula $P \times \dfrac{U}{100} \times \dfrac{2.5}{100} = \$R \text{ per tonne}$ Where P = the gross copper metal price per tonne f.o.b. in Australian currency or its computed equivalent used for the purpose of calculating the actual sale price of copper metal in the nickel by-product (under usual conditions of sale, without special discounts); U = the number of units per hundred of copper metal in the nickel by-product sold; R = the royalty.
Diamond		7 1/2%	

Source: Mining Regulations 1981, Western Australia, as amended.

In contrast to systems that address every mineral type uniquely, the trend in royalty legislation introduced over the past several decades, except in jurisdictions with many mines and a mature tax administration, is to provide a more harmonized approach, with either a uniform system applied to all minerals, or assessment methods that are uniform for a class or group of minerals. The example that follows is from Botswana.

Example of a system with uniform royalties for classes of minerals (trend in newer mining codes where tax administration capacity may be limited)

66. Royalties

   (1) Subject to the provisions of this Part, the holder of a mineral concession shall be liable to pay royalties to the Government on any mineral obtained by him in the course of the exercise of his rights thereunder at the rates and in the manner prescribed under this section.

   (2) The royalties payable shall be the following percentages of gross market value as defined under subsection (3) below –

Mineral Type	Percentage
Precious Stones	10%
Precious Metals	5%
Other minerals or mineral products	3%

   (3) The term "gross market value" shall for the purposes of calculation of royalties be defined as the sale value receivable at the mine gate in an arms length transaction without discounts, commissions or deductions for the mineral or mineral product on disposal.[2]

In nations where the practice is to set a royalty on a mine-by-mine basis, perhaps as negotiated in an agreement, the royalty system can be tailored to fit the unique characteristics of the deposit being exploited. Such an approach is becoming increasingly rare because most investors favor investment in nations that do not practice discriminatory taxation. The examples below are from Angola and China.

Example of a system in which a unique royalty regime is defined for each mine

Article 15. Fiscal Regime

...

(2) An applicable fiscal regime will be established, with precision, for each Mining Title, which will include:
   (a) A tax on the value of run-of-mine mineral resources, where there is no processing, where there is processing, which will be the result of using a perceptual tax on the annual production value, to be established in accordance with the unit value of each mineral resource to be extracted.

   This tax, also referred to as "royalty", may be paid in kind, when this is convenient to the Angolan State. In any case, it is considered as an operating cost and will be paid monthly.[3]

Example of a system in which a royalty regime is defined for each mine, subject to a prescribed range

(1) To mine the mineral deposits listed in these regulations and to produce salt in People's Republic of China the miner (the royalty-payer) has to pay resources royalty. . . .

(3) The specific amount of royalty for royalty-payers within prescribed ranges is decided by the Minister for Finance in consultation with the relevant authority in the State Council, based on the resource situation of the mine, product mined by the royalty payer.[4]

The preceding examples illustrate the diversity of approaches that governments take in applying royalty systems to mineral production. From a policy perspective, a primary objective in selecting an overall approach, that is, systems tailored to each commodity or mine or a uniform system, should take into account the ability of the tax authority to administer the selected approach.

Royalty Types, Definitions, and Attributes

Royalty What is a royalty? This is a more complex question than might be imagined from a cursory examination. Governments are inventive

when it comes to taxation, and some tax approaches are not always amenable to easy classification. Such classification will depend on one's point
of view, and what constitutes a royalty to an accountant may be different
than to a politician or an economist. In this study a broad interpretation
of the term royalty is used to illustrate a wide variety of revenue-captur-
ing mechanisms that one party or another might consider a royalty. The
criteria used in this study to determine whether a tax type is a royalty are
admittedly subjective; the following definition has been applied.

A royalty is any tax type that exhibits one or more of the following
attributes:

- The law creating the tax calls that tax a royalty.
- The intent of the tax is to make a payment to the owner of the mineral
  as compensation for transferring to the taxpayer the ownership of that
  mineral or the right to sell that mineral.
- The intent of the tax is to charge the producer of the mineral for the
  right to mine the minerals produced.
- The tax is special to mines and is not imposed on other industries.

Unit-based royalties   The oldest form of royalty assessment is based on a
fee levied per unit volume or weight and is termed a *unit-based* or *specific*
royalty (the latter used mainly in Australia). For example, the royalty may
be calculated based on $A5.00 per cubic meter or $A2.50 per tonne.
Although volume-based unit royalties used to be applied in some nations,
primarily to industrial minerals and crude oil, they have largely been replaced by weight-based unit royalties that are easier to monitor and assess.
A unit-based royalty is most often applied to minerals that are more or
less homogeneous, such as industrial minerals (sand, gravel, cobbles, limestone, dimensional stone) or sold in bulk (coal, iron ore, salt, phosphate,
potash, sulfur). The most prevalent forms of unit-based royalty are based
on making the measurement (weight or volume) at the mine mouth, before significant treatment or processing takes place. However, the concept
can be applied at any stage of the mineral preparation process.

Unit-based royalties are straightforward compared with most other
assessment methods because parameters subject to dispute, such as price,
value, and costs, do not come into the calculation. However, they are not
without their quirks, and as is said about many things in life, the devil is
in the details. For instance, weight-based measures may change depending on the degree to which the mineral undergoes treatment, such as

dewatering coal. For metallic minerals sold as ore or in concentrate, the weight basis may be linked to the weight of the ore or concentrate, the weight of the metal contained in the ore or concentrate, or the weight of the metal that can be recovered.

Unit-based royalties are not as easily applied to nonhomogeneous mineral products. For example, a typical copper concentrate from a massive sulfide deposit may contain marketable copper, but also zinc, lead, gold, and platinum, each of which has a very different intrinsic value. A unit-based royalty based on copper content alone would not recognize the value potential of by-products or coproducts.

Unit-based royalties are well suited to discriminate between scales of operation, and it is common to see a sliding-scale approach. Smaller operations that tend to be less efficient than larger operations may be assessed at a lower rate than large operations. Such discrimination recognizes that small operations, particularly family- or cooperative-run quarries in the industrial minerals sector, provide substantial employment and service demand that may be of little interest to large operations. In effect, sliding-scale unit-based royalty schemes recognize that too high a royalty may keep small, economically marginal projects from ever developing and that too low a royalty may not adequately compensate the owner of a deposit that is being exploited at a high profit.

Value-based royalties   The most common way in which governments assess a royalty is to calculate the product of a royalty rate times the value of the mineral. Such value-based royalties are sometimes referred to as ad valorem royalties—a term used throughout this study. The royalty rate may be uniform for all sales of that mineral or may vary according to a sliding scale based on the volume or cumulative value of material sold. Value can be determined in many ways, with the most common being the value of the mineral in the following circumstances:

- Contained in the ore at the mine mouth
- Contained in the first product sold (such as a concentrate)
- Recoverable
- Determined by the gross revenues derived from sales
- Determined by the gross revenues derived from sales less certain allowable costs, such as transportation, insurance, and handling
- As reflected in a net smelter return (adjusted for smelter and refining charges)

Like unit-based royalties, value-based royalties are payable irrespective of whether the mine is making a profit or losing money. However, unlike unit-based royalties, value-based royalties fluctuate following commodity prices. Thus, when prices are high, the government will enjoy more revenue than when prices are low.

Value-based royalties should be easy to calculate but often are not. The degree of complexity will depend largely on how value is defined. If value is defined simply as revenue received from a sale (gross value, invoice value, billed value), the calculation is straightforward. However, some governments are concerned that the value received from a sale may be less than the market value. This suspicion may arise from experiences with "transfer pricing" tax avoidance situations, sales to vertically integrated affiliates at abnormally low prices, poor guessing with regard to futures contracts, long-term sales agreements where prices are out of sync with the market, and so forth. Companies may argue that invoice value does not reflect market value, because market value would take into account certain expenses, for example, transportation, insurance, and handling to the point of export. In response, some countries have moved to more complicated systems that take into account a hypothetical market value. Governments define market value in a number of ways. For instance, value may be calculated by first determining the amount of the physical mineral contained in the product and then applying a reference price to that amount. Reference prices, such as a London Metals Exchange daily quotation for copper cathode, are available for some but not all minerals. An inherent problem with reference price systems is that quite often what is being sold, such as a concentrate, is not the same product as is being referenced, such as cathode.

The picture becomes more complicated when the value begins to be adjusted to subtract out specified costs, usually not directly related to mineral extraction or beneficiation. The most common adjustment is to deduct from the sales value all costs such as transportation, insurance, and handling that are incurred from the mine site to the point of sale. Another common value is net smelter return, in which the taxable amount takes into account the return to the producer after smelting and refining charges and penalties are taken out.

Profit-based and income-based royalties   Most investors favor taxation systems that are based on the ability to pay, that is, some measure of profitability or adjusted income. Unit-based and value-based royalties do not take into account the relative profitability of an operation because they simply look at the quantity of mineral produced or at some measure of the value of mineral produced or sold. Ad valorem royalties in their purest forms look only at value, although cost-adjusted valuation methods do to some extent account for some non-production-related costs. Distinct from unit-based and ad valorem approaches are a variety of methods that in some way include deducting a broader set of costs, including production and capital costs, in the royalty calculation. Some nations have moved away entirely from assessing royalty and rely instead only on the general income tax (for example, Greenland, Mexico, Sweden, and Zimbabwe do not impose a royalty).

Many nations have applied to royalty assessment the concept of taxation based on the ability to pay. The approaches vary but are grounded in the concept that both the value of the mineral produced and certain allowable costs (such as capital costs, production costs, marketing costs, transportation costs, handling costs, insurance costs) should be taken into account. One commentator described the ideal approach to royalty assessment as follows (Green, quoted in Faber 1977):

> A mineral royalty is a compensation to the owner for the exhaustion of an asset and ideally, therefore, should be fixed at a figure bearing some relation to the value of the mineral as it lies in the ground, i.e., the sale of the mineral recovered less a reasonable charge for the extraction, treatment and transport to the point of sale, sufficient to cover all costs and overheads including a reasonable return on the capital expenditure, together with the provision for the amortization of that capital. (79)

In other words, some tax experts argue, as Green does, that royalty should bear some relation to the concept of rent that is described fully in Chapter 2 of this study.

In practice, the assessment and auditing challenges posed by a royalty based on the concept of resource rent have proved too great, and today few, if any, governments attempt it. However, simpler profit-based or income-based royalty systems have been adopted that include in the calculation the sales revenues less allowable costs but ignore return on capital. Profit-based royalties go by many names, including net profit royalty, net interest royalty, net proceeds royalty, mining tax, and so forth. The problems inherent in any system that requires taking into account both sales or revenues and costs are explained by Harries in his book detailing private party royalty arrangements (1996).

The net profit royalty is complex and often difficult to understand or confirm, requiring a lot of information and often the services of an accounting professional to calculate and confirm it. It is also open to abuse and is often best avoided . . . Conceptually, and if determined equitably by a payor, the net profit royalty is good for all concerned. The recipient will probably receive a relatively large percentage of net profit (when compared to the small NSR percentages) and so may see a high return from a successful venture. He must, however, be prepared to wait to realize this return and to share with the payor in the risks of the venture by permitting the payor to recoup at least a goodly portion of his costs before sharing. He must also be prepared to spend time and money for expert professional advice to be sure that he receives his proper share. Above all, he must be prepared to run the risk that the project, even if it is brought into commercial production by a generous and equitable payor, may never see a "net profit," in which event he will never see a royalty payment. (109)

In agreements between private parties, royalty rates that apply to net profits are usually higher than rates in agreements in which gross sales value or net smelter returns are used as the basis. The same is true for rates set by governments. For example, many governments that impose an ad valorem royalty on copper will apply a rate of between 1 percent and 4 percent (on value), whereas most jurisdictions with a profit-based system will assess at a rate in excess of 5 percent (on profit).

Most governments that assess royalty are risk averse and prefer simple unit-based or ad valorem systems; however, an increasing number of jurisdictions have successfully implemented systems based on various measures of profitability or income. The difference between profit-based systems and income-based systems is largely one of definition. A pure profit-based system will look at sales revenues from a single mine and deduct from those revenues allowed costs that are pertinent to that mine. An income-based system will not limit revenue to product sales but may include other sorts of revenues, such as the sale of a property, and may allow revenues to be aggregated by the taxpayer for all the taxpayer's mines.[5] Statutes that set out profit- and income-based royalty schemes tend to be lengthy and provide lists of what types of revenue qualify as income and what costs can be deducted from income. Such systems are more prevalent in nations with many mines and where a well-trained and well-equipped tax administration has developed.

Hybrid systems   A variety of approaches combine the concept of profitability with value- or unit-based royalties. For example, a measure of profits can be calculated and, depending on that measure—perhaps a ratio of costs to sales revenue, a rate of return, or a ratio of price per unit to a reference price—the ad valorem royalty rate is adjusted up or down. This type of system thus takes into account profitability and distinguishes low-profit mines from high-profit mines, while maintaining a royalty flow from all mines. (For examples of hybrid systems, see the royalty systems for Ghana and in Michigan, in Appendix A1.)

In another hybrid system, the taxpayer calculates both an ad valorem and a profits-based royalty and then pays the higher of the two, or pays both, but in the latter case is able to credit the ad valorem payment against the profits-based royalty liability. In such systems the ad valorem royalty acts as a minimum tax (as in British Columbia and the Dominican Republic).

Royalty Approaches

Most approaches to royalty assessment fall within the three general categories listed above—unit-based, value-based, and profit- or income-based. In addition, within each category are numerous specialized methods that are used to calculate the amount of royalty payable. Table 3.1 lists some of the approaches for establishing the royalty. The table is not exhaustive; other approaches are used as well. Examples of some of these methods are given later in this report, and Appendix A1 contains selected statutes that implement these and other royalty approaches. Some of the terms that appear in the table, for example, *net value*, are widely used but have different meanings depending on the jurisdiction.

Sample Calculations

The previous sections have described a sampling of the various royalty methods used by nations. The variety is large, and even among a single method, such as an ad valorem royalty, the tax basis can vary. How does a royalty of 2 percent of net smelter return compare to 3 percent of the international market value of contained metal? This section includes examples of the various approaches. Nine different types of unit-, value-, and profit-based royalty calculations are calculated below, assuming U.S. currency. The calculations are similar to the royalties calculated in the

Table 3.1. Examples of Royalty Methods and Basis of Calculation

Unit-based royalties

- Units of volume
- Units of weight
- Graduated fee per unit that increases with the number of units produced

Value-based royalties

Basis of mineral valuation

- Gross sales price as billed (invoice value, billed value)
- Gross market value
  - Refiners certificate and a daily international reference price quotation
  - Government official to determine product value
  - International market price to establish value of metal in ore exiting the mine mouth
  - International market price to establish the value of the metal in the product sold
  - International market price to establish the value of contained metal that is recoverable
  - Government to publish the market price from time to time
  - Minister to determine the market value
  - Valuation expert to set the value (diamonds and gemstones)
- Net market value (adjusted for nonproduction costs such as transportation, insurance, and handling)
- Net smelter return (adjusted for smelting and refining and related costs)
- Best price available within an agreed-upon range (sets a floor)

Royalty rate

- Fixed
- Varies according to the level of profit
- Graduated depending on level of cumulative annual production
- Graduated depending on level of cumulative annual sales

Profit- or income-based royalties

- Net value (market value less allowed capital and operating costs)
- Net profit (realized sales value minus allowed capital and operating costs)
- Net income (realized income less allowed capital and operating costs)

Source: Author J. Otto.

mine models in the first section of Chapter 4 of this study, but variations will exist in the metallurgical aspects of each mine. As described earlier, the applicable royalty unit charges and royalty percentages will vary from country to country and across states and provinces.

The rates in this section have been calculated to generate $20 million in royalty revenues for each of the different royalty calculations. Each royalty is based on the following ore deposit characteristics that relate to the following hypothetical nickel deposit:

Ore body:	30,000,000 tonnes of ore
Mill capacity:	2,000,000 tonnes of ore per year
Average ore grade:	2.85%
Mill recovery:	85.00%
Smelter recovery:	97.00%
Price of smelter return:	$12,500 per tonne or $5.67 per pound
International market price premium:	Assume a 2% premium to the stated price per pound
Capital investment:	$1.0 billion over 30 months

When appropriate, depreciation will be $100 million for the period in question.

Operating costs (per tonne of ore)

Mining	$ 7.60
Milling	$11.20
Overhead	$17.20
Freight	$ 4.00

Total operating costs $40.00 per tonne of ore

(1) **Unit-based royalty**: A set fee (assume $0.19303 per pound) assessed per pound of nickel recovered from the smelter, for which the units are calculated as follows:

2,000,000 tonnes
× 2,204.62 pounds per tonne
× 0.0285 pounds per tonne
× 0.8500 mill recovery
× 0.9700 smelter recovery
103,609,424 pounds of nickel

Unit-based royalty
103,609,424 pounds × $0.19303 per pound = $20,000,000

(2) **Ad valorem royalty—net smelter return times percentage**: Assessed as a percentage of net smelter or refinery return (assumed to be 3.4045% in this example). This royalty might also be described as the net smelter return before any adjustments for freight, handling, or other transportation charges.

2,000,000 tonnes
× 2,204.62 pounds per tonne
× 0.0285 pounds per tonne
× 0.8500 mill recovery
× 0.9700 smelter recovery
_____
103,609,424 pounds × $5.67 per pound = $587,465,434

Net smelter return royalty
$587,465,434 × 3.4045% = $20,000,000

(3) **Ad valorem royalty—metal contained in ore at mine mouth, valued at international reference price, times percentage**: Assessed as a percentage (assumed to be 2.7519%) of the value of the nickel contained in the ore, as determined by the average recovery, adjusted for the international market price premium.

2,000,000 tonnes
× 2,204.62 pounds per tonne
× 0.0285 pounds per tonne
_____
125,663,340 pounds × $5.67 per pound
                 × 1.02 premium = $726,761,361

Mine mouth value royalty
$726,761,361 × 2.7519% = $20,000,000

(4) **Ad valorem royalty—metal contained in concentrate at the mill, valued at international reference price, times percentage**: Assessed as a percentage (assumed to be 3.2376%) of the value of the nickel contained in the concentrate, as determined by the weight of the contained nickel times mill recovery times international market price premium.

2,000,000 tonnes
× 2,204.62 pounds per tonne
× 0.0285 pounds per tonne
× 0.8500 mill recovery
_____
106,813,839 pounds × $5.67 per pound × 1.02 market premium = $617,747,156

Percent of market value royalty
$617,747,156 × 3.2376% = $20,000,000

(5) **Ad valorem royalty—metal contained in smelter product, valued at international reference price, times percentage**: Value of the metal contained in the ore after adjustment for average recoverability from both the mill and the smelter, assuming the commodity traded at the market price adjusted for the international market premium (applicable royalty percentage assumed to be 3.3377).

2,000,000 tonnes
× 2,204.62 pounds per tonne
× 0.0285 pounds per tonne
× 0.8500 mill recovery
× 0.9700 smelter recovery
_____
103,609,424 pounds × $5.67 per pound × 1.02 market premium = $599,214,742

Premium net smelter return (NSR) market value royalty
$599,214,742 × 3.3377% = $20,000,000

(6) **Ad valorem royalty—gross sales, less transportation, handling, and freight, times percentage** (applicable royalty percentage of 3.4515):

2,000,000 tonnes
× 2,204.62 pounds per tonne
× 0.0285 pounds per tonne
× 0.8500 mill recovery
× 0.9700 smelter recovery
_____
103,609,424 pounds
    × $5.67 per pound = $587,465,434 NSR (or gross sales)
less 2,000,000 tonnes
    × $4.00 per tonne freight = $8,000,000 freight cost
_____
Royalty basis $579,465,434

Gross sales (less transportation, handling, and freight)
market value royalty
$579,465,434 × 3.4515% = $20,000,000

(7) **Profit-based royalty—percentage of gross sales, less operating costs, transportation, handling, and freight**: Operating profit includes deductions for mining, milling, processing, and mine overhead. It also includes costs such as interest paid, withholding taxes, local taxes, import duties, and reclamation costs (applicable percentage of 3.9412).

2,000,000 tonnes
× 2,204.62 pounds per tonne
× 0.0285 pounds per tonne
× 0.8500 mill recovery
× 0.9700 smelter recovery

103,609,424 pounds	
× $5.67 per pound =	$587,465,434 NSR (or gross sales)
less 2,000,000 tonnes	
× $4.00 per tonne =	$8,000,000 freight cost
less 2,000,000 tonnes	
× $36.00 per tonne =	$72,000,000 operating costs
Royalty basis	$507,465,434

Gross sales (less transportation, handling, freight, and operating costs) royalty
$507,465,434 × 3.9412% = $20,000,000

(8) **Profit-based royalty—percentage of gross sales, less capitalized costs, operating costs, transportation, handling, and freight**: Operating profit includes deductions for mining, milling, processing, and mine overhead. It also includes costs such as interest paid, withholding taxes, local taxes, import duties, and reclamation costs. The basis is reduced by the allowable noncash deductions for depreciation and amortization of tangible and intangible assets. For this example, a sum of $100,000,000 is used to cover the later noncash deductions (applicable percentage of 4.9084).

2,000,000 tonnes
× 2,204.62 pounds per tonne
× 0.0285 pounds per tonne
× 0.8500 mill recovery
× 0.9700 smelter recovery

103,609,424 pounds	
× $5.67 per pound =	$587,465,434 (gross sales)
less 2,000,000 tonnes	
× $4.00 per tonne =	$8,000,000 freight cost
less 2,000,000 tonnes	
× $36.00 per tonne =	$72,000,000 operating costs
less allowable depreciation	
and amortization =	$100,000,000 capitalized costs
Royalty basis	$407,465,434

Gross sales (less transportation, handling, freight, and operating costs) royalty
$407,465,434 × 4.9084% = $20,000,000

(9) **Ad valorem—sliding-scale percentages of NSR:** Based on an increasing, or sliding, percentage relative to the magnitude of value associated with the NSR. If the NSR is less than $100,000,000, a royalty of 1.17% is applied. If the NSR is greater than $100,000,000 but less than $200,000,000, an additional 1.5% is applied (2.67% on incremental $100,000,000) and any NSR value in excess of $200,000,000 has an additional 1.5% applied (4.17% on NSR above $200,000,000).

2,000,000 tonnes
× 2,204.62 pounds per tonne
× 0.0285 pounds per tonne
× 0.8500 mill recovery
× 0.9700 smelter recovery
103,609,424 pounds of nickel

NSR basis for royalty
103,609,424 pounds × $5.67 per pound = $587,465,434

Incremental royalty based on NSR	
$100,000,000 × 1.17% =	$1,170,458
$100,000,000 × 2.67% =	$2,670,458
$387,465,434 × 4.17% =	$16,159,084
Total sliding scale =	$20,000,000

Using an iterative routine, the actual models change the initial percentage, which causes an incremental change in each of the incremental rates.

Table 3.2 summarizes the royalty rate that will yield the identical royalty tax for the nine royalty bases described above. As can be seen in the table, the definition of the royalty basis is critical to understanding the rate. When comparing royalty rates in different jurisdictions, care must be taken not to compare rates unless the royalty base is identical. The calculation here assumes a single year of production and sale of product. If the same calculation were to be performed for a mine over a period of time, the difference between the ad valorem and the profit-based royalty would broaden, that is, the ad valorem–based tax would be higher, because the profit-based tax would not be paid, or would be low, in the early years of the project.

Government and Investor Royalty Preferences

The advantages and disadvantages of the most common types of royalties from government and investor perspectives are listed in Table 3.3.

Table 3.2. Rate Applied to Nine Royalty Bases That Yields $20 Million in Royalty

Royalty tax basis	Rate (% unless noted otherwise)
(1) Unit-based royalty	$0.19303 per pound nickel
(2) Ad valorem—NSR times percentage	3.40
(3) Ad valorem—metal contained in ore at mine mouth, valued at international reference price times percentage	2.75
(4) Ad valorem—metal contained in concentrate at the mill, valued at international reference price times percentage	3.24
(5) Ad valorem—metal contained in smelter product, valued at international reference price, times percentage	3.34
(6) Ad valorem—gross sales, less transportation, handling, and freight, times percentage	3.45
(7) Profit-based—percentage of gross sales, less operating costs, transportation, handling, and freight	3.94
(8) Profit-based—percentage of gross sales, less capitalized costs, operating costs, transportation, handling, and freight	4.91
(9) Ad valorem—sliding-scale percentages of NSR	1.17 / 2.67 / 4.17

Source: Author J. Stermole.

Table 3.3. Evaluation of Royalty Types Using Selected Government and Investor Criteria

Government criteria

Royalty type	Income generation	Stability of revenue flow	Revenue in early years	Administrative ease and transparency	Affects production decisions	Amenable to multi-party distribution
Unit based	Y	Y	Y	Y	Y	Y
Ad valorem	Y	Y	Y	Y, if gross revenue based ?, if market value based	Y	Y
Profit or income based	?, only if profitable	N	N	N	N	Y
Hybrid (minimum ad valorem floor applies if profits are too low)	Y, stable minimum base plus additional profitable	Partial	Y, but modest	N	Y, slight distortion	Y

Investor criteria

Royalty type	Reduces income	Responsive to profitability	Rapid payback	Responsive to market price	Impact on marginal projects	Supports production efficiency
Unit based	Y	N	N	N	Y	N
Ad valorem	Y	N	N	Y	Y	N
Profit or income based	?, only if profitable	Y	Y	Y	N	Y
Hybrid (minimum ad valorem floor applies if profits are too low)	Y, to a degree	Y, mostly	Y, mostly	Y	Y, modest	Y, mostly

Source: Author J. Otto.

Note: Y = meets most related objectives; N = does not meet most related objectives; ? = may or may not meet most related objectives.

Governments and investors have different objectives. Governments favor methods that are stable, transparent, and equitable and that generate continual revenues, are easy to administer, and are amenable to distribution to a variety of governmental entities and stakeholders. Companies, on the other hand, prefer royalty approaches that are stable and predictable, are based on the ability to pay, allow early recovery of capital, respond to downturns in market prices, do not distort production decisions such as cutoff grade or mine life, can be deducted from taxable income for the general income tax, do not add significantly to operating costs, and are amenable to distribution directly to affected stakeholders.

From a government perspective, all forms of royalty have the potential to generate revenue necessary to fund society's needs. Unit-based and ad valorem–type royalties are certain to be paid in all years when production takes place, whereas profit- and income-based royalties will be paid in years with profits or income. Unit-based and ad valorem royalties also satisfy the objective of providing revenue in the early years of a project, whereas a profit or income type probably will not yield a return. Unit-based and ad valorem royalties are also transparent and easy to administer compared with profit- or income-based royalty taxes. This can be a large advantage if the agency responsible for administration is institutionally weak. Governments have an interest in seeing that minerals are mined efficiently; unit-based and ad valorem royalties are neutral in this regard, neither rewarding nor penalizing improved or degraded efficiency. Unit-based and ad valorem taxes can affect marginal undeveloped and operating mines. On one hand, marginal mines can be an important source of employment in remote regions with few other employment options, but they can also pose problems when cash-flow challenges lead to less than optimal operations with regard to health, safety, and the environment. On the whole, most governments favor imposing some sort of royalty, but there are notable exceptions.

It is often stated that private sector investors favor having no royalty or, if one is imposed, having it based on profit or income. This is true in most circumstances. However, because profit and income types of taxes are not always paid, and are almost never paid in the early years of a project, significant pressures can be brought on a mine where an activist population turns hostile because of perceptions that they are being cheated out of an entitlement. In such an environment, at least some companies prefer to see a reasonable ad valorem royalty, particularly if a portion flows directly to the affected parties. In effect, such a royalty reduces overall project risk. Few investors would see any advantage, other than ease of payment, in a unit-based royalty. Unit-based royalties reduce income, are not based on the ability to pay, prolong payback, do not respond to market conditions, and can affect decisions about whether to mine or to continue mining. At best, use of a modest unit-based royalty may be acceptable for low-value bulk commodities if distorting effects are compensated for by very low compliance costs. Ad valorem–type royalties have most of the same disadvantages as unit-based royalties and, depending on how the value basis is determined, also can be difficult to calculate. However, given a choice between a unit-based and an ad valorem royalty, most companies would prefer an ad valorem method because such methods are sensitive to price changes. Clearly, profit- or income-based royalties satisfy most investors' royalty preferences.

Some regimes use a combination of royalty methods. These entail a profit-based royalty that is subject to a minimum level of ad valorem royalty. This system shifts some but not all of the market and competence or operational risk from the developer to government, and it ensures a modest and stable revenue flow to the government irrespective of project circumstances.

The following two sections focus on regulatory royalty issues—administrative efficiency and the role of government departments—followed by examples of administrative structures in selected jurisdictions.

Consideration of Administrative Efficiency

Trade-offs between administrative efficiency and incompatible objectives Sound formulation of royalty policy should take into account and balance a number of fundamental, but in some cases incompatible, objectives. For example, a high degree of incompatibility exists between the objective of achieving economic allocative efficiency and that of administrative efficiency. Administrative considerations are also influenced by the government objective of maintaining stability in government revenue.

In terms of decreasing administrative efficiency, the most common royalties would be ranked as follows:

1. Unit-based royalties based on units of volume or weight
2. Ad valorem royalties based on value of sales
3. Hybrid royalties
4. Profit-based royalties

5. Resource rent–type royalties (no longer used by governments except in the context of petroleum royalties)

By contrast, in terms of economic allocative efficiency, the ranking would be reversed.

Selecting an appropriate royalty system inevitably represents a compromise between these objectives. The choice is influenced by the size and diversity of mining operations, allowing for greater spreading of administrative costs. In addition, the institutional strength of the country's mining regulatory regimes determines the degree of administrative complexity that can be effectively handled without excessive delays.

The costs of administering royalties fall into one of two categories:

• Fixed costs, which are largely independent of the methodology used to calculate the royalty, of the nature and value of the commodity mined, and of the scale of the operation; or
• Variable costs, which are a function of increasing methodological and administrative complexity and of the potential for ambiguity and disputes, which in turn lead to greater effort for compliance and verification by both the company and the government.

Governments that are intent on balancing administrative and economic allocative efficiency must also consider the following:

• The unit price of the commodity mined, which determines the relative importance of projects of similar size in terms of their contribution to revenue and, therefore, the financial consequences of possible errors in computing royalty payable.
• The price volatility of the commodity mined, which affects the stability of government revenue.
• The size of the mining operation, which, if large, lowers the cost of administration per unit of production.

It is thus not by accident that the majority of regimes apply unit-based royalties to low-value bulk commodities, even though such an approach, although administratively efficient, is generally recognized to be the most disruptive in terms of rational economic decisions. Similarly, there is a strong rationale to shift from unit-based to ad valorem royalties in the case of higher-value commodities or large-volume operations. Both of these two methodologies and, to some degree hybrid royalties, generate above-the-line costs for the mining companies. As such, they influence the size of the mining reserves of a project and, consequently, its value and degree of financial feasibility. They also do not take into account the fact that different operations, which are characterized by very different unit costs of production and therefore different cash-flow margins, may have vastly different capacities to pay royalty. Thus, both unit-based and ad valorem royalties discriminate against less-profitable and marginal projects, even though some of these projects could have been, under a less economically disruptive royalty regime, larger producers and employers. Most low-value bulk commodities, such as gravel or aggregate, serve a local market, and the cost of transportation is a major factor. Prices are often set in the local market, so royalty costs can effectively be passed on to customers. Furthermore, having a unit-based royalty is nearly free of costs from an administrative perspective because the royalty base is the same basis as the charge to customers.

As a consequence, regulatory regimes that use predominantly unit-based and ad valorem royalty systems generally feature provisions for royalty relief in case of cash-flow hardship brought about by, for instance, commodity price cycles. As discussed below, from an administrative point of view, relief provisions inevitably are more complex, result in higher compliance costs, and, in extreme cases, have the potential for abuse. Luckily these complexities are relatively infrequent and do not detract excessively from the general simplicity of these royalty systems.

Some regimes, such as that of the Australian state of New South Wales, attempt to alleviate the adverse impact of ad valorem royalties on less-profitable projects. Companies that mine base and precious metals have the option of choosing between a fixed royalty rate or a variable ad valorem royalty rate that increases linearly as a function of increasing commodity prices within a prescribed range. Beyond this range, minimum and maximum royalty rates apply.

Similarly, the large-scale operations in Ghana[6] and the Chinese[7] regimes provide ranges of royalty rates for each mineral, and the rate applicable to any individual project is set by negotiation with the relevant authority with reference to the financial feasibility of each project. The discretionary nature of these processes, together with the required documentation, introduces additional administrative complexity and, as a consequence, compliance costs.

The distribution of royalty methodologies used across the jurisdictions analyzed in this study is heavily weighted toward the unit-based and ad valorem types (see following section comparing royalty systems in selected nations). To the extent that profit-based royalties are generally thought to be less economically disruptive, the question arises as to why they are grossly underrepresented in most regulatory and fiscal regimes. The explanation clearly rests with the fact that profit-based royalties introduce the following:

- Significant additional administrative costs, which mostly relate to the difficulty and ambiguity in correctly determining the profit measure on which the royalty is to be based. The profit measure used is normally different from the traditional financial accounting measure of profit or that used to levy corporate income tax.
- Difficulties in determining the profit base at a project level rather than at a corporate level. The fact that royalties are normally levied at a project level introduces questions as to which corporate items of expenditure should be legitimate deductions in the context of royalties.
- Exposure of risk-averse governments to:
  ○ the vagaries of commodity prices affecting revenue stability,
  ○ the project risk inherent in different mineral deposits,
  ○ inefficient (higher cost) project operators, and
  ○ risk arising from the higher or lower level of technical and managerial competence of various project proponents.

At the extreme, a combination of cyclically low prices and management incompetence could result in state- or publicly owned mineral resources being depleted, possibly for many years, without the government collecting any royalties or income tax. This situation would hardly represent an economically rational use of the resources.

An effective compromise to address this type of issue is the adoption of a hybrid, profit-based royalty that is subject to a minimum floor-specific or ad valorem royalty. The latter is generally payable out of cash flows irrespective of whether the project makes a profit or the magnitude of such a profit (or loss). Examples of this are the royalties applicable to rough diamonds and to vanadium pentoxide in Western Australia.

With regard to profit-based royalties, a range of issues also arise in assessing the deductibility of many indirect costs and noncash items of accrual accounting, particularly if the prevailing income tax regime includes significant accelerated depreciation expenditures. For example, corporate overheads are apportioned to project costs and capital recovery expenses. Theoretically, in an income tax regime that allows generous levels of accelerated depreciation, a project subject to profit-based royalty may avoid paying any income tax and royalty for a number of years during which the project is unprofitable (using financial accounting measures) even though the project may be generating substantial cash flow.

On the other hand, some capital recovery rules used for calculating royalties will spread capital recovery more evenly over time but also include a measure of cost of capital or interest. For example, in the case of the Australian Northern Territory[8] and some Canadian provinces, this takes the form of a sinking fund, which brings about the need to specify appropriate computational rules and rates of interest. The latter will need to vary over time, depending on the prevailing level of inflation, once again adding to complexity, compliance and auditing costs, and the potential for disputes. The Canadian province of British Columbia provides a variation of a minimum tax based on two different profit-based royalties. A 2 percent annual charge on net current proceeds is determined before any allowances for the capital expended on the project. An additional 13 percent rate is applied to net revenue that does allow the deduction of capital costs. The royalty paid on net current proceeds is fully credited against the net revenue tax so that it truly represents a minimum royalty.

Because the profit base on which royalties are levied is generally very different from the corresponding financial accounting profit calculated according to acceptable accounting standards, companies need to keep a separate set of accounts or have special interrogation and reporting routines in their accounting systems to comply with royalty return requirements. Furthermore, many regimes require submission of royalty returns on the basis of periods of one month or less. These short time frames are not conducive to accurate reporting, resulting in constant readjustment for over- or underpayments.

Furthermore, government departments regulating royalties must carry out labor-intensive, meaningful audits of royalty returns, resulting in a significant number of often intractable disputes. In general, governments do not fully appreciate the value added by their royalty auditors and tend to give too few resources to their royalty administration and collection functions. For instance, only six relatively junior officers are employed in Western Australia, where in 2003/04 they collected a total of more than

$A1 billion (about US$760 million) in state royalties and some $A240 million (about US$183 million) in petroleum royalties on behalf of the commonwealth government. As a result, rigorous audits are limited to a sample of very large mining and petroleum projects or to suspicious situations.

Legal costs resulting from royalty audit disputes can be a significant drain on both corporate and government resources. In an increasingly litigious world, this represents a further incentive for governments to select the less ambiguous unit-based and ad valorem royalty systems in preference to the more litigation-prone profit-based systems. It is thus no surprise that profit-based royalties and the purest forms of resource rent taxes are found primarily in very large projects and in the petroleum arena, where projects generate large economic rents and the authority that administers royalty is generally the same as that enforcing the income tax legislation. Under those conditions, the tidiest and least administratively complex way of levying the desired proportion of economic rent would be the application of resource rent tax and no other impost. In practice, few regimes have adopted this policy. In most cases such as Australia's Petroleum Resources Rent Tax, economic rent is extracted through a combination of royalty and income taxes, which are often levied by different, at times poorly coordinated, authorities.

Procedural steps in royalty administration and collection   The process of royalty administration and collection generally entails the following administrative procedures.

1. To the extent that royalties should not discourage downstream processing, the determination of the final mining products subject to royalty (e.g., bulk crushed and screened ore, concentrate, or metal) must be clearly supported by legislation and regulations. This is generally easy for common mine products such as iron ore, copper concentrate, or gold, but it can become extremely complex for other products. For example, in the case of vanadium pentoxide, the final product is neither a concentrate nor a metallic product. Application of a royalty rate based on concentrate or on the value of contained metal would heavily discriminate against the establishment of the product's capital-intensive processing facilities. Royalty regulations are generally unhelpful in resolving this type of situation.

2. The company must submit a royalty return, generally within one month after the end of the production or royalty reporting period, based on mineral production or sales that have occurred in the preceding peri-

od. The reporting period is normally the preceding semester (e.g., China's mineral royalty), quarter (e.g., Australia, Russia[9]), month (e.g., some of China's resource compensation fees, Cuba, Papua New Guinea). In some cases (e.g., China's royalties[10]) a shorter period may apply (e.g., 1, 3, 5, 10, or 15 days).

3. The return must provide details about the quantity (units of volume or weight) of mineral produced, sales prices, and, where deductible, cost of sales, transport, and insurance. In the case of arm's-length transactions, verifying the accuracy of these details is not difficult, because such costs are eventually captured by the relevant invoices. On the other hand, transactions that are not at arm's length may result in significant issues and disputes over both quantities and values. This is typically the case with minerals that are subject to internal transfer to associated companies. Examples include a company that quarries limestone for use as flux in a smelting process or one that transfers rough diamonds to a related cutting and polishing division.

A range of particularly intractable complexities may arise when the final product is a polymetallic concentrate. These complexities may stem from poor assaying and estimating of relevant recoveries to determine what commodity prices should be applied, whereas the royalty would otherwise have been based on realized net smelting returns. To overcome these types of often-protracted disputes, many regimes use discretionary ministerial powers (embodied in the relevant legislation) in making and enforcing determinations as to the amount of royalty payable. Excessive ministerial discretion, however, may open the way to corrupt and, at best, inequitable practices. Exercising discretion in a specific case is often seen as setting a precedent and creates industry expectations that may not be appropriate in other cases, potentially causing resentment. Ministerial discretion is also not always the end of the dispute. Industry commonly seeks alternative interpretations of the royalty regulations and elevates their grievances to higher courts.

In the case of low-value bulk commodities, which often are subject to unit-based royalties, royalty tax is frequently levied within a given period of production, whether sales have taken place during the period or the product has been stockpiled. However, such levies are often difficult without direct measures (e.g., weigh bridges) and good record keeping to validate the declared production volumes. In many cases quantities are worked out on the basis of the original mine plans and surveys, resulting in very approximate measures. On the redeeming side, the cost to government of possible errors or omissions in assessing royalties for low-value bulk commodities can be assumed to be low, and thorough auditing is unwarranted given cost-benefit considerations.

4. Payment of an appropriate amount of royalty must either accompany the royalty return or follow it within a generally short, prescribed period of time. For arm's-length transactions, the amount of royalty payable is generally calculated either on the basis of provisional sales estimates or on the actual value of sales as displayed on the relevant invoices.

Documentary evidence of sales is eventually required by the administrative authority for auditing purposes. Irrespective of the result of audits, particularly in the case of sales of concentrates, any metal price adjustments, credits, penalties, and other contract variations may result in realized sales being different from those on which the original royalty estimates were based, thus requiring royalty adjustments from estimated to actual amounts. Although many regimes have specific provisions for adjustments and corrections, some legislative regimes are silent about such corrections. Their assumption is that the exact amount of royalty must be tendered in the first instance. Once again, ministerial discretion must be invoked to rectify the situation.

For transactions that are not at arm's length or for internal transfers of mineral products to subsidiaries or associated companies, appropriate procedures must be applied for determining the correct amount of royalty payable. This implies determining the actual mineral content or grade of the product, acceptable estimates of the rate of recovery, and an applicable proxy for the market price of either the product or its metal content at the time of shipment. Unless the relevant legislation is clear and specific, these processes can be fraught with ambiguity and potentially lead to significant disputes and delays.

5. A review of royalty rates may become necessary for a number of reasons:

- A new mining project may plan to extract a new commodity that has not yet been subject to royalty.
- Mining may resume for a commodity that has not been mined in the nation for a significant number of years, and the royalty rate of that commodity has been deleted from the relevant schedule in the regulations.
- Government has come to the conclusion that royalty collections, individually or in aggregate, are not in line with the desired proportion of

economic rent that they originally intended to levy or that the proportion has become inadequate in light of evolving events or emerging needs.

• The royalty rates for specific commodities have moved out of line as an effect of inflationary trends.

The first three points are essentially matters of fiscal policy. The underlying question is: What is an appropriate level of impost that achieves the desired balance of the basic economic objective? Very few nations have developed policy statements that clearly quantify the appropriate level of royalty to be levied. Although Western Australia has a policy framework, it is generally cast in terms of a specific percentage of the value at the head frame or mine mouth, which none of the existing royalty regimes could easily achieve at the individual project level without continuous readjustment of royalty rates.

In the final analysis, royalty rates are set in an empirical process that seeks the maximum revenue at the lowest economic and political cost. In this respect the type and frequency of industry-government communication and consultation are critical. Consultation can be formal (such as through advisory boards or professional and industry lobbying groups) or less formal, at the level of individual companies or influential individuals. Governments need to adopt the fundamental principle of "no surprises" if they are to avoid developing a reputation for sovereign risk, thus affecting investment in their countries.

In the short run, mines are captive to their locations, employ few people, and therefore have little influence at the polls; thus, in theory at least, government could levy a larger proportion of economic rents with impunity. However, in the medium and long run they would suffer the severe consequences that investment in mineral exploration and new mine developments would dry up. It also takes a long time to redress a perception of sovereign risk.

The last reason to readjust royalty rates is an interesting one. In the case of unit-based royalties, it stands to reason that the quantum of royalty per tonne, presumably based on the prevailing prices at the time of introduction, would soon get out of kilter during inflationary periods unless market prices fell at the same rate as the corresponding inflation rate. This problem does not arise with any of the other methods for calculating royalties, for which the amount of royalty payable is a direct function of prevailing commodity prices.

As a consequence, unit-based royalties must be subject to review, which can be either occasional or at regular intervals as specified by law (e.g., India). Regardless of their justification, reviews of unit-based royalty rates tend to affect a large number of royalty payers and invariably engender political heat—so much so that ministers are generally reluctant to embark in indexing exercises, and unit-based royalty rates often are allowed to fall grossly out of line.

6. Currency considerations and hedging can also create ambiguity unless the legislation is clear about how to handle them, which is not frequently the case. Essentially, most regimes require that royalties be paid in the national currency, although in some cases they may require royalty payments in the foreign currency in which sales were denominated. It is a normally accepted principle that governments should not expose themselves to risky speculative foreign exchange hedging operations. Most taxation regimes do not allow the deduction of hedging losses in determining taxable income. This principle is generally inferred but not often explicitly stated in royalty regulations. It is generally regarded as the responsibility of company directors to determine to what extent their operations should be exposed to exchange rate volatility by formulating and adhering to a corporate hedging policy.

The situation is not always as clear-cut when it comes to exposure to commodity price volatility and related hedging losses and gains. In practice, because many companies have programs of at least partial forward sales, the degree of government exposure to price risk is determined by whether the value as it appears on the actual sales invoice is used as the base on which to levy royalties.

If the royalty is based not on actual sales but on the amount that would have been received if the minerals had been sold on the spot market, then the legislation must be clear as to what commodity prices need to be applied to assess the value of the minerals sold forward for royalty purposes. This can be a simple process for metallic commodities that are frequently traded on terminal markets, as, for example, the calculation of nickel, cobalt, and gold royalties in Western Australia, where a large proportion typically is sold forward.

It is a vastly different proposition to calculate royalty payable on less common and more infrequently traded commodities, polymetallic concentrates, and nonmetallic compounds in general, for which prices are determined by consumers' value-in-use, are not frequently quoted, and are sometimes even confidential. In spite of everybody's best efforts, significant ambiguity and disputes arise in this area, resulting in considerable delays of royalty collection, particularly in regimes with low ministerial powers of determination and weak penalty provisions for late payment.

7. Appropriate penalties need to be applied for late or nonpayment of royalties. The ways different regimes handle the question of penalties vary significantly. They range from the relevant regulations only having tenement forfeiture and general fines for breach of tenement conditions (e.g., Western Australia), to fairly general provisions (e.g., Papua New Guinea[11]), to excruciatingly detailed and progressively more severe penalty provisions (e.g., China's mineral resources compensation fee regulations, Australia's Northern Territory[12]). If no specific provisions exist, and in cases of prolonged delays or failure to pay, most regimes rely on forfeiture of the relevant mineral title as the ultimate sanction. In one case (Papua New Guinea) a lofty fine or jail sentence or both are envisaged.

In practice, forfeiture is a measure of last resort. Because a mine closure would entail significant loss of economic benefits and jobs, the process is politically risky and tends to be applied only when the company in default is beyond financial salvation. In most other noncompliance cases, a phone call by a senior officer of the relevant regulatory authority informing the company that a formal notice of intent of forfeiture is pending is sufficient to induce payment. Company executives know that news spreads like wildfire when a formal notice of forfeiture has been issued, and if their company is listed, they must notify the stock exchange, with a disastrous effect on their company's share price. In general, forfeiture of title does not relieve the company of the liability to pay overdue royalties and does not preclude the state's pursuing normal debt recovery processes.

Where specific penalty provisions are in force, they generally take the form of a penalty rate of interest on the outstanding amount, with generally both the interest rate quoted and the penalty compounded on a daily basis. Under some jurisdictions (China's mineral resources compensation fee) the rate of penalty interest is subject to successive increases after the expiry of prescribed periods or in cases of serious default and, in particular, of deceiving behavior. At the extreme, the penalty may blow up to multiples of the outstanding amounts. Seizing of mineral products is in some cases advocated as a possible penalty until the situation is rectified.

In the majority of cases, where royalty tax is administered and collected by the department of mines, penalty provisions are specific to the mining industry and incorporated in the relevant mining acts and related regulations. In some jurisdictions, however, such as the Philippines,[13] where provisions for royalty administration and collection are contained in their internal revenue codes, penalty provisions for late or nonpayment of royalty are generally in common with those relating to default on all other forms of fiscal imposts, such as income tax. This is a rather undesirable state of affairs, as the royalty-collecting authority (in the Philippines the Tax Office) has little knowledge of and empathy for the unique characteristics and needs of the mining industry, particularly of its capital-intensiveness and volatility due to high cash flows

8. Royalty incentives, or relief by way of deferral or reduction of royalty, or exemption from royalty, may also be applied, on a temporary or indefinite basis, in special cases or in case of hardship.

The cyclical nature of commodity prices, combined with the above-the-line impact of specific and ad valorem royalties, can result in severe variations in the level of the annual cash flows produced by a project. If cash flows become negative, the operation is in no position to pay royalties unless its shareholders inject equity funds to cover them. Unfortunately, when companies fail to pay royalties, they are also generally unable to pay other major creditors and are often close to insolvency. Under these circumstances, shareholders are generally unwilling to contribute additional equity. Most of the regimes make provisions for deferral of, and in some cases exemption from, royalty payment.

In most African countries the usual practice is for mines to apply for deferment or reduction of royalties when they experience financial hardship. It is also possible in some nations, for example Ghana, to negotiate a special royalty regime for extraordinary investments. Namibia went as far as to make provision for the refunding of royalties upon application to the minister of finance.

Exemption from royalties is generally infrequent. In China,[14] partial exemption can be obtained for the first few years when investing in the underdeveloped northwestern provinces, in new mining technology, or in marginal projects. By contrast, in most Australian states, deferral, but not exemption, is generally allowed. This is achieved by extending the payment due date, thereby delaying forfeiture action to allow the outstanding royalties to be paid. To qualify, a company must demonstrate that its cash flows are negative and that it does not have sufficient funds to make the royalty payment by the due date. Periods of deferral are generally short (a few months), because the presumption must be that the cash flow difficulties are temporary and capable of being overcome. In practice, many companies do not apply for royalty deferral prospectively but seek it once they actually experience cash-flow problems. Though many operations recover, some do not and end up under administration or in liquidation. The seniority of the royalty debt is not clear in all regulatory regimes, but it is assumed to rank after income tax and before all other creditors. This is primarily because the regulatory authority can prevent the transfer of mining titles that are in default for nonpayment of royalty to a third party if the administrator or liquidator attempts to put in place a scheme of arrangement or to liquidate the company assets.

Shareholders tend to see the responsibility of bailing out companies with cash-flow difficulties as the government's rather than their own and use political pressure and threats of mass retrenchments as their strategy to force government's hand. Administering royalty relief is generally a complex and politically delicate process, because government has to gauge the benefits of maintaining operations and employment against the possibility that things may get worse—the debt and the economic and political cost of an eventual mine closure may increase with time. In addition, the assistance provided through the royalty system is not transparent and for this reason is not favored by some governments.

Most, but by no means all, legislative regimes include regulations and guidelines for addressing these administrative steps. Where the relevant regulations are not sufficiently specific, the administrative authorities, to make the necessary determinations, must rely on discretionary powers conferred by the law on the relevant minister. Although some ministerial discretion is essential, excessive discretionary powers are undesirable, as they may open the way to abuse, controversy, and, at the extreme, corrupt practices.

Role of Government Departments with Regard to Administration, Collection, and Apportionment of Royalties

Whether the government system of a nation is a federation (e.g., Australia, Canada, Malaysia, the United States) or not, nations are generally governed at three levels: central or federal; state, province, or autonomous region; and region, county, locale (regency, shire, city, etc.), or community. There is no consistency, however, among different nations as to which level of government is empowered to manage mineral resources and to legislate and administer royalties.

The simplest administrative systems are found where both legislative and administrative powers are centralized. This is the case for most developing countries, such as most African states, Papua New Guinea, and Mongolia. In other cases, policy-formulation and legislative powers may rest at a higher (generally central) level of government than that handling administration and collection of royalties. For instance, in China and India[15] royalty policy and legislation are in the ambit of central government, whereas administration of the relevant acts and collection of royalties are decentralized mostly at the state and provincial or lower levels of government, respectively.

Extremes of decentralization have been set in Indonesia where, with the introduction of the Regional Administration Law,[16] companies no longer deal with the central government for matters relating to royalty administration. Instead they deal with the relevant provincial government and with several (of some 330) regencies and municipal or city authorities that may be relevant to their project area. There is evidence of a clear and urgent need for institutional strengthening of these administrative structures.

In some federations, such as in all states of Australia, Canada, and Malaysia, the central or federal government has little or no constitutional role in managing land and resources. As a result, provisions for mineral royalties are embodied in a number of different state mining acts and related regulations drafted by state legislators and passed by the individual states' parliaments. In most cases, however, the central or federal governments have undisputed power over offshore mineral resources and over territories under federal jurisdiction (such as Canada's Northwest Territories), and in some cases they have power over strategic minerals, for example, uranium. This does not mean that federal or central governments cannot exercise any power over matters of resources management, but that power is generally exercised indirectly, often through their constitutional power to control imports and exports, customs and excises, foreign investment, exchange rates, and, increasingly, environmental and indigenous affairs.

In Argentina,[17] although management of mineral resources is a role delegated to the provinces (which therefore legislate on and administer royalties), the central government has the power to set a cap on the maximum royalty rate that can be applied (currently 3 percent).

To the extent that the royalty legislation in various states or provinces is different, including different royalty rates and computational methodologies for different minerals, federal systems of government generally result in a very complex and inconsistent conglomerate of regimes at the national level.

Examples of Administrative Structures in a Cross-Section of Nations
The issue of whether royalties are to be considered taxes or, alternatively, compensation for the right to exploit community resources is in many ways intimately involved with the type of institution empowered with the administration and collection of royalties.[18]

Appendix A3, which provides details of the administrative arrangements in a cross-section of nations, shows how policy formulation and administration of royalties may be primarily the task of the following entities:

- The Ministry of Finance, Treasury, and related taxation authorities, or
- The Ministry for Mines, in consultation with the above institutions, or
- Integrated natural resources management and economic planning and development departments.

In the case of Bolivia, China (in the context of royalties but not of the mineral resources compensation fees), Cuba, Nevada (U.S.), Peru, the Philippines, and South Africa, royalties are viewed as excise or complementary taxes, and relevant provisions are embodied within their fiscal codes; however, formulation of royalty policy is dominated by their ministries for finance, and the administration and collection of royalties by the relevant internal revenue or taxation authorities.

By contrast, in nations where royalties are viewed as compensation for the right to exploit state resources, the royalty regime is generally based on the mining acts and related regulations, and the relevant department of mines or equivalent is empowered with their enforcement and administration. In most cases, administration of royalties is carried out in close consultation with the relevant ministry of finance and treasury and other departments concerned with planning, trade, and economic development.

In some cases, such as in Argentina, Michigan (U.S.), Peru, Saskatchewan, and some Australian states, economic planning and development, trade, and resources management are handled by a single megadepartment in an attempt to bring about greater coordination and to cut down on the time required for development approval and implementation. Under such regimes, and particularly in mineral economies, the relevant minister for mines tends to have significant influence in the cabinet and strong political support from industry. Not surprisingly, industry views the department of mines as better informed about the special characteristics and needs of the mining industry and therefore as better attuned to the task than departments dealing with fiscal issues in general.

From an administrative point of view it is also pertinent to consider whether royalties are appropriated in full by the level of government empowered with their collection or whether they are remitted in part or in full to a higher or lower level of government.

The mode of appropriation is also important: royalties may go to the general fund of the state treasury (the *fiscus*) to fund the state's normal budgetary processes, or they may be earmarked for specific applications. Under this system, regions or communities in which mines are located and from which royalties have been raised must compete for budgetary allocations through the normal political processes. This may generate a measure of resentment and political pressure in the regions hosting the mines, which derive no special benefit and, in some cases, may even be disadvantaged by them. In the second system, royalties are "hypothecated," or earmarked; that is, they are allocated to the exclusive benefit of a specific region or community or even to fund specific initiatives, whether at the state, regional, or community level. In the absence of other regional wealth redistribution mechanisms (e.g., Australian Grant Commission process), this approach may result in significant, and at times politically undesirable, disparity in the wealth and standard of living of different parts of a nation.

Appendix A4 gives a general indication of how royalty revenue is appropriated in different nations. The various patterns of revenue distribution and their socioeconomic consequences are also discussed in greater detail in Chapter 5.

Comparison of Royalties in Selected Nations

Royalty Types and Rates in Selected Nations

This section provides a synopsis of royalties in selected nations, organized by the following regions: Africa, Asia and Pacific, Australia, Latin America, and North America. In addition to the summary tables (Tables 3.4–3.8), a brief regional description is provided. Additional detail is provided in Appendix A1, which describes the royalty system for each country and includes extracts from laws and regulations, where available. The information presented in the tables and Appendix A1 should be used with caution. Governments frequently amend tax laws; care should be taken to verify that reported information is current (to aid in this process,

Appendix A1 includes Web sites, where available). The tables indicate the legal origin of royalty (national law, provincial law, or negotiated agreement); the predominant type of royalty imposed on nonindustrial minerals, the range of ad valorem royalty rates, if applicable; whether different mineral types are taxed at different rates, with examples for copper, gold, limestone, and coal; whether mine scale affects the royalty calculation; and whether there is a means to defer or exempt a mine from royalty liability. Royalty rates for minerals other than copper, gold, limestone, and coal can be found in Appendix A1.

Africa   The following observations have been made on royalty systems in African countries:

1. In most African nations, it is standard practice to include royalties as part of the legal framework. Most African nations impose some form of royalty. Two notable exceptions are South Africa and Zimbabwe. South Africa is poised to pass a royalty bill; a draft royalty bill[19] was released in 2003, and the second draft is ready for release as this study goes to press. Zimbabwe is reportedly considering imposing royalties.

2. Many African countries that impose ad valorem–type royalty taxes allow some costs to be deducted from sales revenue when determining the royalty base. It is necessary to allow some discretion in determining which costs may be deducted. These deductions are influenced by policy objectives. For example, countries that want to stimulate the local value added of minerals introduced NSR-type royalties, which allow smelting, processing, and refining costs to be deducted, in addition to off-mine transport and other costs. It is also regarded as important to ensure first that the sales value meets the arm's-length principle, and second that the law allows the minister to intervene when sales prices do not reflect those of unconnected parties in the market.

3. Ad valorem royalty rates vary from 0 to 12 percent for the selected countries. Low or zero royalty rates are not necessarily an investment incentive in Africa. Zimbabwe is a case in point. Despite its zero royalty rate, other factors make investment unattractive: the gross domestic product (GDP) is declining, inflation is out of control, the political situation is not stable, the president exhibits a hostile approach to foreigners, and investment in many sectors has been withdrawn on a large scale.

4. Most countries with older mining laws have different royalty rates for different minerals. This variation flows from national sovereignty issues in which some minerals are perceived as being more important to the host nation. Zambia and Ghana[20] have moved away from this approach by standardizing their regimes across all mineral types. Although standardization is desirable, making frequent changes to the rate when market conditions change may discourage potential future investors concerned about such instability. Ghana has overcome this problem by introducing a sliding-scale mechanism whereby highly profitable ventures pay at a higher ad valorem royalty rate than others, allowing for both flexibility and predictability.

5. Although it is not standard practice to design different royalty regimes for different scales of investment, it seems that holders of artisanal and small-scale (ASM) mining rights are treated differently. This is mostly because of the difficulties associated with formalizing the sector. Zambia's approach, of including royalties in the annual rent of ASM producers, seems like a sensible example of taxing the sector appropriately.

6. Standard practice in the selected countries allows for deferment or reduction of royalties in difficult times. Such a decision in Tanzania and Zambia is linked to the operating margin, and Ghana's sliding-scale royalty principle automatically allows for the reduction of royalties (the only consideration is to decide whether the range of 3 to 12 percent is fair for marginal and loss-making operations).

Asia and Pacific   The following observations have been made on royalty systems in Asia and Pacific countries:

1. The Asia-Pacific region encompasses a rich diversity of nations with widely different cultures and governing systems. In some nations (e.g., China, Malaysia, and Pakistan) provincial governments play an important role in mineral sector administration; in others the central government takes the lead.

2. All Asia-Pacific nations examined in this study levy some sort of royalty, with the prevalent forms being unit-based (mainly for industrial minerals) and ad valorem–based royalty. Ad valorem rates tend to be low, typically 2–3 percent for base metals. The value basis varies from

Table 3.4. Summary of Royalty Practices in Selected African Countries

	Botswana	Ghana	Mozambique	Namibia	South Africa	Tanzania	Zambia	Zimbabwe
Format	National law	National law and negotiated agreement acts	National law	National law	Guidelines	National law	National law	None
Royalty type (nonindustrial minerals)	Ad valorem (NSR)	Ad valorem (sales revenue)	Ad valorem (sales revenue)	Ad valorem (sales revenue)[a]	Variable	Ad valorem (NSR)	Ad valorem (NSR)	n.a.
Royalty rate	3–10%	3–12%	3–12%	5–10%	Variable[b]	0–5%	2%	0%[c]
Variation: Minerals	Yes Precious stones: 10%; precious metals: 5%; other minerals or mineral products: 3%	No Same royalty system for all minerals	Yes 10–12% for diamonds; 3–8% for all other minerals; rate established through negotiation	Yes Uncut precious stones: 10% of market value; dimension stone: 5% of market value; other minerals: max. 5% of market value	Yes Sliding-scale formula for gold; other minerals variable % of either market value or net profit	Yes Diamonds: 5%; cut and polished gemstones: 0%; building materials: 0%; all other minerals: 3%	No Same royalty system for all minerals	n.a.
Copper	3% ad valorem on adjusted gross market value	3–12% ad valorem, graduated on operating ratio	Negotiable within 3–8% ad valorem, on market value	5% ad valorem, on market value	Negotiated within guidelines	3% ad valorem on free on board (FOB) or NSR	2% ad valorem on net back value (NSR)	No royalty, but sometimes applicable in special cases

(continued)

Table 3.4. (continued)

	Botswana	Ghana	Mozambique	Namibia	South Africa	Tanzania	Zambia	Zimbabwe
Gold	5% ad valorem on adjusted gross market value	3–12% ad valorem, graduated on operating ratio (3–4% fixed in recent agreements)	Negotiable within 3–8% ad valorem, on market value	5% ad valorem, on market value	Negotiated within guidelines	3% ad valorem on FOB or NSR	2% ad valorem on net back value (NSR)	No royalty, but sometimes applicable in special cases
Limestone	3% ad valorem on adjusted gross market value	3–12% graduated on operating ratio	Negotiable within 3–8% ad valorem, on market value	5% ad valorem, on market value	Negotiated within guidelines	0%	2% ad valorem on net back value	None
Coal	5% ad valorem on adjusted gross market value	3–12% graduated on operating ratio	Negotiable within 3–8% ad valorem, on market value	Up to 5% ad valorem, on market value	Negotiated within guidelines	3% ad valorem on net back value	2% ad valorem on net back value	None
Variation: Mine size	No	No	Yes ASM exempt	No	Yes[d]	No	Yes[d]	n.a.
Deferment /Reduction	Yes[e]	Yes	No	Yes[c]	No	Yes	Yes	n.a.

Source: Authors, based on information provided in Appendix A1.

Note: n.a. = not applicable. ASM = artisanal and small-scale; NSR = net smelter return, that is, value at the mine gate.

a. The act makes provision for an alternative definition to be negotiated and included in the mineral lease agreement.

b. The royalty rate depends on the base; the percentage increases when more costs can be deducted. The discretionary system will be abandoned upon promulgation of the (currently draft) royalty bill.

c. This situation may change in the future following a series of statements by President Mugabe aimed at "Africanizing" Zimbabwe's mineral resources.

d. Different regime for small-scale sector; small-scale miners are exempt.

e. At ministerial discretion, *other* costs can be deducted before calculating the royalty amount.

country to country but typically looks to a market value rather than an invoice value.

3. Some of the nations in the region that have significant small-scale mining industries provide for specialized taxation of those miners.
4. Although some nations allow deferment or reduction of royalties, or both, in difficult times, many do not.

Australia   The following observations have been made on royalty systems in Australia and its provinces:

1. Most royalties are levied at the provincial level.
2. The royalty systems tend to be highly detailed, with different minerals being subject to different valuation methods or rates. Most provincial- (state-)levied royalties are unit or ad valorem based; however, one state, Northern Territory, has moved to a profit-based system.
3. Western Australia imposes higher royalties on raw minerals (ore) than on products with value added (metal) in an effort to induce local processing.
4. Some states allow for deferment or reduction of royalties; others do not.

Latin America   The following observations have been made on royalty systems in Latin American countries:

1. Two of the most important mineral-producing nations in the region, Chile and Mexico, do not impose royalties, and in Argentina, some provinces do not.
2. Nations imposing royalties rely mainly on ad valorem–based systems, have "reasonable" rates, and tend to distribute them to mandated parties instead of adding them into the central treasury.

North America   The following observations have been made on royalty systems in North American countries:

1. Most Canadian jurisdictions levy a tax on mines based on profits or net revenue. Calculation procedures are complex compared with procedures under most ad valorem or unit-based systems and generally allow for special processing allowances to encourage further processing within the province or territory. Most commodities are

Table 3.5. Summary of Royalty Practices in Selected Asian and Pacific Countries

	China	India	Indonesia (7th generation COW)	Mongolia	Myanmar	Papua New Guinea	Philippines
Format	National law	National law	Model agreement	National law	National law	National law	National law
Royalty type (most non-construction minerals)	Two types: 1. Royalty: unit based plus 2. Mineral resources compensation fee: ad valorem based	Ad valorem or unit based	Unit based	Ad valorem	Ad valorem	Ad valorem	Ad valorem
Ad valorem rate range	1: Various ranges for each mineral, expressed in yuan/tonne ore, plus 2: 1–4% depending on mineral	0.4–20.0%	n.a.	2.5%, except placer gold at 7.5%	1.0–7.5%	2.0%	2.0%
Variation: Minerals	Yes, 1: Ranges of unit charges for each mineral, plus 2: ad valorem rate for each mineral	Yes, Ad valorem rate or unit-based charge for each mineral	Yes, Unit-based rate for each mineral	No, Except gold	Yes, Gemstones: 5.0–7.5%; precious metals: 4–5%; industrial minerals: 1–3%; other minerals: 3–4%	No	No, Except coal

(continued)

Table 3.5. (continued)

	China	India	Indonesia (7th generation COW)	Mongolia	Myanmar	Papua New Guinea	Philippines
Copper	2% ad valorem plus 0.4–30.0 yuan/tonne ore	3.2% ad valorem of London Metals Exchange value of copper in ore	< 80,000 tonnes, US$45.00 per tonne; (80,000 tonne, US$ 55.00 per tonne	2.5% ad valorem on sales value	3 to 4% ad valorem, inter-national refer-ence price	2% NSR	2% ad valorem on market value
Gold	4% ad valorem plus 0.4 to 30 yuan/tonne ore	1.5% ad va-lorem; London Bullion Market Association price of gold in ore	If from placer 7.5% ad valor-em; otherwise 2.5% on sales value	4–5% ad valorem, international reference price	2% realized FOB	2% ad valorem on market value	
		< 2,000 kg, US$225/kg; >2,000/kg, US$235/kg					
Limestone	2% ad valorem plus 0.5–20.0 yuan/tonne or yuan/m³ ore	55 rupees/ tonne	< 500,000 tonnes: US$0.14/tonne; (500,000 tonnes: US$0.16/tonne	2.5% ad valorem on sales value	1–3% ad valorem, international reference price	2%	2% ad valorem on market value
Coal	1% ad valorem plus 0.3–5.0 yuan/tonne	65 to 250 rupees/tonne	13.5% FOB or of sales revenue	2.5% ad valorem on sales value	—	2%	10 pesos/ tonne

(continued)

Table 3.5. (continued)

	China	India	Indonesia (7th generation COW)	Mongolia	Myanmar	Papua New Guinea	Philippines
Variation: Mine size	Yes, Unit-based royalties set mine-by-mine	No	Yes, Different rates for miners with COWs than miners with mining law licenses	No	No	No	Yes, Special treatment of small-scale operations
Deferment /Reduction	Yes	No	No (under most COWs)	No	Yes	No	No

Source: Authors, based on information provided in Appendix A1.
Note: — not available; n.a. not applicable; FOB = free on board.

Table 3.6. Summary of Royalty Practices in Selected Australian Jurisdictions

	New South Wales	Northern Territory	Queensland	Western Australia
Format	Provincial law	Provincial law	Provincial law	Provincial law or negotiated agreement act
Royalty type (nonindustrial minerals)	Ad valorem[a]; but profit-based royalty in the Broken Hill District	Profit based (% of net back value)	Ad valorem or unit based	Mostly ad valorem or unit based, and profit based or hybrid for diamond and Vanadium
Royalty rate (most nonindustrial minerals)	4–7% ad valorem	18%	2.7% of value, or a variable royalty rate if price exceeds a reference price	2.5–7.5% ad valorem
Variation: Minerals	Yes, Coal: 5–7%; industrial minerals $A 0.35–0.70/tonne; other minerals: 4%	No	Yes[b], Most metallic minerals: 2.7% of value or a variable royalty rate; industrial minerals: $A0.25–1.00/tonne; coal: 7%	Yes[c], Metallic: metal 2%; concentrates 5%; ore 7%, depending on degree of processing; industrial minerals: generally $A0.30–0.50/tonne
Copper	4% ad valorem on value minus allowable deductions	18% on net back proceeds less production and other costs	2.7% of value or a variable royalty rate if price exceeds a reference price	Concentrate: 5% of royalty value; metal: 2.5% of royalty value
Gold	4% ad valorem on value minus allowable deductions	18% on net back proceeds less production and other costs	2.7% of value or a variable royalty rate if price exceeds a reference price	2.5% of invoice value minus deductions such as transport value

(continued)

Table 3.6. (continued)

	New South Wales	Northern Territory	Queensland	Western Australia
Limestone	$A0.40/tonne	18% on net back proceeds less production and other costs	$A 0.30/tonne	$A 0.30/tonne
Coal	5–7% ad valorem	18% on net back proceeds less production and other costs	7% of value	7.5% of value if exported
Variation: Mine size	No	Yes, Mines with net back value less than $A50,000 are exempt	Yes, Generally if sales are less than $30,000 the producer is exempt	No
Deferment /Reduction	Yes, Discretion is very limited	No	Substantial reductions allowed if base metals are processed in the state	Yes

Source: Authors, based on information provided in Appendix A1.

a. Several special cases deviate from the norm. See Appendix A1 for details.

b. Special rates apply to bauxite, mineral sands, oil shale, phosphate, silica, and some other minerals. See Appendix A1 for details.

c. Information in the table is general. For details on any mineral see Appendix A1.

Table 3.7. Summary of Royalty Practices in Selected Latin American Countries

	Argentina	Bolivia	Brazil	Chile	Dominican Republic	Mexico	Peru	Venezuela, R. B. de
Format	Provincial law	National law	National law	None	National law	None	National law	National law
Royalty type (nonindustrial minerals)	Most provinces: no royalty; others: ad valorem	Ad valorem, sliding scale based on ratio	Ad valorem	n.a.	Ad valorem, creditable against income tax	n.a.	Ad valorem, sliding scale based on annual cumulative sales	Ad valorem
Royalty rate	0–3%	1–6% based on sales price position relative to reference price bands	0.2–3.0%	n.a.	5% of FOB export	n.a.	0–3% (exported mineral 1–3%; if no international price 1%; small scale 0%)	3–4%

(continued)

Table 3.7. (continued)

	Argentina	Bolivia	Brazil	Chile	Dominican Republic	Mexico	Peru	Venezuela, R.B. de
Variation: Minerals	No	Yes	Yes, 1: Aluminum ore, manganese, salt, phosphorus: 3%; 2: iron, fertilizer, coal, and remaining minerals: 2% (except for 3); 3: precious stones, diamonds, and noble metals: 0.2%; 4: gold: 1%	n.a.	No, Unless there is a negotiated agreement or minerals are not exported	n.a.	No	Yes, Gold, silver, platinum and its associated metals: 3%; diamonds and precious jewels: 4%; other minerals: 3%
Copper	Catamarca: 3% ad valorem on sales value less allowable deductions	1–5% ad valorem: reference bands not known	2% ad valorem on sales value less commercial taxes, transportation, and insurance	None	5% ad valorem, FOB export	None	Up to US$60 million 1%; from US$60 to US$120 million 2%; over US$120 million 3% on gross value	3% of commercial value

(continued)

Table 3.7. (continued)

	Argentina	Bolivia	Brazil	Chile	Dominican Republic	Mexico	Peru	Venezuela, R.B. de
Gold	Catamarca: 3% ad valorem on sales value less allowable deductions	More than US$700: 7%; $400–$700: 0.1% of price; below $400: 4%	1% ad valorem on sales value less commercial taxes, transportation, and insurance	None	5% ad valorem, FOB export; if not exported, no royalty	None	On gross value: up to US$60 million: 1%; US$60–120 million: 2%; over US$120 million: 3%	3% of commercial value
Limestone	Catamarca: 3% ad valorem on sales value less allowable deductions	3–6% ad valorem: reference bands unknown	2% ad valorem on sales value less commercial taxes, transportation, and insurance	None	25% ad valorem, FOB export; if not exported, no royalty	None	If not exported: 1%	3% of commercial value
Variation: Mine size	Catamarca: No	No	Yes, Sales by Garempeiros are exempt	n.a.	No	n.a.	Yes, Cumulative revenue slides the rate	No
Deferment /Reduction	Catamarca: No	If sold for domestic use royalty is 60% of the normal royalty	No	n.a.	No	n.a.	No	Yes, Can reduce the rate to 1%

Source: Authors, based on information provided in Appendix A1.

taxed at the same rate and tax basis within any given jurisdiction. Graduated rates are applied in some jurisdictions; others have minimum profit thresholds above which a uniform rate of tax applies. In Ontario, new mines are offered a three-year tax holiday, subject to a Can$10 million limit on taxable profits. Remote mines in Ontario are taxed at half the rate of other mines and are given a 10-year tax holiday subject to the same Can$10 million limit on taxable profits. Saskatchewan offers the most diversity in royalty assessment, with a general profit-based system for most metallic and nonmetallic minerals and a sales-based royalty for uranium, potash, and coal.

2. Mine taxation in the United States is highly complex and is often tied to the type of land where minerals occur—federal, state, Native American, or private land—and to the mineral type. Because the mineral estate can be severed from the surface estate in some cases, determining the appropriate party is not always straightforward. The federal government does not levy royalty tax on most minerals in federal lands (with important exceptions, such as coal obtained through bidding). States often levy royalties on minerals in state-owned lands. These are usually ad valorem or unit-based approaches, although profit-based systems are also used. Nevada applies a sliding-scale rate based on net proceeds, with a floor value to implement the highest rate. Michigan has flat rates for coal and limestone but sliding-scale rates for metallic minerals.

Examples of Selected Royalty Types and Rates as Defined by Law

Governments that impose a royalty have a variety of methods to choose from, with the principal approaches being unit based, value based, or profit or income based. Hybrid systems that combine several methods are also in use. Each of these approaches has a number of choices for calculating the royalty basis (Otto 1995). The characteristics of a variety of assessment methods and examples drawn from historical and current laws and agreements are provided below.

Selected examples of unit-based royalties   The examples provided are intended only to illustrate the methods used. In some cases, the laws and agreements from which the examples have been extracted have been amended, repealed, or terminated. For current royalty legislation in selected nations, see Appendix A1 on the CD.

Table 3.8. Summary of Royalty Practices in Selected North American Jurisdictions

	Arizona (U.S.)	British Columbia (Canada)	Michigan (U.S.)	Nevada (U.S.)	Northwest Territories (Canada)	Ontario (Canada)	Saskatchewan (Canada)
Format	Provincial law	Provincial law	Provincial law	Provincial law	National regulations	Provincial law	Provincial law
Royalty type (nonindustrial minerals)	Ad valorem	Profit based (net revenue) and ad valorem (net proceeds)	Ad valorem; sliding scale	Profit based (net proceeds); sliding scale	Profit based; sliding scale	Profit based	Mixed ad valorem and profit based
Royalty rate	At least 2%, commissioner to determine rate	13% (of net revenue) or 2% (of net proceeds)	2–7% sliding scale	2–5% sliding scale	5–14%	10%	5% of net profit (increases to 10% with life-time production thresholds)
Variation: Minerals	Yes	No	Yes	No	No	No	Yes
Copper	At least 2% of market price	More than 13% of net revenue less 2% of net proceeds, or 2% of net proceeds	2–7% of adjusted sales value	5% of net proceeds (above US$4 million per year)	5–14% of output value	10% of defined profits	5% of net profit (increases to 10% with life-time production thresholds)
Gold	At least 2% of market price	More than 13% of net revenue less 2% of net proceeds, or 2% of net proceeds	2–7% of adjusted sales value	5% of net proceeds (above US$4 million per year)	5–14% of output value	10% of defined profits	5% of net profit (increases to 10% with life-time production thresholds)

(continued)

Table 3.8. (continued)

Limestone	At least 2% of market price	More than 13.0% of net revenue less 2% of net proceeds, or 2% of net proceeds	5% of sales value	5% of net proceeds (above US$4 million per year)	5–14% of output value	10% of defined profits	5% of net profit (increases to 10% with life-time production thresholds)
Coal	At least 2% of market price	More than 13% of net revenue less 2% of net proceeds, or 2% of net proceeds	7% of sales value	5% of net proceeds (above US$4 million per year)	5–14% of output value	10% of defined profits	15% of gross sales adjusted by resource allowance
Variation: Mine size	Yes, Commissioner to set rate	No	No	Yes, Highest royalty rate paid on mines above US$4 million in net proceeds	Yes, Operations with incomes below Can$10,000 pay no tax	Yes, Operations with incomes below Can$500,000 pay no tax	Yes, Uranium operations eligible for small-producer credit
Deferment/ Reduction	No	No, But losses can be carried forward	No	No	No	Yes, Mines in remote regions enjoy substantial reduction; tax holiday for first Can$10 million in profits for mining tax subject to three-year maximum period in non-remote areas and 10 years in remote areas	Yes, Capital recovery based on 150% of expenditures

Source: Authors, based on information provided in Appendix A1.

Example of a unit-based royalty (weight calculated based on mine mouth production)

6. On lignite, 1 1/2 d. a ton[ne] mined
7. On coal, other than lignite, six shillings a ton[ne] mined[21]

Example of a sliding-scale unit-based royalty (weight calculation based on mineral content or actual total weight sold)

Annex F Royalty on Mineral Production[22]

No.	Mineral	Total production per calendar year	Unit	Royalty tariff per unit (US$)	Weight basis
5	Copper	< 1,250 ˆ 1,250	Tonne	70.00/tonne 78.00/tonne	Contained metal in the product sold
9	Gold	< 2,000 ˆ 2,000	Kg	225.00/kg 235.00/kg	Contained metal in the product sold
19	Chromite	< 15,000 ˆ 15,000	Tonne	0.35/tonne 0.45/tonne	Weight of concentrate sold
27	Bauxite	< 200,000 ˆ 200,000	Tonne	0.40/tonne 0.50/tonne	Weight of ore sold

Note: Should a mine exceed the quantity cutoff, it pays the lower royalty tariff on the amount up to the cutoff and the higher royalty tariff on all production above that cutoff.

Example of a unit-based royalty (weight based, calculated on the basis of exported shipments)

Royalty is payable at the rate of 1s 6d per long ton (2,240 lb.) of bauxite exported.[23]

Example of unit-based royalty (weight based, calculated on the basis of exported shipments, sliding scale)

Royalty: Payable annually on all shipments of titanium bearing and associated minerals as follows:

Leones 3 per tonne on the first 25,000 tonnes,

Leones 4 per tonne on the next 25,000 tonnes,

Leones 5 per tonne on any amount in excess of 50,000 tonnes.[24]

Selected examples of value-based royalties

Example of ad valorem royalty based on value of mineral contained in ore at the mine mouth

12. Copper   Three point two per cent of London Metal Exchange Copper metal price chargeable on the contained copper metal in ore produced.[25]

Example of ad valorem royalty based on recoverable mineral

5. The mineral resources compensation fee is calculated in the following way: Mineral resources compensation fee = sales income times rate of compensation fee times coefficient of recovery rate

• Coefficient of recovery rate = appraised recovery rate/actual recovery rate, where appraised recovery rate is the rate determined during mine design according to national regulations; according to national regulations if there is only a mining plan without a mine design, the appraised recovery rate is determined by the Geology and Mineral Resources Administration in conjunction with other relevant administrations at County or higher levels of government. For other mineral types where [the] mineral resources compensation fee cannot be calculated in the way mentioned above, other ways of calculating the mineral resources compensation fee are decided by the Geology and Mineral Resources Authority in conjunction with Finance Authorities within the State Council.[26]

In many nations the value of the mineral for royalty purposes is adjusted by deducting certain allowable nonproduction costs from the sales revenue.

Two examples of an ad valorem "cost-adjusted" royalty

104. Interpretation of Part XI.
In this part unless the contrary intention appears –
"f.o.b. revenue" means
(a) in the case of a delivery of mine products made pursuant to sale by the miner, other than a sale to which paragraph (b) of this definition applies, the whole of the consideration receivable by the miner for the mine products less the costs, charges and expenses bona fide incurred or suffered by the miner in respect

of them from the time when the mine products are loaded on board a ship or aircraft in the country until the mine products are delivered to and accepted by the purchaser including, without limiting the generality of the foregoing –

   i.   taxes, dues, duties, excise, tariffs and other levies imposed on the export of the mine products from the country, and

   ii.   trimming costs, and

   iii.   ocean freight, and

   iv.   marine insurance premiums, and

   v.   port and handling charges at the port of discharge, and

   vi.   delivery costs from the port of discharge to any place for the purpose of further processing, and

   vii.   weighting, sampling, assaying, inspection, representation and selling agency costs and charges, and

   viii. shipping agency charges, and

   ix.   tax, dues duties, primage duties, tariffs and other levies imposed in country of port of discharge on the import of the mine products, and

      . . .

"net smelter return" means –

  (a) in the case of a miner who is also a processor in the country the value of the products of his smelter or his smelter and refinery, as the case may be, less the costs, charges and expenses bona fide incurred or suffered by the miner in respect of those products from the time when the mine products are delivered to a smelter until the time when the smelter or refinery products are delivered to and accepted by the purchasers, including, without limiting the generality thereof –

   i.   smelting and refining costs that may include a reasonable profit element but that shall be no greater than amounts that are or would be charged to any other person for the smelting or smelting and refining, as the case may be, of similar mine products, and

   ii.   realisation costs, and

   iii.   the costs itemised in the definition of "f.o.b. revenue" to the extent they are payable by the miner in respect to the transporting of the smelter or refinery products to the point of delivery to the purchaser; and . . .

105. Royalty.

Notwithstanding Section 202, every miner shall pay to the State royalty at the rate of 1.25% of the value of –

(a) the f.o.b. revenue applicable to deliveries of mine products by the miner pursuant to sales or other dispositions where the mine products are directly or indirectly for export from the country; and

(b) the net smelter return applicable to deliveries of mine products where the mine products are smelted or smelted and refined in the country.[27]

66. (1) The holder of a large-scale mining licence shall, in accordance with his licence, this Act and the terms of any relevant development agreement, pay to the Republic a royalty on the net back value of minerals produced under his licence at the rate of three per centum.

(2) In this section-

"net back value" means the market value of minerals free-on-board at the point of export from Zambia or, in the case of consumption within Zambia, at the point of delivery within Zambia, less–

(a) the cost of transport, including insurance and handling charges, from the mining area to the point of export or delivery; and

(b) the cost of smelting and refining or other processing costs, except such other processing costs as relate to processing normally carried out in Zambia in the mining area;

"market value" means the realised price for a sale free-on-board at the point of export from Zambia or point of delivery within Zambia.[28]

Example of an ad valorem "price-adjusted" royalty

Artículo 98.- La alícuota del Impuesto Complementario de la Minería se determina de acuerdo con las siguientes escalas:

- Para el oro en estado natural, amalgama, preconcentrados, concentrados, precipitados, bullón o barra fundida y lingote refinado
- Cotización oficial del oro ALICUOTA (%)
- Por onza troy (CO) (en dólares americanos)
- mayor a 700.00 7
- desde 400.00 hasta 700.00 0.01 (CO)
- menor a 400.00 4[29]

Unofficial translation

For gold in its natural stage, its amalgamates, preconcentrated, concentrated, stud, its sweeps, smelted and refined, and ingot

Price per troy ounce in U.S. dollars Higher than $700: 7% $400–700.00: 0.01% of price; below $400: 4%

Example of an ad valorem "sliding scale" royalty based on cumulative sales

Art 5°.- Ranks for the payment of the mining royalty
The ranks for the payment of the mining royalty are over their concentrating value or its equivalent:

a) first rank: up to US$60 million annually, pays 1%.
b) second rank: for higher than US$60 million up to US$120 million annually, pays 2%.
c) third rank: for over US$120 million annually, pays 3%.[30]

Profit- and income-based royalties   Governments seeking to attract mineral sector investment may wish to consider a royalty based solely on profit or income. Most investors will prefer a profit-based royalty to one based on production or sales value. Generally, if a government plans to adopt a profit- or income-based system, it may want to consider a higher royalty rate than would be selected if the royalty basis is strictly revenue. The higher rate is justified, given that royalties will begin to be generated later in the project and may be absent in times of low prices. Of key importance is the need to carefully define what constitutes "revenues" and "allowable deductions from revenues" when determining the profit or income basis. If such deductions are already defined for determining income tax, a government may want to simply reference the appropriate income tax provisions to calculate royalty. The government could consider assessing the royalty based on taxable income as calculated for income tax (a type of surcharge). The main objections that may be raised regarding the latter approach would be problems arising from ring fencing principles, and the recognition that mining is a specialized business, and the cost treatment of exploration, development, depreciation, and so forth may require special treatment.

The examples below show three approaches that use profitability or income as part of the criteria for determining royalty. In the first example, the diamond royalty in Botswana, the approach is a straightforward, defined percentage of profit. The second example is from a private party agreement and provides an itemized list of what may be deducted from income. The third example, from British Columbia, illustrates the income-type royalty approach that is used by most Canadian provinces. In each example, production costs are included in the calculation. It should be noted that both Botswana and the Canadian provinces have sizeable mining industries that attract foreign investment.

Example in which realized profit is used as the royalty basis

Additional Diamond Royalties

54 (1) In addition to such royalties as may be payable in terms of section 53 the State shall be entitled to one-quarter of the annual realized profits from the working of any diamond pipe, and such one quarter shall be paid within six months of the termination of the financial year of the holder of the mining right.

(2) For the purposes of sub-section (1) the realized profit shall be the excess of revenue from the sale of diamonds over expenditure, including capital expenditure, incurred in working the pipe and in the production and realization of diamonds. If there is a loss in any one year, it shall be carried forward as an addition to expenditure in the following year.

(3) For the purpose of sub-section (2) "expenditure" shall include such expenses as may be prescribed.[31]

Detailed accounting rules, as are required for profit- or income-based taxes, are familiar to oil-producing governments that use production sharing agreements (PSAs). Such agreements usually contain lengthy descriptions of which costs are allowed and which are not allowed for calculating the basis for the government share. The following language, drawn from a private party mining royalty agreement reported by Harries (1996), illustrates how cost allowances can be specified with regard to mining.

Example of "net profit" definition

(a) "Net profit" shall be calculated for each year after the right to receive the Royalty has arisen and means the aggregate of the revenues received during such year from or in connection with carrying on the business relating to mining, milling and/or other treatment of any ores or concentrates and/or marketing of any Product resulting from operations upon the Property including, without limitation, any cash proceeds received upon the sale of capital assets in the ordinary course of such business or upon, or in anticipation of, the termination of such business or from the investment of moneys retained with respect to such operations, less:

(i)   all or part of the aggregate amount (if any) by which operating costs for any prior year or years exceed such revenues received during such prior year or years;

(ii)   the aggregate of all operating costs allocable to such year;

(iii)   the aggregate of all preproduction expenditures incurred by a Property Owner until deducted in full;

(iv)   such amount as may be required to maintain working capital at an amount considered by the Operator to be advisable in order to carry on operations on the Property in a proper and efficient manner;

(v)   reserves for contingencies which are confirmed by the auditors of the Operator to be reasonable in the circumstances;

(vi)   the aggregate cost (or reserves contemplating such cost) of any major improvement, expansion, modernization and/or replacement of mine, mill or ancillary facilities until deducted in full (for the purposes hereof, a major improvement, expansion, modernization or replacement is one which involves an aggregate cost of more than $500,000, lesser amounts being considered to be part of the operating costs);

(b)   "operating costs" means, for any year, the amount of all expenditures or costs (other than those expenditures or costs herein excepted and those that have been included as preproduction expenditures hereunder) incurred in connection with carrying on the business related to the mining, milling and/or other treatment of ores or concentrates and/or marketing any Product resulting from operations upon the Property, including, with limitation, the following costs:

(i)   all costs of or related to the mining, crushing, handling, concentrating, smelting, refining or other treatment of such ores or concentrates, the handling, treatment, storage or disposal of any waste materials and/or tailings arising with respect thereto, and the operation, maintenance and/or repair of any mining, milling, handling, treatment, storage or ancillary facilities related to the carrying on of such business or the use of any property, asset, process or procedure with respect thereto;

(ii)   all costs of or related to marketing any Product, including, without limitation, transportation, commissions and/or discounts;

(iii)   all costs of or related to taking to lease and/or maintaining in good standing or renewing from time to time the Property and/or the taking of any steps considered advisable by the Operator or a Property Owner to acquire, protect or improve any interest of a Property Owner in the Property and/or in properties or property rights considered by the Operator or the Property Owner necessary or advisable for the purposes of carrying on such business;

(iv)   all costs of or related to providing and/or operating employee facilities, including housing;

(v)   all duties, charges, levies, royalties, taxes (other than taxes computed upon the basis of the income of any of the parties hereto) and other payments imposed upon or in connection with such business or the carrying on of such business or any related business by any government or municipality or department or agency thereof;

(vi)   all reasonable cost and fees payable for providing technical, management and/or supervisory services (including to the Operator);

(vii)   all costs of or related to financing arrangements relating to operations upon the Property and/or bringing the same into commercial production, including, without limitation, the payment of interest (including interest as set forth in paragraph 6.07 hereof) and/or standby or other fees;

(viii) all costs of consulting, legal, accounting, insurance and other services or protection in connection with the carrying on of such business;

(ix)   all amounts expended in doing work;

(x)   all costs of construction, equipment, mine development after commencement of commercial production, including maintenance, repairs and replacements, except capital expenditures relating to a major improvement, expansion, modernization and/or replacement of mine, mill or ancillary facilities;

(xi)   all costs for pollution control, shutdown or any other similar costs incurred or to be incurred as a result of any governmental regulations or requirements (including reasonable reserves relating to such costs);

(xii) any royalties or similar payments made to any third party (save for the Royalty);

(xiii) any costs or expenses incurred or estimated to be incurred relating to the termination of such business, including, without limitation, disposal of assets, termination of employees, reclamation and rehabilitation;

(c) "preproduction expenditures" means the aggregate of all cost (whether capital or otherwise) incurred after the date upon which the right to receive the Royalty arose and related to the exploration or development of the Property and/or the bringing of the Property into commercial production, and/or the construction of facilities and/or services (whether located on or off the Property) related thereto, including, without limitation

(i) all amounts expended in doing work but only until the Property has been brought into commercial production;

(ii) all costs of or related to the construction of any mine or mill buildings, crushing, grinding, washing, concentrating, waste storage and/or disposal and/or other treatment facilities and/or any facilities ancillary thereto;

(iii) all costs of or related to exposing and mining any orebody or orebodies situated in whole or in part on the Property, but only until the date upon which the Property is brought into commercial production;

(iv) all costs of or related to the construction of storage and/or warehouse facilities; the construction and/or relocation of roads; the acquisition and/or development of waste and/or tailings areas and/or systems;

(v) all costs (including the costs of acquiring and transporting thereof) of or related to transportation facilities for moving ore, concentrates and/or any products derived therefrom, electric power including power lines and equipment, water pipelines, pumps and wells or any other utilities;

(vi) all costs of or related to employee facilities, including housing;

(vii) all costs of or related to the supplying of management, marketing, supervisory, engineering, accounting or other technical and/or consulting services or personnel, whether to the Operator or otherwise;

(viii) all costs of or related to taking to lease and/or maintaining of the Property in good standing and/or the taking of any steps considered advisable by the Operator or a Property Owner to acquire, protect and/or improve any interest a Property Owner may have or acquire in the Property and/or in properties or property rights considered by the Operator or a Property Owner to be necessary or advisable for the purpose of carrying on such business, but only until the date upon which the Property is brought into commercial production.

(ix)   All costs of or related to feasibility, marketing, economic, reclamation, rehabilitation and/or technical evaluations, plans, studies or reports.

(x)   All costs of consulting, legal, insurance, marketing and other services in connection herewith, but only until the date upon which the Property is brought into commercial production.

(xi)   All costs of or related to financing arrangements relating to bringing the property or any part thereof into commercial production, including, without limitation, the payment of interest ... and/or standby or other fees or charges, but only until the date upon which the Property has been brought into commercial production.

Most Canadian provinces have successfully replaced traditional ad valorem and other royalty tax types with a tax based on net income. In some provinces the tax is termed a royalty, but in others it has a different name. In effect, it is a specialized income tax that uses a different income and deduction scheme than used by the general federal income tax. Extracts from the British Columbia statute are shown below. Income-based royalties are similar to profit-based royalties but are not necessarily tied only to mineral sales. For example, the sale of a property might be included in income.

Example in which net income is used as the royalty basis

... "income" includes

(a)   the gross amount received or receivable as the product of capital, labour, industry or skill,

(b)   all money earned and all gratuities and annuities, and

(c) all income, fees, revenue, rent, interest, dividends or profits arising from any source, including the federal, British Columbia and
municipal governments

but nothing in paragraphs (a), (b) and (c) is to be construed as limiting the generality of any other of those paragraphs;

Imposition of tax on net income from mining operations

2 (1) As provided in this Act and for the raising of a revenue for Provincial
purposes, every owner of a mine is to be assessed and taxed on the
owner's net income derived from mining operations.

(2) For the purposes of determining net income derived from mining
operations, any income derived from the acquisition, storage or transportation of materials used in the manufacturing of mineral ore or
processed mineral ore into any product must be included.

(3) If the net income for the fiscal year exceeds
(a) in the case of the fiscal year being a full year, $50 000, or
(b) in the case of the fiscal year being less than a full year, the proportion of $50 000 that the number of days in the fiscal year bears to
the number in the full year,

the tax must be assessed, levied and paid at the rate of 12.5% of the
entire net income.

. . .

Determining net income for tax purposes

4 (1) The net income derived from mining operations must be ascertained
for the purposes of taxation by deducting from the total net income
of a taxpayer from all sources all of the following:

(a) the net income, if any, derived from dividends, interest or other
similar payments from stock, shares, bonds, debentures, loans or
other similar investments;

(b) the net income, if any, derived by the taxpayer from, and attributable in accordance with sound accounting principles to, the
carrying on of a business or derived from and so attributable to a
source other than mining operations, and other than as a return
on investments mentioned in paragraph (a);

(c) an amount by way of return on capital employed by the taxpayer in processing or manufacturing mineral ore or products

derived from it, equal to 8% of the original cost to the taxpayer of the depreciable assets including machinery, equipment, plant, buildings, works and improvements, owned by the taxpayer and used by the taxpayer during the fiscal year in the processing or manufacturing of mineral ore or products derived from it, but the amount to be deducted under this paragraph must not be less than 15% nor more than percentages, not exceeding 70%, prescribed by or calculated in accordance with regulations, of that portion of the total net profit remaining after deducting the amounts specified in paragraphs (a) and (b);

(d) the net income, if any, derived from mining operations outside British Columbia.

. . .

Determining total net income for taxation purposes

5 (1) For the purposes of section 4, the total net income of the taxpayer must be ascertained by deducting from the taxpayer's gross income all expenses incurred in its production, but no deduction by way of expenses must be allowed for any of the following:

(a) disbursements not wholly, exclusively and necessarily laid out or expended for the purpose of earning the income;

(b) an outlay, loss or replacement of capital or a payment on account of capital or any depletion or obsolescence;

(c) the annual value of property used in connection with the business, except rent actually paid for the use of the property;

(d) amounts transferred or credited to a reserve, contingent account or sinking fund, except the amount for bad debts as is allowed at the discretion of the minister;

(e) carrying charges or expenses of unproductive property or assets not acquired for the purposes of the business or of a liability not incurred in connection with the business;

(f) an allowance for depreciation, except the amount as is allowed at the discretion of the minister for depreciation of vehicles, machinery, plant and buildings used in the production of the income if the depreciation has been actually charged by the taxpayer to the taxpayer's profit and loss account;

(g) a loss or expense recoverable under an insurance policy or contract of indemnity;

(h) the domestic or personal expenses of the taxpayer and the tax-payer's family;

(i) the net loss, if any, incurred in any business referred to in section 4 (1) (b) or (d).[32]

Hybrid system-based royalties   Some nations combine attributes of profit-based and ad valorem–based systems. The following two examples, from Ghana and Jamaica, use a measure of profit in order to establish the parameters of the ad valorem royalty. Ghana uses a ratio of costs to revenues to determine which ad valorem rate to apply.[33]

Example of royalty in which profit ratio is used to determine the ad valorem sliding-scale royalty rate

Payment of royalty

1. Every holder of a mining lease shall be liable to pay royalty to the Republic in respect of his mining operations at the rate specified in the Schedule to these Regulations.

Variation of rate of royalty

2. (1) The rate of royalty payable under these Regulations shall be based on the profitability of the mining operations.

(2) Such profitability shall be determined by the application of the operating ratio, being the ratio as expressed in terms of percentage which the operating margin bears to the value of the minerals won from the mining operations during the yearly period.

(3) For the purpose of determining the operating margin of any mining operation, the operational cost shall be deducted from the total value of minerals won from such mining operations.

3. . . . "Operational Cost: in relation to any period means –

a. the current expenditure wholly and exclusively incurred by the holder of the mining lease during that period for the purpose of mining, transporting, processing or sale of minerals won; provided that such current expenditure shall not include -

i. any royalty payable under these Regulations;

ii. any income tax or other tax on profit whether imposed in Ghana or elsewhere;

iii. any payment under any agreement between the Republic and any person on the value of, or receipts from, minerals won;

iv. in the case of a company any expenditure incurred in respect
of the management and control of the company which in the
opinion of the Commissioner are not directly related to the
operations of mining, transporting, processing or sale of the
minerals won;

(b) capital allowances for the period deductible under the provisions
of section 26 of the Minerals and Mining Law, 1986 (P.N.D.C.153)

. . .

(c)

Operating Ratio	Rate of Royalty
(i) where the operating ratio is 30% or less	3%
(ii) where the operating ratio is more than 30% but less than 70%	3% plus 0.225 of every 1% by which the operating ratio exceeds 30%
(iii) where the operating ratio is 70% or more	12%

Example of profit-based royalty in which profit is used to determine both the ad valorem royalty basis and rate

In Jamaica, except for bauxite and clay, royalty was payable as follows[34]

(i) where yield is not greater than 15% of value, 5% of yield;

(ii) where yield is greater than 15% of value, but is not greater than
30% of value, 5% of yield plus 1/5% of yield for each increase
of one unit in the percentage of yield to value above 15% of
value;

(iii) where yield is greater than 30% of value, 8% of yield plus 2/5%
of yield for each increase of one unit in the percentage of yield to
value above 15% of value.

Provided that where the royalties payable aforesaid in any year is
less than 1/2% of value, royalties payable shall be 1/2% of value.
For the purpose of the foregoing
"value" means -

(a) the actual amount paid to the mining lessee for the mineral
at the mine; or

(b) where the Minister is satisfied that such amount is not a fair
valuation having regard to the current price of the mineral on
leading world markets, either:

   (i) the value determined by the Minister by agreement with the mining lessee; or

  (ii) in default of such agreement the value determined by the Minister having regard to the current price of the mineral on leading world markets.

"yield" means the amount obtained after deducting from value the permitted expenditures and amortisation allowances.

"permitted expenditure" means such sum as the Commissioner of Mines is satisfied the mining lessee has expended for the purpose of mining, treating and transporting the product, but excluding

  (a) any interest paid on borrowed capital; and

  (b) any head office expense (including staff salaries), Director's remuneration, dividend distribution costs and rent incurred whether within or outside Jamaica;

"amortisation allowance" means an allowance to amortise expended capital by the reducing balance method being 25% per annum on both expended capital not amortised in the previous year and such additional capital, if any, expended since the previous year.

In other words, the Jamaican royalty was calculated as a percentage of the sum of the value of the minerals sold in a given period less allowable costs, including mining costs incurred during that period. To ensure that some royalty is paid in times of high costs and low prices, a minimum royalty is substituted based on the value of minerals sold without taking costs into account.

Example of hybrid system where highest of ad valorem or profits-based royalty is payable

In another hybrid system the taxpayer calculates both an ad valorem and a profits-based royalty and pays the higher of the two, or pays both but receives a credit in the amount of the ad valorem royalty as an offset against the profit-based royalty. The following example is from British Columbia, Canada.

2 (1) A person who is an operator must, for each mine of which that person is an operator, pay a tax in respect of each fiscal year of the mine equal to the aggregate for that mine of the following:

  (a) the amount, if any, by which 13% of the net revenue of the operator derived from the operation of the mine exceeds the aggregate of

(i) the balance of the cumulative tax credit account at the end
of the immediately preceding fiscal year of the mine,

(ii) the amount of imputed interest determined under section
3(b) for the current fiscal year of the mine, and

(iii) the amount determined under paragraph (b);

(b) 2% of the net current proceeds of the operator derived from the
operation of the mine for the current fiscal year of the mine.[35]

Example of royalty as income tax deduction or credit

In almost all nations imposing royalty, such royalty is allowed as a deduction when computing income subject to income tax. However, some nations allow royalty to be directly credited against the amount of income tax payable. The following example is from the Dominican Republic.

> ARTICLE 120.- The five percent (5%) royalty on export may be credited against the payment of the income tax of the same fiscal year. Any excess of the royalty over the income tax of a given year may not be credited against the payment of the income tax of successive years.[36]

In summary, policy makers have many royalty methods to choose from. Simple methods, such as unit-based royalties, are fairly easy to administer. Ad valorem methods are able to differentiate between the intrinsic value of the minerals being sold, but determining the value basis can pose a challenge. Companies prefer methods that are based on profitability or income, and although these methods are the most difficult to administer, they reduce the probability that a mine may close prematurely and permanently during a short-term price downturn, thus reducing long-term tax revenue.

Royalty Exemptions and Payment Deferral

The specter of a mine closing because of a short-term cash-flow situation, such as may result from a natural disaster, strike, commodity price reduction, or other circumstance, should be of concern to taxation policy makers. In particular, mineral prices are cyclical, reflecting the changes in demand that occur as demand rises and falls. In times of low prices, newly discovered deposits may not be developed and existing marginal operations will come under pressure to close down. This process is how the marketplace keeps a balance between supply and demand. Royalty methods that are not based on income or profitability may aggravate a cash-flow problem, resulting in permanent closure. However, governments may have socially important reasons for partially insulating an operation from the market or for deferring royalty payments or exempting a marginal mine from royalty liability, both of which temporarily diminish cash flow, in order to keep the mine operational. For instance, a marginal mine may be the major employer in a district or essential to that district's economy, and by forgoing the royalty, the nation may be able to preserve jobs and lessen costly economic impacts. It should be noted that royalty systems that are based on profitability or income do not need to provide for a deferment or exemption option.

Although the power to grant royalty relief was common in most earlier mining laws, it is less common in newer ones. This may reflect a recognition that such discretionary power is subject to abuse and that once a temporary exemption or deferral has been granted, it may be politically difficult to remove it. Examples from a variety of nations are provided below.

Two examples of the power to grant a temporary royalty liability exemption to a mineral title holder

20. The Ministry may – . . .
    (b) exempt in whole or in part, any royalty payable on any mineral by the holder of a permit for such period as may be determined with a view of promoting production of mineral . . .
    (d) defer payment of royalty due for such period it may determine.[37]

55 . . . (3) The Minister may remit wholly or in part the royalty payable on any specified mineral or specified deposit of minerals for such period as he may determine whenever he deems it expedient to do so in the interest of the production of such mineral or as an inducement to the commencement or continuation of mining operations:
Provided that where the State does not hold the mineral rights such remission shall not be made save with the consent of the holder of the mineral rights.[38]

Two examples of temporary deferral of royalty

15(3) The Minister may defer payment of royalty on any mineral for a specific period as in his discretion becomes necessary, by publication in the Gazette.[39]

22(3) Notwithstanding the provisions in subsections (1) and (2), the Secretary may in consultation with the Secretary for Finance and Economic

Planning and on the advice of the Minerals Commission defer wholly or in part the royalty payable on any mineral for such period as he may determine where he is satisfied that it is in the national interest and in the interest of the production of such mineral so to do.[40]

Example in which a specific operation or locality is exempted from royalty

86B. Tenement within Carnarvon Irrigation District

Notwithstanding regulation 86(2) the holder of a mining tenement within the Carnarvon Irrigation District established under section 28(1)(a) of the Rights in Water and Irrigation Act 1914, is exempt from the payment of royalty on sand obtained from that mining tenement. . .

86D. Exemption in respect of certain clay, gravel, limestone, rock or sand

Notwithstanding regulation 86, the holder of a mining tenement who uses in the course of mining operations clay, gravel, limestone, rock or sand which is not —

(a) sold; or

(b) used for processing or manufacturing purposes,

is exempt from the payment of royalty in respect thereof.

86E. Exemption in respect of rock for the Eyre Highway

Notwithstanding regulation 86, no royalty is payable on rock sold by Central Norseman Gold Corporation Ltd to the department principally assisting the Minister to whom the administration of the Main Roads Act 1930 is committed in the administration of that Act, where that rock is to be used in the upgrading of the Norseman section of the Eyre Highway.[41]

Example in which the amount of royalty payable can be reduced

86F. Royalty relief

(1) If the Minister is satisfied in a particular case that there are circumstances justifying royalty relief, the Minister may determine that in that case the rate of royalty payable —

(a) under regulation 86, for any mineral produced or obtained while the determination is expressed to apply;

(b) under regulation 86AA, for gold metal produced while the determination is expressed to apply; or

(c) under the Mining (Ellendale Diamond Royalties) Regulations 2002, for diamond obtained while the determination is expressed to apply, is to be on the basis of a portion only, as specified in the determination, of the royalty base. . . .

(3) In this regulation —

"circumstances justifying royalty relief" means circumstances that meet criteria for the giving of royalty relief that the Minister has published in the Gazette; . . .

"royalty base" means —

(a) in the case of gold metal, the realised value of the gold metal in respect of which the rate of royalty is payable;

(aa) in the case of diamond obtained from the Ellendale mining lease as defined in the Mining (Ellendale Diamond Royalties) Regulations 2002, anything by reference to which those regulations fix the rate of royalty payable for that mineral;

(b) in the case of any other mineral, anything by reference to which regulation 86 fixes the rate of royalty payable for that mineral.[42]

In recognition that the collection and analysis of specimens and samples are necessary parts of establishing whether or not there is economic ore, the taking of specimens and samples are either automatically or by administrative decision exempt from royalty. The following examples are from Nigeria and Ghana.

Two examples of discretionary exemption for minerals taken as specimens and samples

15(2). The Minister may reduce or waive royalty on any mineral which the Minister is satisfied is being exported solely for the purpose of analysis or experiment or as a scientific specimen, not being in greater quantity than in his opinion is necessary for that purpose.[43]

22(4) Samples of minerals required for assay, analysis or other examination may be exempted from liability for royalties at the discretion of the Secretary.[44]

Determination of the Rate and Type of Royalty Imposed in Jurisdictions

Effect of mineral, mine size, or deposit type on royalty types and rates   As evidenced by the summary of royalty systems in the world (Appendix A1), the only common thread among royalty types is "variability." This variability extends to different minerals, deposit types, and mine size. Furthermore, variability across jurisdictions can occur within countries as well, where individual states or provinces may have constitutional rights to impose royalties on mineral production. In this sense, individual jurisdictions within countries are competing for investment. In Canada, for example, changes to mining tax and royalty rates in one province often lead to changes in other provinces competing for the same exploration and development investment. Australia provides other examples in which the royalty rates vary significantly across states and commodities. For instance, the royalty rate on gold production varies from 4 percent in New South Wales to 0 percent in some states.

With respect to variation in royalty rates, commodities with high unit values, such as diamonds and other precious stones, have a general tendency to carry higher charges. On the other end of the spectrum, many countries will exempt small-scale or artisanal miners from paying royalties. In general, the cost of administering and collecting royalty payments on these operations is perceived to be higher than the economic benefits. Even in countries where small mining operations are highly regulated, operators may be given a break on royalty payments. For example, many Canadian provinces charge no mining taxes on operations that record a minimum threshold of income during the tax year.

Correlation between royalties and a lack of diversity in the mineral sector of a jurisdiction   Across the jurisdictions considered in this study, no apparent connection exists between either type or rate of royalties and the diversified nature of the mineral economy. Highly diversified mineral producers such as Mexico have no royalty charges, whereas others such as Australia and Canada have complex and highly variable royalty structures. In jurisdictions where mineral production is focused on commodities with a high unit value such as diamonds, royalty rates are generally higher, but there is no evidence to suggest that this is the result of the lack of diversity of mineral production.

Likelihood of lower or higher royalties in countries with world-class mines World-class mines are exceptionally high quality mines that fall in the upper decile of discounted value for all mines of a specific deposit type. Thus, certain porphyry copper mines in Chile, uranium mines in Saskatchewan, sedex deposits in Australia, gold deposits in Peru, and nickel mines in Russia would be considered world-class. Although there is no apparent systematic trend—Chile and Mexico, for instance, currently impose no royalty for exceptional deposits, whereas Australia, Canada, and the United States do—special royalty agreements are often negotiated on the basis of unique deposits. In Australia, for example, separate royalty agreements have been negotiated between owners and states for the development of exceptionally big or rich deposits—for example, Olympic Dam, Mount Isa, and Broken Hill. This practice is common in African nations that have relatively small economies but large mines (for example in Angola, Botswana, Democratic Republic of Congo, Ghana, and Namibia). In Canada, Saskatchewan has developed special royalties for commodities in which the province has a major competitive advantage from an endowment perspective: potash and uranium. Again, the richness and size of deposits in this jurisdiction allow the governments to capture a higher share of the profits (rents) from the deposit.

Relationships between broader economic indicators and royalty types and rates across countries With respect to the type of royalty imposed within given jurisdictions, it has been noted in previous sections of this study that nations with well-developed tax administrations tend to use either profit-based systems or complex systems in which different minerals are subject to different royalty rates and valuation methods. In contrast, many nations with less-developed tax administrations apply simpler systems that are uniform for all minerals within defined categories. Thus, to the extent that economic measures such as per capita GDP are broadly indicative of the complexity of the tax systems in a given jurisdiction, a correlation can be expected between the economic well-being of a country and the type of royalty structure.

Royalties imposed by governments on mining operations are usually only part of the overall taxation on mineral deposits. Income taxes, withholding, and any number of local and mandated taxes are imposed as well. So, although mining royalties make mining operations stand out

from other types of economic activities in the same jurisdiction, the royalty rate needs to be considered in the context of overall level of taxation
and the base against which the royalty rate is applied. Is a 2 percent ad
valorem royalty more onerous than a 4 percent net profits royalty? This
question is difficult to answer because in reality each mineral deposit is
different and the tax system will affect it differently. The only way to
really compare across jurisdictions is to look at a range of deposits and
commodities on the basis of the overall level of taxation or on their effective taxation rate. Royalty rates are one determinant of the overall level
of taxation.

As part of an analysis of mining countries' competitive position, Otto,
Cordes, and Batarseh (2000) determined the effective rate of taxation for
gold and copper models in 24 jurisdictions based on a range of discount
rates. At a zero discount the effective tax rate varied from less than 40
percent to more than 90 percent of before-tax profits. This section attempts to correlate these effective tax rates with broader measures of
economic activity in the various jurisdictions. Figure 3.1 plots effective
tax rates against per capita GDP for the 24 jurisdictions. The GDP values
indicate that mining takes place in jurisdictions covering a wide range in
economic well-being. It is clearly shown in the figure, however, that the
effective rate of taxation is not linked to the relative wealth of the country as measured by per capita GDP. This lack of correlation suggests that
no systematic tendency exists for poorer nations to have a higher or lower incidence of taxation in their mineral industries. Figure 3.2 plots the
effective tax rate in a country against the mineral industry's contribution
to the overall economy. The idea is to see if there is a correlation between
the importance of the mining industry in the economy and the overall
incidence of taxation. Again, no correlation, either positive or negative, is
exhibited by the points in the figure, which suggests that countries where
mining is a major contributor to economic activity do not systematically
exhibit higher or lower rates of taxation.

Overall, the type and level of taxation (including royalties) need to be
considered on a case-by-case basis. The type of legal system, mining and
cultural traditions, and government ideology all contribute to the mining
royalty and taxation structure. Furthermore, the assessment of royalty
types and levels carried out here is a static picture of a highly dynamic
policy environment. In nearly all of the jurisdictions studied, significant
changes to royalties have occurred over the life of large mining operations, and such changes are likely to occur in the future.

Figure 3.1. Effective Tax Rate vs. per Capita GDP for 24 International Mining Jurisdictions

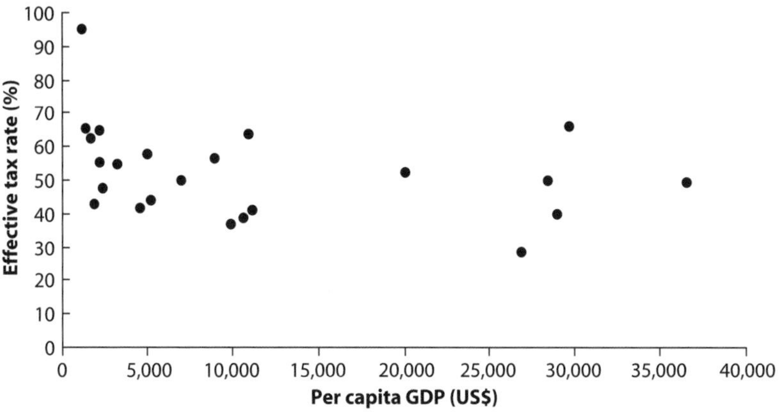

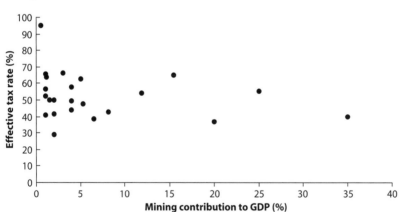

Sources: GDP—CIA World Factbook (2004); effective tax rates—Otto, Cordes, and Batarseh (2000).

Figure 3.2. Effective Tax Rate vs. Contribution of Mining to GDP for 24 International Mining Jurisdictions

Sources: Contribution to GDP—Mineral Commodity Summaries. U.S. Geological Survey. http://minerals.usgs. gov/minerals/pubs/mcs/ (accessed March 17, 2005); effective tax rate—Otto, Cordes, and Batarseh (2000).

Why Each Country's Tax Structure Is Unique

The rich diversity of royalties described in the preceding sections raises the question of why. Why do many countries have royalties but other countries don't? Why, in those countries with royalties, do the taxes differ in so many ways? Why are royalty taxes in some countries based on tonnes of output, in others on the value of sales, and in still others on some modified measure of profits? Why are royalty rates high for some countries and low for others? And why do royalty rates vary from one mineral commodity to another in some countries but not others? Why can royalties be deducted from corporate income taxes in most but not all countries? Why do royalties in some countries rise with the level of output? Why do certain but not all countries give government officials the authority to excuse firms from royalties when times are difficult?

The simple answer, of course, is that every country is unique, with its own legal system, history, political institutions, interest groups, levels of economic development, and dependence on mineral production. In some cases, royalties are designed along with the other taxes that are imposed on mineral firms and imposed as an integrated package. In other countries, such as Peru, royalties are introduced separately, as an add-on to existing mineral taxation. So it is not surprising that the size and nature of royalties are tailored to meet the special needs of each country.

Perhaps the best way to illustrate the unique forces responsible for the diversity of royalties in mining countries is to examine one country in depth. A good case study is Chile, a country that is currently in the throes of (perhaps) introducing a royalty. To understand why the country is now considering a royalty, and the proposals under consideration, one needs some historical perspective.

Foreign mining companies developed the Chilean copper industry in the early part of the 20th century. After World War II, two U.S. companies, Anaconda and Kennecott, controlled the four major mines that accounted for the lion's share of the country's copper mine output. During the 1960s, Chile undertook a number of steps that increased the country's control and equity interest in these companies, a process that culminated in 1971 with the complete nationalization of these properties under the government of Salvador Allende. The ownership and operation of the two companies were at that time consolidated within Codelco, a state mining company that was completely owned by the Chilean government.

Following the military overthrow of the Allende government in 1973, the Pinochet dictatorship moved away from socialism and toward more market-oriented economic policies. During the late 1970s and early 1980s, the country liberalized its investment policies to attract private investment into mining. Although Codelco retained control of the old Anaconda and Kennecott properties, private investment, largely direct foreign investment, played an increasingly important role in the Chilean copper industry.

The first major development in this direction occurred in 1978, when Exxon bought the Disputada Company from the Empresa Nacional de Mineria (ENAMI), another state-owned company with properties in the mineral sector. Exxon paid about US$98 million for the company, which was doing poorly and was nearly bankrupt. Then private mining companies developed a number of new projects during the 1980s and 1990s (see Table 3.9). As a result, over this period Codelco's share of Chilean copper production declined from more than 70 percent to less than 33 percent.

Table 3.9. Ownership and Output of Chilean Copper Mines, 2003

Company	2003 output[a]	First production	Ownership
Codelco			
Chuquicamata	601	pre-1980	Government of Chile
El Teniente	339	pre-1980	Government of Chile
Radomiro Tomic	306	1998	Government of Chile
Andina	236	pre-1980	Government of Chile
Salvador	80	pre-1980	Government of Chile
Output-Codelco	1,563		
Other producers			
Escondida	995	1990	BHP Billiton, Rio Tinto plc, Mitsubishi, IFC
Collahuasi	395	1998	Anglo American, Noranda, Mitsui, Nippon Mg Hold
Los Pelambres	338	1999	Antofagasta
Disputada	278	pre-1980	Anglo American
El Abra	227	1996	Phelps Dodge, Codelco
Candelaria	213	1994	Phelps Dodge
Zaldivar	151	1995	Placer Dome
Mantos Blancos	147	pre-1980	Anglo American
Cerro Colorado	132	1994	BHP Billiton Gr
Enami	122	pre-1980	Government of Chile
El Tesoro	92	2001	Antofagasta, Equatorial
Quebrada Blanca	80	1994	Aur Resources Inc.
Lomas Bayas	60	1998	Noranda
Michilla	53	1994	Antofagasta
Others	61		
Output, other	3,342		
Total output	4,904		

Source: Government of Chile, Comisión Chilean de Cobre.

a. Output is measured in thousands of tonnes of contained copper.

The economic reforms introduced during the last half of the 1970s and the 1980s, coupled with the rapid rise of Chilean copper production, stimulated the country's economy. For nearly two decades, Chile enjoyed rapid economic growth. This success in turn created expectations for the future.

Over the past five or six years, however, a growing sense of public disappointment and frustration with the private mining companies has emerged, fueled by several developments. First, in the early years of the current decade, economic growth slowed markedly as the global copper industry stagnated, copper prices declined, and new investment largely ceased.

Second, with the exception of Escondida, the new private mines have paid little or no taxes. This is in part because low copper prices depressed profits, but also because the government instituted a favorable investment climate to attract new foreign investment. Chile has no royalty on mineral production, and the corporate income tax allows companies to defer their taxes by accelerating the depreciation of their capital and other ways. Escondida has voluntarily decided to forgo the use of accelerated depreciation, suggesting a political acumen not found among other private investors. Still, the company will almost certainly be subjected to the same changes in the tax laws as all other private companies. The fact that Codelco continues year after year to contribute great sums to government coffers, in the form of taxes and dividends, has not helped the deteriorating public image of the private sector.

Third, and perhaps most damaging of all, is the legacy of Disputada, the company Exxon bought in 1978 and then sold in 2002 to Anglo American (as described in Aguilera 2004). During the 24 years that Exxon owned Disputada, the company's two mines produced ore containing more than 3 million tonnes of copper. During that period, the company paid no income tax, in part because the mine had to stop production for a year after the concentrator at the company's Los Broncas mine was buried by an avalanche. However, there were other reasons as well. The ability under Chilean law to carry losses forward allowed the firm to avoid taxes even during those years when it did make a profit. Also the unusually high debt-to-equity ratio used to finance the company meant that revenues that would otherwise have been profits were repatriated abroad as interest payments, a cost of production that was not taxed. Finally, Exxon invested heavily in Disputada, and like other Chilean companies enjoyed the benefits of accelerated depreciation.

Thanks to the investment that Exxon had poured into the company and to Anglo American's keen interest in acquiring the company, Exxon sold Disputada for US$1.3 billion. The book value of the company at the time was US$500 million, which left US$800 million in capital gains. The capital gains tax in Chile is 35 percent, which works out to a liability of some US$280 million for Exxon, but the company claimed that under its agreement with the government it did not have to pay capital gains. After a drawn-out dispute, Exxon paid US$39 million (of which US$27 million was for capital gains), a fairly modest amount.

Ultimately, of course, Exxon's management has a statutory responsibility to serve the interests of its shareholders. The welfare of the Chilean people is presumably the responsibility of the Chilean government. So it is not surprising that the company took full advantage of the favorable investment environment provided by the government. The result, however, has been to leave many in Chile feeling that their country's current tax regime with respect to the foreign mining sector is in need of revision. Currently the benefits from the exploitation of the country's mineral wealth seem to many to be flowing largely to the private companies and their owners, most of whom are not even Chilean.

Finally, the dramatic recovery of the global copper industry in 2004 reinforced this impression. The near doubling of copper prices greatly increased the revenues of the copper mining companies. Although this produced a jump in the taxes the companies paid, the increase accounted for only a small portion of the huge rise in overall profits. Again, the behavior of Codelco, which as a state enterprise contributes all of its profits to the government either as taxes or dividends, accentuated the situation.

The result of the growing frustration with the private companies in the mining sector—a national sense of disinheritance—was the legislative proposal introduced by the government of Ricardo Lagos in 2004 to impose a royalty on the private mining companies. Codelco was exempt, presumably because the company already pays 10 percent of its total revenues directly to the Chilean Armed Forces under the Chilean constitution. Small and medium-size mining operations were also exempt, since many of these companies—largely Chilean owned—were going through difficult times and had successfully lobbied for public assistance. The proposed royalty was a type of profit royalty, in that companies could deduct wages and certain other production costs from total revenues. However, companies were explicitly enjoined from deducting capital costs, including interest payments, management fees, and a number of other indirect costs. The idea clearly was to ensure that companies exploiting the country's mineral wealth pay some taxes, regardless of how profitable or unprofitable they are.

The mining industry managed after considerable effort to defeat the proposed legislation. The government, however, sees the proposal as a win-win political issue, because most Chileans feel that the mining industry should be contributing more to the country. The potential negative effects of additional taxation on the country's mining sector over the long run are largely overlooked. As a result, the government recently introduced similar legislation. Whether it will ultimately pass is not yet known. However, what is clear is how the particular circumstances described above—and the sense of injustice that those circumstances have created—have shaped the particular royalty proposals that the government has put forward.

Private Party Royalties

Royalties are not restricted to the levy of a charge on the private sector by government and, in fact, royalties between private parties are common. The principal distinction is that in the first instance the levy is, in most cases, a unilateral exercise of a nation's inherent ability to impose taxes, whereas royalties between private parties are the result of a bilateral, consensual process. Government royalties tend to be uniform for like types of mineral rights holders, but private party royalties are diverse, reflecting the respective negotiating strengths and objectives of the affected parties.

Private Party Mining Royalties

Private party royalties on mining properties exist among individuals, government agencies, private companies, public companies, consortiums of landowners, and native or community groups. Many private party royalty arrangements arise out the situation in which a company specializing in exploration discovers a deposit and then transfers, in exchange for a royalty interest, its right to develop that deposit to a company specializing in mining. Another common situation occurs when a company that both explores and mines has a mineral property that is not a good strategic fit, that is, it's too small or large or the wrong mineral, and transfers its mining right for a royalty interest. Depending on the scale of an operation, a number of firms may find it advantageous to form a joint venture or joint operating company to spread costs, risks, and expertise and to share at least a portion of the rewards through royalty distribution schemes. Notwithstanding the large numbers of artisanal miners in many parts of the developing world, the majority of mineral commodity production is derived from larger-scale operations developed by public or private corporations. Legal, technical, and financial obligations put the development and production of mineral commodities beyond the reach of many mineral rights owners.

In addition to the transfer of mining rights are situations in which a corporation may have a mining right but lack the right to use the land in which the mineral occurs and therefore, in order to gain access, pays the landowners or users a royalty interest. As a result of these and other circumstances, a market exists for the buying, selling, and optioning of mineral properties and rights. Mineral property and rights agreements are highly varied and complex, but many contain some type of private party royalty provision.

The types of royalties arising under private party arrangements are diverse but generally can be categorized in the same way as royalties imposed by governments, namely, unit based, value based or profit or income based. The type agreed to by the parties is apt to reflect the contracting parties' appetites for risk. Table 3.10 indicates the respective risk of the parties for the three principal royalty types. Clearly, production type royalties appeal more to owners of mineral rights while profit-based royalties appeal more to investors.

The following examples of private party mineral royalties in Canada and South Africa highlight the two endpoints of the relationship between private party and government royalties. In the South African case, private party and government royalties are seen as being mutually exclusive. The

Table 3.10. Exposure to Risk with Periodic Mineral Royalties

Description	Production royalties (unit based)	Net smelter return royalties (value based)	Profit- or income-based royalties
		Exposure to risk	
Owner of the mining right	Low risk	Medium risk	High risk
Investor	High risk	Medium risk	Low risk

Source: Cawood 1999.

producer of a mineral commodity will pay a royalty to either a private landowner or a public (government) landowner. This situation also is common in many state jurisdictions in the United States. In the Canadian example, private and government royalties are not usually mutually exclusive. A producer of mineral commodities in Canada will pay provincial mining tax and royalties, regardless of whether private parties have negotiated a royalty on production. The private royalty may be acknowledged in the treatment of income for mining taxes as an allowable deduction. The only exceptions to the combined private and public royalty payment occur where Aboriginal groups have negotiated with the government to collect royalties on their ancestral lands.

Private Party Mineral Royalties in Canada

Canada is a major producer of mineral commodities and therefore a favored destination for mineral exploration and mine development. Exploration in Canada historically has accounted for 15 to 25 percent of global exploration expenditures.[45] A large portion of this expenditure occurs with properties that have some type of joint-venture agreement that contains a royalty provision. These private royalties reflect a shared ownership interest in the property and are in addition to government royalties rather than in lieu of them. In general, the royalties fall into two broad categories.

Net smelter return (NSR) royalty   This type of royalty is determined as a percentage of the value received from the sale of the product produced at the mine site. Costs associated with further downstream processing are deducted before calculating the base value for the NSR royalty. In the case of high-unit-value commodities such as gold or diamonds, these downstream costs are relatively insignificant, because the mine produces a nearly pure product. In mines that produce a highly impure form of the salable metal, the royalty received is truly a net value. In the case of base metal concentrates, the net smelter value would be net of smelting charges, refining charges, transportation charges, and any profits generated along this chain. For example, a company producing a concentrate containing 30 percent copper may receive payment equivalent to 65 percent of the value of the copper in the concentrate. This payment would represent the NSR base or net smelter revenue for the calculation of the royalty payment. None of the direct capital or operating costs at the mine site are deducted in the calculation of the royalty base.

The NSR royalty is by far the most common type of royalty in Canadian exploration and mine development agreements. As Table 3.10 shows, this stems from the fact that property owners and investors are convening on the medium risk royalty instrument. Furthermore, the definition of the base for determining NSR royalties is generally well accepted within the industry and in the case of public companies can be readily checked against earnings statements in quarterly and annual reports. Although NSR royalty rates as high as 5 percent have been noted in the past, values in more recent years tend to range from 1 to 3 percent of net smelter revenue (also see Harries 1996). Examples of NSR royalty provisions can be seen in many recent mine developments. For example, the Diavik diamond mine in the Northwest Territories has two residual NSR royalties of 1 percent each. The Voisey's Bay mine, under development in Newfoundland and Labrador, has an NSR royalty of 3 percent.

The structure of NSR royalty provisions can be complicated by the incorporation of sliding rates based on production levels or mineral prices, advance payments, minimum payments, maximum payments, and so forth. In nearly all cases, however, the base for the determination of the royalty payment is the net smelter revenue.

It is not uncommon for existing NSR royalties to be converted to a lump sum payment when mine development proceeds. The sale of the royalty may be to the developer of the property or to a third party and is usually offered at a discount to the present value of the anticipated royalty payments over mine life. The royalty holders (Archean Resources) at Voisey's Bay have carried out three transactions to sell off their 3 percent interest in the mine. This comprised two sales of 0.15 percent NSR to a junior company (Altius Minerals[46]) followed by the sale of all shares of Archean Resources to a public company (International Royalty Corporation).[47]

Net profit interest (NPI)   Net profit interest is paid on the basis of profit from the mine rather than on sales revenue from the mine. As such, capital expenditures, operating costs, interest payments, and any other costs associated with producing, selling, and moving the mine product are deducted from revenues in determining the base for the royalty. The direct result is that the existing property owner does not share in the profits from the mine until the partner company has recovered all of its costs. NPI payments, therefore, tend to be at a much higher rate than NSR royalties and range from 10 percent up to 50 percent. NPI agreements are much less common than NSR agreements because they are difficult to monitor and are less transparent. Existing property owners are, to some extent, at the mercy of the accounting practices of the mine operator. As a result, NPI is often facetiously referred to as "no payment intended."

Joint-venture agreements that initially have existing property owners as equity partners will have provisions to dilute their interest as the partner assumes more of the costs of exploring or developing the property. The NPI provision in these cases is often the sole remaining interest in the property for the existing property owner. Another term occasionally seen in mining agreements is *net proceeds royalty*. In most cases, it is not clear how (or if) this differs from NPI royalty.

Private Party Mineral Royalty Instruments in South Africa

The instruments and rates for collecting private party mineral royalties vary significantly internationally. Private party mineral royalties are payable to owners of mineral rights when mining rights are granted over such properties. In contrast with the discussion of Canadian agreements above, the South African focus is on agreements between private property mineral rights owners and private mining companies. Very few countries, outside of those in South America, allow mineral rights ownership to be registered as private property. However, this arrangement was standard in South Africa until recently, and this section uses the South African experience, before the promulgation of the Mineral and Petroleum Resources Development Act (MPRDA)[48] in April 2004, to demonstrate the differences between private party and government-owned mineral royalties. Other types of private party royalties along the lines of the Canadian examples are less common in South Africa. This stems from the traditional structure of the mining sector whereby several large mining houses controlled a large proportion of mineral production. The lack of a well-established junior mining and exploration sector, such as evidenced in Canada or Australia, retarded the development of joint-venture and farm-in type agreements, which contained NSR or NPI provisions. As the mineral sector in South Africa is transformed by internationalization, these types of private party royalties are becoming more common.

When the MPRDA came into effect, private party mineral rights were the norm in areas underlain by Witwatersrand gold reefs. Historically, the state had no royalty claim to privately owned mineral rights and was excluded from the commercial deal entered into between the registered owner and the mining company that wanted to develop the minerals. The royalty arrangement decided upon for private party mineral rights could have been any of the standard methods used by states, or a combination of those methods, but was not limited to the traditional methods. Private-ly owned South African mineral rights included a category called *trust land*, which allowed for community-owned mineral rights. This category required separate registration in the name of such tribal communities. Before the 1994 elections brought about the end of apartheid policies in South Africa, these black communities were not allowed to contract with mining companies. The president of South Africa, or the appropri-ate head of the Transkei, Bophuthatswana, Venda, or Ciskei (TBVC)[49] state in which the lease area occurred, acted as trustee for black com-munities to negotiate leases and mineral royalties. The result was a great similarity between state and community royalties, both of which were usually payable on profits and at low rates.

After 1994, the trusteeship was abandoned, which allowed these com-munities to negotiate new agreements on their own terms. The best pub-licized example was the conversion of Impala Platinum royalties payable to the Royal Bafokeng into a 21 percent profit-based royalty, which was subject to a minimum royalty of 1 percent of the sales revenue derived from platinum group metals. Table 3.11 shows a sample of typical min-eral royalties between private parties in South Africa, as recorded in min-eral lease agreements from 1990 to 2004.

Comparison between State and Private Party Royalties

For the most part, mining royalties are determined in a similar fashion whether they are paid to private sources or to the government. The dif-ferences relate to the sources' propensity for using certain types of roy-alties and the range of royalty rates demanded. To a large extent, these differences stem from varying risk preferences and objectives of private and public mineral rights holders. The private owner has only his or her own good in mind, whereas government officials have the common or public good in mind. *Own good* implies narrow personal economic gain resulting from legal ownership of a wasting asset that is capable of earn-ing extraordinary wealth. On the other hand, public policy defines the common good, which is aimed at broad public gain, as being gain re-sulting from the exercise of national sovereignty over natural resources and the management of mineral wealth. Government royalties must also take into account the political will, the need for investment, and interna-tional competitiveness, issues that are of little concern to private owners of mineral rights.

In the Canadian context, the majority of private royalties are negoti-ated on the basis of units of production or value of production. With the

Table 3.11. Private Party Mineral Royalties in South Africa, 1990–2004

Property	Year	Mineral	Royalty
Sea area	1990	Diamonds	25% of profits
Mooifontein	1992	Coal	R 0.23/tonne sold, escalation 1/2 PPI plus additional above threshold
Cato Manor	1992	Tilite	Royalty 2–7.5% of revenue
Bethesda	1995	Iron	4% of revenue plus land rent
Haverklip	1996	Coal	Royalty R 1.00/tonne ROM mined and removed plus PPI
Klipfontein	1997	Clay	Royalty R 4.00/tonne clay
Hamburg	1997	Diamonds	5% of gross sales
Spitskop	1997	Quartzite	Royalty R 0.58/tonne mined and removed
Blesbokfontein	1998	Coal	Royalty R 0.37/tonne mined and sold, escalation 1/2PPI
Roodepoort	1998	Coal	Royalty R 1.00/tonne sold
Schoongezicht	1998	Diamonds	5% of gross sales
Marsfontein	1998	Diamonds	R 75,000,000 plus royalty 5% gross income
Buffelsfontein	1998	Gold	R 4,000/month plus R 30.00/m³ ore mined
Rietkuil	1999	Diamonds	5% of gross sales
Ingonyama Trust	2000	Anthracite	2% of gross revenue plus R 0.70/tonne sold (meant as land rent)
Somkele	2000	Anthracite	Can$50,000 plus 3.25% free-on-mine value
Wonderheuwel	2004	Coal	R 1.20/ROM tonne mined, escalating at 5% compound interest

Source: Cawood, F. T. Personal database of transactions and valuations compiled from various sources, 1990–2005.

Note: ROM = run of mine, PPI = producer price index.

exception of production royalties on potash and uranium in Saskatchewan, most government royalties are based on profit.

In the case of South Africa, the following points highlight similarities and differences between private party royalties and state mineral royalties for the corresponding period:

- Profit-based royalties were much higher than revenue-based royalties, which was also the case for state-owned mineral rights.
- Production royalties on units of production were based on either units mined or sold, whereas government royalties tended to be based on units sold.

- Both state and private party mineral royalties were often escalated using the annual producer price index (PPI) for mining and quarrying, as published by Statistics South Africa.
- State mineral royalties were not increased according to preestablished threshold rates of production, whereas this was recorded for private party mineral royalties.
- Private owners often negotiated a fixed fee in addition to the mineral royalty, whereas state officials insisted on a minimum royalty per annum.
- Not all private party royalties were concluded in local currency.

Instead of using the standard practice of charging an annual rent in South African rand per hectare for land use, the Ingonyama Trust negotiated a production royalty as payment for land use. This rental fee was linked to a monthly minimum payment. The Ingonyama example developed from the notion that surface mines and areas that are underlain by minerals at shallow depths give landowners negotiation powers tantamount to those of owners of mineral rights, even when mineral and land ownership are severed in law. Legally, landowners have no royalty entitlement, but the nature and extent of surface mines require that the surface owner not be allowed to continue with normal land use once mine development starts. The result is that a premium is added to land value, which could be considered a once-off royalty payment for the benefit of the landowner.

The government of South Africa had for many years reserved the right to mine certain strategic minerals for itself.[50] This right to mine could best be described as a separate blanket of ownership over and above the civil law system introduced by Dutch occupiers. The state leased its right to mine reserved minerals to companies and, in return for the grant, received a lease consideration from the lessee, the payment of which was based on profits. The rate of payment was calculated using a unique lease formula for each mine, which could slide between predetermined minimum and maximum rates depending on the annual profitability ratio (Van Blerck 1992). The lease consideration was payment in addition to the usual mineral royalty payable to the owner of the mineral rights.

Although most private owners of mineral rights preferred outright sales agreements, the government of South Africa preferred to enter into mineral lease agreements, allowing for the payment of periodic mineral royalties as consideration for its permission. Table 3.12 illustrates the

Table 3.12. Differences between State and Private Mineral Royalties in South Africa

State mineral royalties				Private mineral royalties			
Lump sum	*Production related*	*Revenue related*	*Profit related*	*Lump sum*	*Production related*	*Revenue related*	*Profit related*
Least popular	Frequently a rate per unit sold	Never above 5%	Rarely above 15%	Most popular	Frequently a rate per unit mined	Rarely below 5%	Rarely below 15%

Source: Author F. Cawood.

differences between state and private party mineral royalties, as recorded in South African mineral lease agreements. When private owners decided to enter into periodic mineral royalty agreements, the rates were much higher than those recorded in mineral lease agreements with the state. This demonstrates that, first, South African private owners had less tolerance for mineral development risk, and second, when they were prepared to take this risk, they would do so only at a significant premium.

Although theory suggests that the special qualities of the mineral resource should be the deciding factor in the selection of the royalty instrument and corresponding rate, this section demonstrates that the identity of the owner and his or her risk profile are the most important factors. Outright sale of the mineral rights for a fixed amount works well when mineral rights are privately owned and when there is an established market for mineral rights that actively trades these rights. Owners who prefer this approach are normally risk averse and have less bargaining power than the mineral company to contract favorable terms and conditions. Periodic royalties, on the other hand, are favored by states because these allow, first, systematic compensation as depletion occurs over time, second, a degree of risk sharing in exchange for a bigger reward when the mineral deposit yields extraordinary returns, and third, demonstration by government that its natural resources are developed for the public good.

References

Aguilera, Roberto F. 2004. "Exporting Mineral Wealth? The Case of Chile's Disputada de Las Condes." Unpublished paper. Santiago, Chile: Universidad Católica de Chile, Centro de Minería.

Barberis, Danielle. 1998. *Negotiating Mining Agreements: Past, Present and Future Trends*. Kluwer Law International, Dordrecht, the Netherlands.

Cawood, F. T. 1999. "Determining the Optimal Rent for South African Mineral Resources." PhD diss., University of the Witwatersrand, Johannesburg, South Africa.

———. 2004. "Will the New South African Mineral and Petroleum Royalty Bill Attract or Deter Investment?" Research paper, Centre for Energy, Petroleum and Mineral Law and Policy, University of Dundee, Scotland.

Commonwealth Secretariat. 1992. *A Study on the Legislative Framework, Agreements and Financial Impositions Affecting Mining Industries in Commonwealth Caribbean Countries*, 174–75. Commonwealth Secretariat, London.

Green, F. R. H., quoted by Mike Faber. 1977. *The Fiscal Regime, Some Policy and Legal Issues Affecting Mining Legislation and Agreements in African Commonwealth Countries*, 79. Commonwealth Secretariat, London.

Harries, Karl. 1996. *Mining Royalties Between Private Parties*, 109, 117–21. Centre for Resource Studies, Queens University, Kingston, Canada.

Mineral Commodity Summaries. U.S. Geological Survey. http://minerals.usgs.gov/minerals/pubs/mcs/ (accessed March 17, 2005).

Ministry for Land and Resources, State Development Planning Commission, State Economic and Trade Commission, Ministry of Finance, Ministry of Foreign Trade and Economic Co-operation, and State Administration for Industry and Commerce. 2000. "China Encourages Foreign Investment in the Exploration and Development of Non-oil/gas Mineral Resources." Announcement. December 14.

Otto, James. 1995. "Legal Approaches to Assessing Mineral Royalties." In *The Taxation of Mineral Enterprises*, ed. James Otto. London: Graham & Trotman/Martinus Nijhoff.

Otto, James, and John Cordes. 2002. *The Regulation of Mineral Enterprises: A Global Perspective on Economics, Law and Policy*. Rocky Mountain Mineral Law Foundation, Westminster, CO.

Otto, James, John Cordes, and Maria Batarseh. 2000. *Global Mining Taxation Comparative Study*. Institute for Global Resources Policy and Management, Colorado School of Mines.

Van Blerck, M. C. 1992. *Mining Tax in South Africa*, 2nd ed. Taxfax CC, Rivonia, South Africa.

Western Australian Department of Industry and Resources. 2005. *Statistic Digest–Mineral and Petroleum Resources–2003/04*. http://www.doir.wa.gov.au (accessed March 17, 2005).

World Facts and Figures. http://www.worldfactsandfigures.com/gdp_country_desc.php (accessed March 17, 2005).

Notes

1. Nigeria, Minerals Ordinance Cap. 121, repealed.
2. Botswana, Republic of Botswana Mines and Minerals Act No. 17 of 1999, assented to September 1, 1999, promulgated by Gazette dated September 17, 1999. In addition to royalty, for some types of mines, particularly diamond mines, the government may assess a profit-sharing scheme.
3. Angola, Mining Law, Law No. 1/92 of January 17, 1992.
4. China has two royalties on minerals, one ad valorem based and one unit based. The unit-based royalty is set on a mine-by-mine basis within the statutorily defined range. Resources Royalty Regulations (Temporary) People's Republic of China, December 25, 1993, by the State Council. Document no. 139; unofficial translation.
5. The ability to aggregate income and expenses from all operations within the taxing jurisdiction indicates a lack of ring fencing. *Ring fencing* refers to a situation in which each of the taxpayer's operations is treated independently, for tax purposes, from all of the taxpayer's other operations.
6. In Ghana, the Mineral (Royalties) Regulations of 1986 provide for a sliding-scale type of royalty, with the final royalty rate determined through negotiation.
7. In China, Resources Royalty Regulations (Temporary), N. 139, 1993.
8. Northern Territory, Mineral Royalty Act 1982.
9. In Russia, although Article 341 of Federal Law N. 126 – FZ deems the quarter to be the tax (royalty) period, royalties are levied in advance on a monthly basis. The monthly amount is set at one-third of the total payments for the preceding quarter.
10. China, Royalty Regulations (Temporary), N. 139, 1993 – Article 13.
11. Papua New Guinea, Mining Act 1992, Part XI, Provisions relating to mineral returns and royalty, Section 111 (Penalty).
12. Northern Territory, Mineral Royalty Act 1982 – Part IV, Collection and recovery of royalty, Sections 42 to 44.
13. Philippines, National Internal Revenue Code of the Philippines as amended by Republic Act N. 8424 (Tax Reform Act 1997).
14. From an announcement by China's Ministry for Land and Resources and others, 2000.
15. India, Sections 9(3) and 9A(1) of the Mines and Minerals (development and regulation) Act, N. 67 of 1957, as amended.

16. Indonesia, Regional Administration Law 22/1997, Article 1, 2 (subarticle 2), and particularly Article 10 (subarticle 2), whereby "a region shall be authorised to manage natural resources available in its territory."

17. Argentina, Article 22 of the Mining Investment Law N. 24196, as amended.

18. The distinction can be important. For example, under Peruvian tax stabilization agreements, taxes are stabilized but nontax fees are not. The introduction of royalties in Peru has brought into question whether mines operating under stabilization agreements are subject to the royalty. If the royalty is a tax, most likely they are not liable to pay it, but if it is a nontax fee, they may need to.

19. Mineral and Petroleum Royalty Bill, March 10, 2003, National Treasury, Pretoria, South Africa (not in gazette).

20. For most mines, royalty rates are imposed under the mining code. However, for very large projects a negotiated royalty may be set out in an agreement that is passed as an act by parliament.

21. Nigeria, 4th Schedule to the Mining Regulations, repealed.

22. Indonesia, 7th Generation Contract of Work, Mine and Energy Ministerial Decree No. 1166.K/M.PE/1992, dated September 12, 1992.

23. Sierra Leone, Bauxite Mineral Prospecting and Mining Agreement 1961 (between Government of Sierra Leone, Sierra Leone Ore and Metal Company, Aluminum-Industrie-Aktien-Gesellschaft), ratified by Act No. 35 of 1962.

24. Sierra Leone, Sierra Leone Rutile Agreement 1972 (between Government of Sierra Leone and Sierra Rutile Limited), ratified by Act No. 1 of 1972.

25. India, Second Schedule, GSR N. 677 (E). Amendments to the Second Schedule of Mines and Minerals (Development and Regulation) Act, 1957 (No. 67 of 1957), October 14, 2004.

26. China, Regulations for the Collection and Administration of Mineral Resources Compensation Fee. Released by the State Council on February 27, 1994. Document no. 150. Unofficial translation.

27. Papua New Guinea, Mining Act 1977.

28. Laws of the Republic of Zambia (Volume 13 of 26) Act No. 31 of 1995.

29. Bolivia, Mining Code, Law 1777, 03/17/1997 Sup dec 24780 of July 31, 1997.

30. Peru, Law of Mining Royalty No. 28258. June 24, 2004.

31. Botswana, Mines and Minerals Act of 1967.

32. British Columbia, Canada, Mining Tax Act (Revised Statutes of British Columbia [RSBC] 1996) Chapter 295.

33. Ghana, Minerals (Royalties) Regulations L.I. 1349 of 1987.

34. As reported in *A Study on the Legislative Framework, Agreements and Financial Impositions Affecting Mining Industries in Commonwealth Caribbean Countries* (Commonwealth Secretariat, London 1992), pp. 174–75.

35. British Columbia, Canada, Mineral Tax Act (RSBC 1996), Chapter 291. Sections in the law establish *net revenue* as revenues less allowable costs, that is, profit, and *net proceeds* as adjusted gross proceeds, that is, the ad valorem basis.

36. Dominican Republic, Mining Law of the Dominican Republic, Law No. 146.

37. Myanmar, the Myanmar Mines Law, September 6, 1994.

38. Botswana, Mines and Minerals Act of 1967.

39. Nigeria, Mineral and Mining Decree No. 34 of 1999.

40. Ghana, Part IV, Article 22, Mining and Mineral Law 1986, PNDCL.153.

41. Western Australia, Mining Regulations 1981.

42. Western Australia, Mining Regulations 1981.

43. Nigeria, Mineral and Mining Decree No. 34 of 1999.

44. Ghana, Part IV, Article 22, Mining and Mineral Law 1986, PNDCL.153.

45. For discussions of Canada's position in global exploration see Natural Resources Canada, *Canadian Minerals Yearbook*, 1990–2002.

46. For details of the sale of royalty interest, see Altius Minerals press release July 14, 2003 on the Sedar Web site at http://www.sedar.com/DisplayCompany-Documents.do?lang=EN&issuerNo=00008222, accessed February 15, 2005.

47. For details of the International Royalty purchase of Archean Resources, see http://www.newswire.ca/en/releases/archive/February2005/23/c7556.html (accessed February 28, 2005).

48. Mineral and Petroleum Resources Development Act 28 of 2002, 3 October 2002, Government Gazette, Vol. 448, No. 23922 (Date of commencement 1 April 2004). This act allows for state custodianship of all mineral rights in South Africa and has put an end to registering mineral rights ownership as immovable private property.

49. Transkei, Bophuthatswana, Venda, and Ciskei were independent territories called homelands.

50. This practice was ended by the Minerals Act 50 of 1991, May 15, 1991, Government Notice 3082 of 1991 (date of commencement January 1, 1992), repealed by the Mineral and Petroleum Resources Development Act 28 of 2002.

CHAPTER 4

Impact of Royalties on a Mine— Quantitative Analysis

In the preceding chapter, types of royalties were introduced and specific examples were provided from a wide cross-section of jurisdictions. The focus was on regulatory options available to governments. This chapter further explores types of royalties but does so from a project economics perspective. Different types of royalties will have different impacts on project economics and government take. In the first section, three hypothetical mine models illustrate the impact of a number of selected royalty types on cash flow, profitability, effective tax rate, and government fiscal receipts. Next, a mine model is introduced that demonstrates the impact royalties can have on production decisions, such as cutoff grade, mine life, and reserves. The final section discusses what can be learned from using a quantitative analysis as an aid when considering changes to royalty policy design and implementation.

Impact of Selected Royalty Types on Three Mines

To demonstrate royalty effects, three hypothetical mine models were developed: an underground gold mine, an open-pit copper mine, and an open-pit bauxite mine. These three mine types were selected to provide and illustrate a cross-section of different cost and pricing structures. The data used are not drawn from any one mine but instead reflect what the authors believe to be reasonable assumptions. The cash flows for the three mines were modeled at a level of detail that might be used by a company at the prefeasibility study stage of project analysis. (Sample spreadsheets for the three mine models are presented in Appendix A2.) The intent of the models is to illustrate the impact that a number of royalty types will have on the project's cash flow. Four measures are used: internal rate of return (IRR), investor net present value (NPV), effective tax rate (ETR), and gross government royalty receipts and taxes.

NPV is a measure of value created by measuring the sum of the cash flows when discounted at an interest rate to adjust for the time value of money. NPV can be calculated for various perceived investment opportunities to provide a means to allocate a capital budget. When a project IRR is greater than the investor's minimum rate of return, or discount rate, the project adds value to the investor portfolio as reflected by the NPV. Though it is common industry practice to calculate NPV in measuring the potential creation of wealth, it is equally common for governments in many countries to neglect the time value of money. The models in this section calculate NPV using both an assumed discount rate and a discount rate of zero to illustrate possible company or government preferences. The NPV of a project may be calculated using the following equation:

$$NPV = \sum_{n=o}^{n} \frac{Rn - OCn - Tn - Kn}{(1+i^{*})^{n}}$$

Where:

NPV = the expected present value of all project annual after-tax cash flows discounted at the investor's desired minimum rate of return.

Rn = the expected annual gross revenue from the sale of each product, determined using the expected product price taken times the expected tonnage, grade, and appropriate recovery factors necessary for the metallurgy employed.

OCn = the expected annual operating costs associated with the sale of product produced and sold.

Tn = the expected annual taxes from all sources (for this study, taxes include royalties, withholding taxes, and income taxes). Implicit in the calculation is the assumption that all allowable capitalized deductions are included in the taxable income figure.

Kn = capital expenditures required for exploration, development, mine equipment, processing equipment, and related infrastructure.

n = the year from the base year (measurement of time).

i^* = the minimum rate of return required from invested capital budget dollars.

IRR is used to measure the compound interest received on the unpaid portion of an investment over its life (Stermole and Stermole 2006 [11th Ed.]). It may also be defined as the compound interest rate that causes a project NPV to equal zero. The IRR of a project may be calculated using the following equation:

$$NPV = 0 = \sum_{n=o}^{n} \frac{Rn - OCn - Tn - Kn}{(1+i)^n}$$

Where:

i = the project rate of return or compound interest rate causing the NPV to equal zero.

Projects will most commonly be described using NPV from the corporate perspective and as a measure of cumulative wealth when the focus is on the government take. IRR and NPV are used by many private and public sector mining companies to determine the economic viability of a proposed mining operation. They are integral to optimizing the design of a mine and to setting basic interrelated parameters such as mine life, reserves, cutoff grade, and extraction profile. The sensitivity of IRR and NPV to selected royalty types is demonstrated for each of the three hypothetical mines.

ETR is defined as the undiscounted value of all amounts paid to the government, divided by the undiscounted value of the project's before-tax cash flow (Otto, Cordes, and Batarseh 2000, 92). Using the previous variables, the ETR of a project may be calculated using the following equation:

$$ETR = \frac{\sum_{n=0}^{n} Tn}{\sum_{n=0}^{n} Rn - OCn - Kn}$$

In this study's models, values paid to the government include the royalty, withholding taxes on dividends and interest, and income taxes. (The models do not include other possible taxes and fees, such as import and export duty, value-added taxes, excise, and so forth.) The cumulative before-tax cash flow includes gross revenue less all cash expenditures, including transportation or freight and handling; mining, milling, and other processing costs, including smelter fees; overhead and capital costs, including working capital expenditures; and all borrowed money considerations, including interest paid.

Variations in the magnitude and timing of capital and operating costs, plus prices of commodities, will affect some types of royalty. For that reason, the costs and prices have been varied for several of the models to illustrate the relative sensitivity of some royalty types to variations in these parameters among the different mine models. In actuality, costs will vary widely from mine to mine.

The three models represented in this study are based on different economic and physical characteristics that might be subject to different aspects of the royalty equation. Such characteristics include the cumulative capital investment, which approaches US$1.8 billion for the bauxite model, with a three-year construction period, and under US$500 million for the underground gold model with a shorter development time frame. Production characteristics include an underground scenario for the gold model and an open-pit scenario for the copper and bauxite models, along with different inferred stripping ratios. Metallurgical differences are assumed to exist because the gold model considers the production of gold from concentrate whereas the bauxite model involves the refining of bauxite to alumina, which is assumed to be sold to an existing smelter. The copper model is based on the use of solvent extraction electrowinning to represent recent advances in the science of copper ore refining. The purpose of using three different models is to determine if royalty structure would offer any unique benefit or cost to the various models.

The authors purposefully created the models in a simple prefeasibility study level of detail. The hope is that the simplicity will allow for a greater focus on the royalty issues without losing the economic qualities that make each model unique. The models are based on a generic tax scenario not based on any particular country. Instead, the models are intended to represent a composite of the way various expenditures might be handled and to address some common financial scenarios, such as ring fencing.

The details on each model are summarized and then followed by a discussion of assumptions that are consistent in each model.

Gold Model

The initial parameters for this large underground gold mine were obtained from a 1999 study by Cawood (1999), which used actual data as extracted from the original feasibility study and subsequent annual reports of a specific mining company. The information was updated using statistics published by Statistics South Africa, Department of Minerals and Energy and South African Chamber of Mines. Although care was taken to accurately reflect the real-life situation, certain assumptions were necessary to simplify the cash-flow parameters. These assumptions should not affect the validity of cash-flow results over the life of the mine. Although certain parameters are described as today's dollar values, the model assumes all costs escalate at 2.0 percent per year. Therefore, all cash flows are described as nominal values in U.S. dollars. The assumed parameters for the model are presented below and are based on the concept that exploration has been going on for some period of time, the deposit is taking form, and development is imminent.

Gold Mine Parameters

Annual rated capacity	4,500,000 tonnes of ore
Average grade of gold	6.0 grams per tonne
Average mill recovery	85.0%
Average smelter recovery	98.0%

Over the past 11 years the average price of gold per troy ounce in U.S. dollars has been approximately $335 (Lown 2004). However, the current contango of futures market prices on the NYMEX through December 2009 results in an average price of approximately $455 per troy ounce at the time of this study.[1] This model is based on a uniform forecasted price of $400 per ounce. That price does not escalate over the project life but remains flat in the base model. Sensitivity analysis is then conducted for gold prices of $440 per ounce and $380 per ounce.

Capital outlays include exploration, development, equipment, and working capital, all of which are described in current U.S. dollars. All capital costs, including sustaining capital and replacement costs in the middle of the mine life escalate at the assumed inflation rate of 2.0 percent per year. Although inflation is often the basis for such escalation, the argument could easily be made that escalation is currently far greater in light of recent increases in steel and energy. However, for simplicity, 2.0 percent is retained for this study. The following are summarized in today's U.S. dollars.

Gold Mine Capital Expenditures

Mine exploration	$60,000,000
Mine development	$120,000,000
Mine and plant equipment	$330,000,000

Sustaining capital is estimated at 2 percent of the mine and plant equipment costs and escalates at the inflation rate (2.0 percent) each year. Working capital is estimated at 30 percent of the first full year of operating costs. That cost is returned in the final year of the project.

Gold Model Operating Expenses (per tonne of ore mined)

Mining	$12.00
Milling	$10.00
Overhead	$7.20
Freight	$0.80

These costs are assumed to escalate 2.0 percent per year and are further assumed to be fully deductible against revenues in the year incurred. No explicit detail is provided concerning yearly changes in the related requirements for working capital at the mine, from the perspective of cost of goods sold.

The parameters described above were incorporated in a Microsoft Excel spreadsheet of the base-case gold model. This base-case model was used as the platform model for the application of selected royalty methods. Appendix A2.1 contains an illustrative part of the model gold mine spreadsheet.

Copper Model

The deposit in this model is not specific to any known deposit. The model may resemble Chilean mines, but is different from most of the enriched blanket porphyry deposits of the northern region of the Atacama Desert. The deposit is assumed to be part of a basement unconformity buried under gravels that will require increased stripping ratios in the early years to expose the ore bodies. It is assumed that development of the resource would involve conventional preproduction stripping and subsequent mining by truck and shovel. Milling will use solvent extraction and electro-winning technology to produce pure copper cathode that would then be shipped a short distance by existing rail routes to an existing port facility. Although certain parameters are described in today's dollars, the model assumes all costs escalate at an assumed inflation rate of 2.0 percent per year. Therefore, all cash flows are described as nominal values in U.S. dollars. The assumed parameters for the model are presented below and are based on the concept that exploration has been going on for a period of time, the deposit is taking form, and development is imminent.

Copper Mine Parameters

Annual plant capacity	18,235,294 tonnes of ore
Initial grade (Cu)	1.5% (declines over time)
Average grade (Cu)	1.32%
Average leaching recovery	80%
Average solvent extraction and electro-winning recovery	90%

The base-case model assumes the average price of copper to be $1.10 per pound.

Although somewhat capital intensive at approximately $1 billion in today's U.S. dollar costs, the project enjoys the benefit of some existing infrastructure to speed development of the property over a period of two years. All capital costs, including sustaining capital and replacement costs in the middle of the mine life escalate at an assumed inflation rate of 2.0 percent per year. Although inflation is often the basis for such escalation, the argument could easily be made that escalation is currently far greater in light of recent increases in the cost of steel and energy. For simplicity, 2.0 percent escalation is retained for this study. The following are summarized in today's U.S. dollars.

Copper Mine Capital Expenditures

Mine exploration	$75,000,000
Mine development	$90,000,000
Mine and plant equipment	$900,000,000

Sustaining capital is estimated at 2 percent of the mine and plant equipment costs and escalates at the inflation rate of 2.0 percent each year.

Working capital is estimated at 30 percent of the first full year of operating costs. This cost is returned in the final year of the project.

Copper Mine Operating Expenses (per tonne of ore mined)

Mining	$2.80
Milling	$3.80
Overhead	$1.50
Freight	$0.50

These operating costs escalate at the same rate of 2.0 percent per year and are assumed to be fully deductible against revenues in the year incurred. No explicit detail is provided concerning yearly changes in the related requirements for working capital from the perspective of cost of goods sold.

The parameters described above were incorporated in an Excel spreadsheet of a base-case copper model. This base-case model was used as the platform model for the application of selected royalty methods. Appendix A2.2 contains an illustrative part of the model copper mine spreadsheet.

Bauxite Model

Although a number of bauxite deposits occur in the tropical and subtropical regions of the world, the profile of the deposit modeled is not specific to any known deposit. Bauxite is generally located near the surface and is extracted using open-pit mining techniques. In most cases stripping is not extensive and reclamation may be ongoing in the deposit, depending on its location. Truck and shovel operations will be used both for stripping overburden and for mining the bauxite ore. Alumina will be refined from the constructed refinery associated with the mine and then sold to an existing smelter.

Bauxite Mine Parameters

Annual refinery capacity	2,297,188 tonnes
Moisture	7%
Plant recovery	95% of wet tonnes
Percentage refinery extraction of alumina	45%
Percentage extraction efficiency	90%

The following calculation illustrates the application of these parameters and the annual alumina produced when operating at rated capacity.

Annual bauxite mined (tonnes)	6,000,000
Moisture	7%
Net annual wet tonnes to beneficiation plant	6,420,000
Beneficiation plant recovery	95%
Net annual tonnage to refinery	6,099,000
Refinery moisture adjustment	7%
Net tonnes processed	5,672,070
Percentage extracted alumina	45%
Net annual tonnes of alumina	2,552,432
Percentage extraction efficiency	90%
Net annual refinery output in tonnes	2,297,188

The market price per tonne for aluminum was multiplied by 20 percent to approximate the equivalent value of alumina per tonne. The project base case assumes a price of US$340 per tonne of alumina. At the time of this writing, the average futures prices for aluminum through 2006, adjusted by the 20 percent factor, are higher than this value.

This project is capital intensive, at approximately US$1.7 billion in today's dollars, and requires a three-year construction period to complete the refinery and related work. All capital costs, including sustaining capital and replacement costs that occur approximately every nine years of the mine's life, escalate at an assumed inflation rate of 2.0 percent per year. Although inflation is often the basis for such escalation, one could easily argue that escalation is currently far greater in light of recent increases in the cost of steel and energy. However, for simplicity, 2.0 percent is retained for this study. The following expenditures are summarized in today's U.S. dollars.

Bauxite Capital Expenditures

Mine exploration	$50,000,000
Mine development	$90,000,000
Mine equipment and infrastructure	$360,000,000
Refinery	$1,200,000,000

Sustaining capital is estimated at 2 percent of the mine and plant equipment costs and escalates at the inflation rate each year. Working capital is estimated at 30 percent of the first full year of operating costs. This cost is returned in the final year of the project.

Bauxite Operating Expenses (per tonne of ore mined)

Mining	$5.00
Beneficiation	$0.80
Refining cost per tonne milled	$98.00
Overhead	$1.00
Freight	$0.50

These operating costs are assumed to escalate at the rate of 2.0 percent per year and are to be fully deductible against revenues in the year incurred. No explicit detail is provided concerning yearly changes in the related requirements for working capital.

The parameters described above were incorporated in an Excel spreadsheet for the base-case bauxite model. This base-case model was used as the platform model for the application of selected royalty methods. Appendix A2.3 contains an illustrative part of the model bauxite mine spreadsheet.

Assumptions Common to All Models

Income tax assumptions   Income taxation systems differ from nation to nation. What constitutes taxable income will generally be calculated as revenues received by the project less various costs. These will typically include costs that are expensed in the year incurred (such as salaries, replacement parts, and other costs that reoccur annually, that is, operating costs) and those that are capitalized through various amortization and depreciation methods (such as exploration costs, development costs, feasibility study costs, and equipment costs). The income tax assumptions used in the three mine models comprise a generic set of deductions that are not specific to any country but are consistent overall with parameters found in the *Global Mining Taxation Comparative Study* (Otto, Cordes, and Batarseh 2000), which include the following:

- **Mine exploration.** These costs are considered to have been incurred in the past and in economic terms are considered to be sunk, although all tax deductions remain and will be taken beginning in the year the mine commences production. Exploration costs are assumed to be amortized using the straight-line method over a five-year life.
- **Mine development.** These costs are charged to the project as capital and deducted using the straight-line depreciation method over a

10-year life beginning in the year the mine commences production. A full-year deduction is realized in the first year.

- **Mine, mill equipment, and sustaining capital.** All such costs are depreciated over a seven-year life using the straight-line method with a full-year deduction beginning when the mine commences production. All residual book values are written off in the final year and used against income in that year or earlier years using an amended return. Replacement costs are included in the model and, along with sustaining capital, are depreciated in a manner similar to the initial capital expenditures.

- **Financial position of mine investors.** It is assumed that no other income exists against which to use deductions that result in negative taxable income in the year incurred. Therefore, all losses are carried forward and used against future project income. The only exception to this rule is the final year of the project, when write-offs are taken if a loss is generated (it is assumed that the loss can be used to offset previous taxable income and reduce the actual tax paid in earlier years by filing an amended return, so tax savings are recognized in that final period). Loss-forward deductions are not subject to a limitation of the time over which deductions must be used.

- **Reclamation costs.** The final year of the project includes an allocation for reclamation of the project site but is not sufficient to backfill the open pit. This cost is assumed to be deductible in the final year as an operating expense. It should be mentioned that no allocation has been made in the early years for the escrowing of funds to satisfy this future liability. Such an inclusion and its annual imputed interest income, which is generally taxable, would diminish the economics by transferring more capital costs and taxes to the early years of the project. This issue may be economically substantial, but it is neglected in this model for simplicity.

- **Income tax.** The tax rate is 30 percent, which is assumed to be an effective rate incorporating the relevant federal and state or provincial taxes, except for royalties and withholding taxes. (In actuality, this effective rate will vary dramatically from country to country and may involve different bases of taxable income, which are assumed to be equivalent in each model for this study.)

Other taxes The models include a 10 percent dividend withholding tax based on positive after-tax cash flow generated in the preceding year. Furthermore, a loan interest withholding tax of 15 percent is also included and is based on the interest paid in that year. In practice, withholding rates may be more or less than 10 to 15 percent and may vary for any one country, depending on the existence of tax treaties. No other withholding or excise taxes are considered. Value-added tax is ignored since such taxes, if applicable, often are passed through, and although they may add a small component to the project working capital, the cumulative effect would be negligible in most projects; therefore, it is neglected in this study. No import or export duty is applied, reflecting the current trend in many mining countries.

Borrowed money   The models assume the inclusion of 60 percent borrowed funds from escalating capital expenditures incurred in the first years of mine development. Although accrued annual interest is paid beginning in the first year following the occurrence of any debt, the line of credit (loan amount) is paid off over a period of eight years, with a series of uniform principal payments along with the accrued annual interest beginning in the year initial production commences. The nominal loan interest rate is 6.0 percent per year, compounded annually.

Projects are often evaluated on a cash basis to avoid the distortion in value caused by leverage on an analysis. The inclusion of borrowed money is based on the assumption that the project has already been deemed viable from a cash perspective. Next, the effects of the financial parameters are addressed to fully understand the implications for cash flow when additional taxes are created, such as interest withholding. Sustaining and replacement capital costs are assumed to be financed out of the project's positive cash flow or cash.

Economic parameters   The project economics are based on nominal after-tax minimum rates of return of 12, 15, and 18 percent to analyze the effects of discount rate changes on the project economics. In general, leveraged project economics based on borrowed-dollar funding always have higher rates of return than project economics based on equivalent cash investment (100 percent equity), assuming the after-tax cost of borrowing is less than the cash investment rate of return. Therefore, a range of higher discount rates is justified for the leveraged project analyses in this study. With 60 percent borrowed money, a 15 to 20 percent minimum discount rate requirement may be considered appropriate by many companies. The 18 percent discount rate is used for the leveraged gold and copper models, and a 15 percent rate is used in the leveraged bauxite model. A 12 percent discount rate is used for the sensitivity analysis of the cash investment gold model.

Minimum rate of return (discount rate)   The minimum rate of return, or discount rate, will vary dramatically from company to company and depends on a number of factors. These may include (1) the location in the world of the deposit being evaluated and the associated political or environmental risks, (2) the size of the capital investment, (3) corporate growth objectives, (4) the handling of inflation and whether it is expressed in nominal or real terms, and (5) in some cases, the cost of borrowing money.

Economic decision criteria   Economic criteria include NPV based on after-tax cash flows, which are assumed to be discrete end-of-period values, and on the corresponding rate of return or IRR, which is the discrete compound interest rate that makes the after-tax NPV equal zero. For situations in which project cash flows create a cost-income-cost situation, the model uses a modified IRR that (1) considers the present worth of all negative cash flows at the minimum rate of return and (2) assumes the reinvestment of the positive cash flows, also at the minimum rate of return, and the resulting future value. The modified IRR is the compound interest rate that causes the escrowed initial investment to grow to the single future value from reinvested cash flows. For each of the criteria, after-tax cash flows are treated as escalated or nominal values that are realized discretely at the end of each year.

Model Results and Discussion

Using the three models, the study applied nine royalty methods and calculated the economic measures. To illustrate the differences that result from using different tax bases, a royalty rate of 3 percent or the dollar per unit equivalent were used in eight of the methods and applied to the different tax bases. The results clearly demonstrate the dangers inherent in comparing royalty tax rates between nations when the tax basis is not identical. The royalty methods applied are described in the section of Chapter 3, "Types of Royalties and Assessment Methods," which also gives sample calculations. The royalty methods modeled were selected because they illustrate the methods that are currently in use and that are often the subject of debate between companies and government tax policy makers.

Companies often calculate project economics based on both a leveraged and a nonleveraged project finance basis. The following summary tables and analysis are based on models that incorporate the leveraged assumptions, described above, except for the gold model, for which both a leveraged and a nonleveraged analysis are illustrated.

Table 4.1 addresses various aspects of the gold model with leveraged financing, and Table 4.2 looks at the difference in the economic measures without the effects of leveraging. (The leveraged data in Table 4.1 are based on the assumption that 60 percent of the up-front capital requirement is borrowed at a nominal interest rate of 6 percent per year, and the cash investment data in Table 4.2 assume the investor is paying 100 percent of the expenditures with zero borrowed money.) The IRR and NPV columns are based on the definitions given earlier in this section (the IRR is a compound interest rate measure of performance; NPV is a measure of value added relative to investing elsewhere). The gold model NPV calculations use a 12 percent minimum rate of return on cash investment and a corresponding 18 percent minimum rate of return for the leveraged model.

The ETR is based on the cumulative royalty, withholding, and income taxes as a percentage of net smelter return (NSR) less all cash costs, as previously described. The ETR percentage is then broken down into the cash equivalent figures for the royalty and cumulative tax revenue generated for the host government. The results are summarized for three pricing scenarios (medium, high, and low), with corresponding gold values (in U.S. dollars) of $400, $440, and $380 an ounce, respectively. The cost-per-unit royalty is based on a value of 3.0 percent of the product selling price for each scenario, so the cost per unit and NSR royalties are identical in each model. The sliding scale royalty assumes the first incremental rate is 1.0 percent. This amount increases by 1.5 percent per $100,000,000 in NSR, up to 4.0 percent. No overall annual percentage limitation exists in the sliding-scale calculations.

As a comparison of the magnitude of impact of leveraged and cash model assumptions, Table 4.3 summarizes a simple arithmetic average of the cumulative royalties the government would receive using the nine different royalty methods, along with the overall government fiscal receipts. The cash and leveraged gold models realize almost identical average royalties over the mine life. The average of profit-based royalties

Table 4.1. Gold Model (leveraged) Summary of Royalty and Tax Calculations[a]

Royalty type and basis	IRR (%)	NPV at 18% (US$ millions)	ETR (%)	Cumulative royalty (US$ millions)	Cumulative royalties and taxes (US$ millions)
Medium profit scenario ($400/oz.)					
(0) No royalty	22.79	41.2	33.50	0	350
(1) Unit based ($12/oz.)	20.38	19.7	42.05	135	439
(2) NSR	20.33	19.7	42.05	135	439
(3) Mine mouth value plus premium	19.76	14.8	43.96	165	459
(4) Mill value plus premium	20.23	18.8	42.40	140	443
(5) NSR plus premium	20.28	19.2	42.22	138	441
(6) NSR less freight	20.37	20.0	41.92	133	438
(7) NSR less all cash costs	21.85	32.9	36.58	48	382
(8) NSR less cash cost less capital deductions	22.50	38.3	35.18	27	368
(9) NSR sliding scale (1% plus Δ1.5%)	21.06	25.7	40.16	105	420
High profit scenario ($440/oz.)					
(0) No royalty	30.23	112.0	33.63	0	503
(1) Unit based ($13.20/oz.)	27.89	88.8	40.19	148	601
(2) NSR	27.89	88.8	40.19	148	601
(3) Mine mouth value plus premium	27.35	83.6	41.67	182	623
(4) Mill value plus premium	27.79	87.9	40.46	155	605

(continued)

Table 4.1. *(continued)*

Royalty type and basis	IRR (%)	NPV at 18% (US$ millions)	ETR (%)	Cumulative royalty (US$ millions)	Cumulative royalties and taxes (US$ millions)
(5) NSR plus premium	27.84	88.3	40.33	151	603
(6) NSR less freight	27.92	89.1	40.10	146	600
(7) NSR less all cash costs	29.19	101.8	36.30	61	543
(8) NSR less cash cost less capital deductions	29.85	107.2	35.18	39	528
(9) NSR sliding scale (1% plus Δ1.5%)	28.51	94.1	39.06	123	584
Low profit scenario ($380/oz.)					
(0) No royalty	18.62	5.1	33.4	0	274
(1) Unit based ($11.40/oz.)	16.03	(16.0)	43.74	182	359
(2) NSR	16.03	(16.0)	43.74	182	359
(3) Mine mouth value plus premium	15.42	(20.9)	46.05	157	378
(4) Mill value plus premium	15.92	(16.9)	44.16	133	362
(5) NSR plus premium	15.98	(16.5)	43.95	131	360
(6) NSR less freight	16.07	(15.7)	43.57	126	357
(7) NSR less all cash costs	17.70	(2.5)	36.83	43	302
(8) NSR less cash cost less capital deductions	18.37	3.1	35.18	21	287
(9) NSR sliding scale (1% plus Δ1.5%)	16.82	(9.6)	41.17	97	338

Source: Authors John Stermole and Frank Stermole.

a. Results based on a 3.0% royalty rate except for the unit based and sliding scale.

Table 4.2. Gold Model (100% equity) Summary of Royalty and Tax Calculations[a]

Royalty type and basis	IRR (%)	NPV at 12% (US$ millions)	ETR (%)	Cumulative royalty (US$ millions)	Cumulative royalties and taxes (US$ millions)
Medium profit scenario ($400/oz.)					
(0) No royalty	14.59	59.3	34.19	0	393
(1) Unit based ($12/oz.)	13.26	28.0	41.95	135	483
(2) NSR	13.26	28.0	41.95	135	483
(3) Mine mouth value plus premium	12.95	21.0	43.69	165	503
(4) Mill value plus premium	13.20	26.7	42.26	140	486
(5) NSR plus premium	13.23	27.4	42.10	138	484
(6) NSR less freight	13.28	28.4	41.83	133	481
(7) NSR less all cash costs	14.03	46.2	37.13	51	427
(8) NSR less cash cost less capital deductions	14.35	53.3	35.86	29	413
(9) NSR sliding scale (1% plus Δ1.5%)	13.61	35.9	40.23	105	463
High profit scenario ($440/oz.)					
(0) No royalty	18.59	163.1	34.11	0	546
(1) Unit based ($13.20/oz.)	17.33	128.8	40.24	148	644
(2) NSR	17.33	128.8	40.24	148	644
(3) Mine mouth value plus premium	17.04	121.2	41.62	182	666
(4) Mill value plus premium	17.28	127.4	40.49	155	648
(5) NSR plus premium	17.31	128.2	40.37	151	646

(continued)

Table 4.2. *(continued)*

Royalty type and basis	IRR (%)	NPV at 12% (US$ millions)	ETR (%)	Cumulative royalty (US$ millions)	Cumulative royalties and taxes (US$ millions)
(6) NSR less freight	17.35	129.3	40.16	146	643
(7) NSR less all cash costs	18.00	147.2	36.72	63	588
(8) NSR less cash cost less capital deductions	18.29	154.3	35.81	41	573
(9) NSR sliding scale (1% plus Δ1.5%)	17.62	135.8	39.18	123	627
Low profit scenario ($380/oz.)					
(0) No royalty	12.33	7.1	34.26	0	317
(1) Unit based ($11.40/oz.)	10.92	(22.9)	43.42	182	402
(2) NSR	10.92	(22.9)	43.42	182	402
(3) Mine mouth value plus premium	10.59	(29.6)	45.47	157	421
(4) Mill value plus premium	10.86	(24.1)	43.79	133	405
(5) NSR plus premium	10.89	(23.5)	43.60	131	404
(6) NSR less freight	10.94	(22.4)	43.27	126	400
(7) NSR less all cash costs	11.79	(4.6)	37.48	45	347
(8) NSR less cash cost less capital deductions	12.12	2.6	35.91	23	332
(9) NSR sliding scale (1% plus Δ1.5%)	11.32	(14.4)	41.14	97	3,810

Source: Authors John Stermole and Frank Stermole.
a. Results based on a 3.0% royalty rate except for the unit based and sliding scale, as indicated.

Table 4.3. Comparison of the Gold Model Average Cumulative Royalties and Average Cumulative Overall Taxes for the Cash and Leveraged Models

Average gold price	Cash investment model (US$ millions)		Leveraged investment model (US$ millions)	
	Total royalties	Total of all taxes	Total royalties	Total of all taxes
$400/oz.	103	623	103	579
$440/oz.	108	462	107	418
$380/oz.	116	381	115	338

Source: Authors John Stermole and Frank Stermole.

is different because the interest expense and interest withholding taxes are included in the measure of operating profit. The cumulative tax paid varies between the cash and leveraged models because interest paid on borrowed money is included in the withholding tax. The deductibility of that interest influences the overall magnitude of taxable income and, therefore, income taxes, especially in the early years. In the model, when dollars are taxed at 15 percent under a withholding tax and that tax is deductible, income is sheltered from taxation at the higher rate of 30 percent.

To clarify, the cash model creates more cumulative tax, on average, for several reasons. First, income tax is paid earlier, since allowable deductions for interest paid and the corresponding withholding tax on interest do not exist. This exposes more project revenues to income taxation at the proportionally higher rate (30.0 percent) in the early years. Depending on the royalty methodology used and the pricing of the commodity, the cash model routinely begins paying income taxes by years two through four of the project, whereas leveraged models often begin paying income tax by years four through eight. Second, as a result of no principal payments being incurred, cash flow is greater in the earlier years despite higher income taxes, and the withholding tax grows in magnitude as a result of the larger cash flow, resulting in more tax.

Although profitable at $400 per ounce, under the structure of this set of assumptions, the cumulative tax is far in excess of NPV generated. However, the two models are not directly comparable, and one misleading aspect under the low pricing scenario is the inclusion of all cumulative royalty and cumulative tax realized over the mine life. The data suggest that for a government to collect those taxes, a mine operator would have to be willing to develop and continue operations while realizing an unsatisfactory measure of overall project economics, which does not seem likely. This would result in closure, or at least deferral, of overall value while waiting for higher commodity prices.

Table 4.4 summarizes findings regarding the copper model and is based solely on leveraged results. The IRR and NPV columns are based on the previous definitions contained in this section. To compute the NPV in the copper model, an 18 percent leveraged minimum rate of return has been used. As with the gold model, the ETR is based on the cumulative royalty, withholding, and income taxes as a percentage of NSR, less all cash costs, as previously described. This ETR percentage is then broken down into the cash equivalent figures for the royalty and cumulative tax revenue generated to the host government. The results are summarized for three pricing scenarios described as medium, high, and low, with corresponding values of $1.10, $1.45, and $0.85 per pound. The unit-based royalty is based on a value of 3.0% of the product selling price for each scenario, so the unit-based and NSR royalties are identical in each model. The sliding-scale royalty assumes the first incremental rate is 1.0 percent, and this amount increases by 1.5 percent per $100 million in NSR up to 4.0 percent. No overall percentage limitation exists in the sliding-scale calculations. The marginal economic aspects of this project for copper prices below $1.00 per pound make some of the low profit royalty and tax data meaningless, since few companies would accept such a low return and corresponding negative NPV on invested capital.

Table 4.5 summarizes findings regarding the bauxite model and is focused on the leveraged results. The IRR and NPV columns are based on the definitions contained in this section. To calculate NPV in this model, a 15 percent leveraged minimum rate of return has been used. There are a variety of reasons for choosing to use a different discount rate. One reason might be the willingness to accept a smaller rate of return on a larger investment, in which case a large cash flow base might be perceived as financially desirable. Also, the project might be located in a country with a more stable political and tax history, allowing for reduced financial risk from the venture. As in the gold and copper models, the ETR is based on the cumulative royalty, withholding, and income taxes as a percentage of gross revenue reduced by cash expenditures of all types. This percentage is then broken down into the cash equivalent figures for the royalty and

Table 4.4. Copper Model Summary of Royalty and Tax Calculations[a]

Royalty type and basis	IRR (%)	NPV at 12% (US$ millions)	ETR (%)	Cumulative royalty (US$ millions)	Cumulative royalties and taxes (US$ millions)
Medium profit scenario ($1.10/lb)					
(0) No royalty	24.26	98	36.97	0	846
(1) Unit based ($0.033/lb)	21.93	61	44.23	252	1,012
(2) NSR	21.93	61	44.23	252	1,012
(3) Mine mouth value plus premium	20.94	46	47.26	358	1,082
(4) Mill value plus premium	21.61	56	45.20	286	1,035
(5) NSR plus premium	21.88	60	44.38	257	1,016
(6) NSR less freight	21.98	62	44.03	245	1,008
(7) NSR less all cash costs	23.08	80	40.35	117	924
(8) NSR less cash cost less capital deductions	23.87	92	38.88	67	890
(9) NSR sliding scale (1% plus Δ1.5%)	23.38	85	39.31	81	900
High profit scenario ($1.45/lb)					
(0) No royalty	46.38	487	35.53	0	1,765
(1) Unit based ($0.0435/lb)	43.81	439	39.93	333	1,983
(2) NSR	43.81	439	39.93	333	1,983
(3) Mine mouth value plus premium	42.72	419	41.76	471	2,074
(4) Mill value plus premium	43.46	433	40.52	377	2,012
(5) NSR plus premium	43.75	438	40.02	339	1,987

(continued)

Table 4.4. *(continued)*

Royalty type and basis	IRR (%)	NPV at 12% (US$ millions)	ETR (%)	Cumulative royalty (US$ millions)	Cumulative royalties and taxes (US$ millions)
(6) NSR less freight	43.85	440	39.84	326	1.978
(7) NSR less all cash costs	44.77	459	38.06	192	1,890
(8) NSR less cash cost less capital deductions	45.53	469	37.39	141	1,857
(9) NSR sliding scale (1% plus Δ1.5%)	45.38	472	36.65	84	1,820
Low profit scenario ($0.85/lb)					
(0) No royalty	4.63	(205)	51.38	0	94
(1) Unit based ($0.025/lb)	2.34	(240)	85.50	195	323
(2) NSR	2.34	(240)	85.50	195	323
(3) Mine mouth value plus premium	1.37	(256)	99.75	276	376
(4) Mill value plus premium	2.03	(245)	90.05	221	340
(5) NSR plus premium	2.30	(241)	86.18	199	325
(6) NSR less freight	2.42	(239)	84.28	188	318
(7) NSR less all cash costs	3.85	(218)	62.64	64	236
(8) NSR less cash cost less capital deductions	4.52	(205)	53.73	14	203
(9) NSR sliding scale (1% plus Δ1.5%)	3.71	(220)	65.09	78	246

Source: Authors John Stermole and Frank Stermole.
a. Results based on a 3.0% royalty rate except for the unit-based and sliding-scale royalties, as indicated.

Table 4.5. Bauxite Model Summary of Royalty and Tax Calculations[a]

Royalty type and basis	IRR (%)	NPV at 12% (US$ millions)	ETR (%)	Cumulative royalty (US$ millions)	Cumulative royalties and taxes (US$ millions)
Medium profit scenario ($340/tonne Al_2O_3)					
(0) No royalty	21.45	360	35.76	0	3,437
(1) Unit based ($10.40/tonne)	20.19	287	41.67	867	4,006
(2) NSR	20.19	287	41.67	867	4,006
(3) Mine mouth value plus premium	19.94	272	42.85	1,039	4,119
(4) Mill value plus premium	20.03	277	42.46	982	4,082
(5) NSR plus premium	20.17	285	41.76	884	4,017
(6) NSR less freight	20.20	287	41.63	861	4,002
(7) NSR less all cash costs	20.82	324	38.20	328	3,672
(8) NSR less cash cost less capital deductions	21.14	340	37.70	285	3,624
(9) NSR sliding scale (1% plus Δ1.5%)	20.03	277	42.47	985	4,083
High profit scenario ($390/tonne Al_2O_3)					
(0) No royalty	27.26	722	35.38	0	4,904
(1) Unit based ($11.70/tonne)	25.94	638	40.08	994	5,556
(2) NSR	25.94	638	40.08	994	5,556
(3) Mine mouth value plus premium	25.68	621	41.01	1,192	5,685
(4) Mill value plus premium	25.76	626	40.70	1,127	5,643
(5) NSR plus premium	25.92	636	40.17	1,014	5,569

(continued)

Table 4.5. *(continued)*

Royalty type and basis	IRR (%)	NPV at 12% (US$ millions)	ETR (%)	Cumulative royalty (US$ millions)	Cumulative royalties and taxes (US$ millions)
(6) NSR less freight	25.95	638	40.05	988	5,552
(7) NSR less all cash costs	26.52	675	37.63	476	5,217
(8) NSR less cash cost less capital deductions	26.85	692	37.28	402	5,168
(9) NSR sliding scale (1% plus Δ1.5%)	25.74	624	40.83	1,155	5,661
Low profit scenario ($290/tonne Al$_2O_3$)					
(0) No royalty	14.91	(5)	36.81	0	1,974
(1) Unit based ($8.20/tonne)	13.60	(72)	45.85	7	2,459
(2) NSR	13.60	(72)	45.85	7	2,459
(3) Mine mouth value plus premium	13.32	(86)	47.66	887	2,556
(4) Mill value plus premium	13.41	(81)	47.06	838	2,524
(5) NSR plus premium	13.57	(73)	46.04	754	2,469
(6) NSR less freight	13.61	(72)	45.78	733	2,455
(7) NSR less all cash costs	14.37	(33)	39.74	240	2,131
(8) NSR less cash cost less capital deductions	14.68	(16)	38.87	168	2,085
(9) NSR sliding scale (1% plus Δ1.5%)	13.47	(78)	46.78	815	2,509

Source: Authors John Stermole and Frank Stermole.
a. Results based on a 3.0% royalty rate except for the unit-based and sliding-scale royalties, as indicated.

cumulative tax revenue generated for the host government. The results are summarized for three pricing scenarios for alumina and are described as medium, high, and low, with corresponding values of $340, $390, and $290 per tonne. The unit-based royalty is based on a value of 3.0 percent of the product selling price for each scenario, so the unit-based and NSR royalties are identical in each model. The sliding-scale royalty assumes the first incremental rate is 1.0 percent, and this amount increases by 1.5 percent per $100 million in NSR up to 4.0 percent. No overall percentage limitation exists in the sliding-scale calculations.

Finally, Tables 4.6 and 4.7 summarize the findings from a different perspective. Here the focus is on the percentage or value per unit that could be applied to the royalty definition and still provide the investor in each mine model the minimum rate of return. Once again, the gold model is used to address the added sensitivity of financing from the perspective of cash investment. In solving for the breakeven royalty rate, the objective is to change the royalty rate to make the overall project NPV equal zero at the desired minimum rate of return. This is accomplished using an iterative routine in the spreadsheet models for the medium pricing scenario.

Any calculation is subject to the unique qualities of the parameters that make up the model. This is certainly true of the findings represented here. The breakeven results above are a function of the magnitude and timing of all costs and revenues as well as of the methodology used to deduct various expenditures and the ability, or lack thereof, to use deductions when incurred. Table 4.7 demonstrates these same characteristics for the copper and bauxite models, which are based solely on leveraged methodology.

Note that for profit-based royalty methods 7 and 8 (based on NSR minus cash costs and capital deductions), the leveraged breakeven royalty rates are higher than the equivalent cash investment breakeven royalty rates. This is because tax deductions for interest and interest withholding reduce the royalty basis from that of the equivalent cash investment. Therefore, to achieve breakeven economics, a higher royalty rate must be applied to the smaller leveraged royalty basis compared with the cash investment royalty basis.

Many governments use models such as these to investigate what type and rate of royalty to levy. The breakeven royalty rates (such as calculated and reported in Tables 4.6 and 4.7) for a model mine that represents

Table 4.6. Gold Model Breakeven Royalty Rates That Achieve the Minimum IRR

Royalty type and basis	Royalty rate yielding minimum IRR (%)[a]		Cumulative royalty (US$ millions)[b]	
	Cash	Leveraged	Cash	Leveraged
Gold, medium profit ($400/oz.)				
(0) No royalty	n.a.	n.a.	n.a.	n.a.
(1) Unit based ($/oz.)	$22.71	$22.77	255	256
(2) NSR	5.68	5.69	255	256
(3) Mine mouth value plus premium	4.64	4.65	255	256
(4) Mill value plus premium	5.46	5.47	255	256
(5) NSR plus premium	5.57	5.58	255	256
(6) NSR less freight	5.76	5.78	255	256
(7) NSR less all cash costs	13.51	14.53	232	238
(8) NSR less cash costs less capital deductions	29.47	41.67	292	377
(9) NSR sliding scale (1st rate plus Δ1.5%)	4.44	4.53	260	264

Source: Authors John Stermole and Frank Stermole.
Note: n.a. = not applicable.
a. Minimum cash internal rate of return is 12.00 percent; leveraged IRR is 18.00 percent (% except where noted).
b. Cumulative royalties reflect 12.00% (cash IRR) and 18.00% (leveraged).

average mines in the country would often not be used by governments to set the rate for all mines. The royalty rate selected would almost always be less than the breakeven rate for the model mine because of the recognition that many mines would be economically less robust than an average mine.

The tables in this section clearly show that the definition of the tax basis plays a significant role in the amount of royalties generated. The distinction is particularly clear when comparing ad valorem royalties

Table 4.7. Breakeven Royalty Rates Necessary to Achieve the Minimum IRR in the Copper and Bauxite Models

Royalty type and basis	Royalty rate yielding minimum IRR (%)	Cumulative royalty (US$ million)
Copper, medium profit ($1.10/lb; minimum IRR of 18.00%)		
(0) No royalty	n.a.	n.a.
(1) Unit based ($ /lb)	$0.0871	666
(2) NSR	7.79	666
(3) Mine mouth value plus premium	5.59	666
(4) Mill value plus premium	6.99	666
(5) NSR plus premium	7.77	666
(6) NSR less freight	8.12	664
(7) NSR less all cash costs	15.69	619
(8) NSR less cash cost less capital deductions	42.10	957
(9) NSR sliding scale (1st rate plus Δ1.5%)	8.42	650
Bauxite, medium profit ($340/tonne; minumum IRR 15.00%)		
(0) No royalty	n.a.	n.a.
(1) Unit based ($/tonne)	$49.35	$4,194
(2) NSR	14.51	4,194
(3) Mine mouth value plus premium	12.11	4,194
(4) Mill value plus premium	12.81	4,194
(5) NSR plus premium	14.23	4,194
(6) NSR less freight	14.59	4,188
(7) NSR less all cash costs	28.68	3,480
(8) NSR less cash cost less capital deductions	51.14	5,001
(9) NSR sliding scale (1st rate plus Δ1.5%)	12.13	4,200

Source: Authors John Stermole and Frank Stermole.

(methods 2 through 6 and method 9) with those based on profit (methods 7 and 8). For that reason, nations using profit-based royalty methods assess at rates significantly higher than applied by nations using ad valorem–based systems.

The arguments for implementing each royalty method vary. In general, mining companies might prefer a profit-based royalty that limits the mine's financial and economic exposure. This can be achieved by allowing for, at least in part, the calculation of the royalty basis using the recovery of invested capital and operating expenditures incurred in extracting, processing, transporting, and selling the final product. The mitigation of project financial and economic risk and the sharing of the profits with the host government also increase the complexity of verifying relevant numbers. Given the added complexity in audits and economic modeling of investment alternatives, some investors might be willing to accept a smaller percentage ad valorem– or NSR-based royalty, which is easily calculated. It also will reduce the likelihood of litigation related to measuring profit or other aspects of profit-based royalty in future years. Such posturing will, at least in part, depend on the perceived overall economic viability of the deposit at the feasibility study stage. The economic acceptability of an ad valorem royalty system will likely also depend on the perceived stability in a tax system imposed by the host government. This is true in any industry, not just mining. Communities grow in a stable job environment that is in part commensurate with a stable tax system that businesses can estimate in their economic models.

Obviously, the more economically robust a mine might be, the more likely it is that such projects contain the ability to incur a royalty at almost any level. Economically marginal projects brought on line during cycles of higher commodity prices will obviously be more susceptible to the imposition of new or additional taxes, which might take the form of new royalties that reduce available after-tax cash flow needed by investors seeking a return on capital.

As mentioned earlier in this section, a government may attempt to model the type of deposits likely to exist in a country to understand which system might generate the desired level of royalty income. However, it is difficult to foresee a royalty system or measure of taxation that would impose the same relative tax effect across the economic spectrum of possible projects and that would not place a bigger burden on some projects compared with others.

Royalty and Tax Effects on Mine Cutoff Grade

Discussions between companies and government decision makers regarding royalty types and methods usually include the topic of royalties' impacts on interrelated production parameters such as cutoff grade, reserves, and mine life. Mines are operated to generate profits, and their designs are optimized to generate maximum profits within assumed cost and price scenarios. The imposition of a royalty in any form is a cost and thus will influence production parameters that are set to optimize mine profitability. This section begins with a general discussion about how production parameters are decided using economic tools and then illustrates the impact of royalties on cutoff grade using a version of the copper model described in the preceding section of this study.

Economic Considerations Affecting Production Parameters

Evaluation of alternatives to determine economically optimum design
Evaluating alternative mine plans to determine the economically optimum design involves analyzing a number of mutually exclusive alternatives. Generally, this can be achieved by maximizing NPV. Incremental analysis is the key to correctly evaluating mutually exclusive alternatives in any industry situation and is necessary with any economic measure of profitability other than NPV. In addition to the economic considerations, other parameters also will influence the optimization decision, including decisions imposed by regulating authorities such as the Securities and Exchange Commission in the United States or the equivalent authorities in other markets, as well as by the analysts who use the same financial numbers to measure corporate value. Another consideration concerns the internal parameters that a company's management deems appropriate to ensure that the company focuses on those projects that create the maximum overall wealth for shareholders. Therefore, a project that creates positive NPV may not be of sufficient magnitude to affect the overall value of the firm and might be overlooked. Other considerations might include accounting for environmental effects and social or religious implications of investments to the indigenous people of the region.

Use of NPV to evaluate alternatives   NPV is the present worth of a project's after-tax cash flows, discounted at a compound interest rate that reflects the other opportunities thought to exist for the use of available funds, over the project life. Economically speaking, all costs and revenues affect the after-tax cash flows that are the basis for analyzing optimum mine plans using a criterion like NPV. Royalties, withholding taxes on interest and dividends (cash flow), income taxes, excise taxes, value-added taxes, and local taxes are government-imposed costs that must be accounted for in mine plan cash flows, and in effect they are economically equal to operating expenses and capital costs. If overall costs are too high compared with the projected future revenues, thus causing the NPV to be negative for a specified discount rate, the project will not be undertaken. The imposition of higher costs in an otherwise economically viable project may cause both the investor and the government to incur opportunity costs equal to the investors' forgone potential profit and to the government's take in the form of royalty, income taxes, and so forth. Both the investor and the government must understand this and work together to find a set of mine plan parameters that create an economically viable project for both the investor and the government.

A very important area of mine plan analysis involves determining the economically optimum cutoff grade, again for a set of assumed mine plan parameters. Important inputs to cutoff grade analysis include government royalties and other taxes, as well as operating costs, capital costs, and projected grade, recovery, and product sale prices.

Cutoff grade analysis will affect the quantity of ore reserves that can be economically produced, which will affect the optimization of annual production rates. Production rate changes can affect a variety of characteristics, including most mining costs, mining methods, and transportation of waste and ore. Other costs include capital expenditures related to the mine equipment, development costs, mill size and its overall cost, working capital costs, and operating expenditures. More specifically, changing the cutoff grade in a surface mine may affect stripping ratios, which may affect the cost of mine equipment needed to move a given tonnage per day, week, month, or year. Cutoff grade may also affect the metallurgical recovery and the desired design and cost of milling facilities, along with the cost of tailings and mine waste considerations. Changing the cutoff grades in an underground mine affects the block model and thus the timing and continuation of production.

This royalty study is intended to demonstrate that royalties and taxes of all types affect the cash flows upon which cutoff grade analysis is based. Decisions might be based on the marginal revenues and costs that will give the investor a desired rate of return on invested capital, thus making all costs relevant to the cutoff grade decision. A lower cutoff grade means bigger reserves and either longer mine life or bigger annual production rates, both of which are very positive project considerations for investors and governments alike. In the perfect theoretical world, the investor and government would work together to develop a royalty and other tax structure that would result in optimum development of an ore body and maximize value to both the producer and the government from all revenue sources.

Up to this point the discussion in this section has been related to pre-production mine plan analysis based on the optimum cutoff grade. Once a mine is in production, changes in parameters such as product price, operating costs, royalties, or taxes can necessitate reconsideration of the economic cutoff grade. Increases in energy costs have the same over-all impact as the imposition of new royalties or other taxes; such costs squeeze profitability from the extraction, processing, and transporting of any product. Once mining production becomes economically marginal for a given average ore grade, both the investor and the government must recognize that changing the cutoff grade affects reserves and mine life, which in turn affect project economics and the royalty and taxes paid to the government. The indirect economic factors, such as mining and re-lated jobs, are affected by the expansion of mine production by a reduced cutoff grade that increases reserves, or by shutting down a mine because the current cutoff grade has become uneconomic.

On the financial side, changes in cutoff grade have a direct impact on the ability of the company to grow reserves, which is a key consideration in measuring the financial and economic viability of any resource com-pany. Financial implications in many companies today are at least as im-portant as the economic implications measured by cash flow. Wall Street and analysts from all the financial markets of the world place a heavy pre-mium on reserves and net income, along with before-tax operating prof-its, which some refer to as "earnings before interest, taxes, depreciation, and amortization," or EBITDA. Any negative changes to these numbers can be devastating to a public company's financial ability to raise capital through the stock market and to undertake the projects in question.

Determination of project viability   The imposition of a new cost (such as a royalty) in an existing mine cash-flow model may influence the deci-sion of when is the appropriate time to consider shutting down an opera-tion. How should management consider the point in the life of a project when it has reached its economic limit? Many companies and financial analysts suggest that it is appropriate when the price of a product drops to the level that net income is less than zero. But is net income the appro-priate measure? Some analysts might prefer the use of operating profit or before-tax cash flow based on revenue received, less the cash costs incurred in a period. Others may prefer the use of after-tax cash flow, which would further account for the various tax aspects of the project, which are also real costs and benefits that directly affect economic criteria such as NPV.

Variable costs may often be identified as operating expense in economic evaluation cash-flow models. *Operating expense* is a summation of the cash costs associated with producing and selling products. However, accountants use various methodologies for valuing inventory, and these can cloud the true cash expenditures in a period, at least from the viewpoint of the net income statement. In other words, if units are drawn from inventories, the cost of those items may have been incurred in an earlier period and, therefore, do not represent true cash costs in the period the units are finally sold.

At issue is whether a true economic breakeven should reflect the non-cash charges related to depreciation, depletion, amortization, and write-offs. Or should cutoffs be determined by after-tax cash flow? Other issues might include the long-term prospects for a project versus short-term cyclical issues and whether the analysis is of an ongoing operation or a project yet to be determined. Once a company invests millions or billions for a project, the costs are sunk, but given the cyclical nature of commodity pricing, companies won't want to walk away until they are convinced the project is no longer capable of adding economic value to its shareholders. In most instances the due diligence of evaluating the economic potential is built into the mine model and development scheme, so it's the extraordinary items, such as the imposition of unexpected taxes or higher energy costs that might force a mine into early closure.

The industry to which these concepts are applied really doesn't matter; all investors must determine when it is no longer economically viable to continue producing and selling a product. Economic theory would suggest that this occurs when the incremental revenues received are just sufficient to cover the incremental costs, or marginal revenues are equal in magnitude to the marginal costs. However, it is also important to recognize that a low-cost producer may still not be an economic producer.

Many gold companies advertise their low cash cost of producing an ounce of gold, but does that mean that the operations are profitable in the long run? It certainly helps, but depending on the magnitude of the capital structure of the operation, long-term economics may vary from very profitable to something less so. Hence, many would argue that the depreciation related to preproduction development, capital improvements, research and development, and general and administrative cost (which may or may not be included as a cash cost according to a company's definition) must always be included in any breakeven calculation.

On the other hand, depreciation and amortization deductions are non-cash items and, as such, are always added back to net income to determine after-tax cash flow. Many times companies may see profitability squeezed to the point that net income is zero (or negative) while the operating or project cash flow is still positive. Doesn't positive cash flow add to the value of a company or shareholder? If so, what magnitude of value is necessary for shareholders to realize an increase in the share price? In other words, positive cash flow of $1 million per year may add value to a project, but it may do very little to contribute to the overall value of a large mining company, given the overhead required to realize that figure.

All of this discussion simply points to the complexities of establishing the basis of the breakeven calculation or the economic cutoff point for a mine. Whether investors are evaluating replacing haul trucks or a pump, expanding a chemical plant, creating a new product line, or developing a mine, the concept of the economically optimum life of an investment opportunity should be one of the first issues evaluated in the economic analysis. Because cash is what really drives value for any investment, these calculations should, in a perfect world, be based on the after-tax cash flow generated from an operation. In reality, often the U.S. Securities and Exchange Commission and equivalent authorities of financial reporting around the world dictate the calculation be based on net income and the corresponding definitions of an economical product. In the breakeven cutoff grade analysis presented here, the economic mine life is the mine life with the maximum NPV based on after-tax cash flow. When annual after-tax cash flow becomes negative as a result of increased costs, royalties, taxes, and so forth, or because of decreased revenue from declining ore grade or product price, it is arbitrarily considered that the investor will terminate production. In practice of course, many mitigating factors could defer the cutoff point to a later time.

To illustrate some of these complex considerations, the simple example in Table 4.8 is based on a single capital investment of $480,000, which is assumed to be straight-line depreciable over six years. A 40 percent overall income tax rate is assumed.

The project depicted has positive net income each year, so the indication is that since the marginal revenues exceed the marginal costs (based

Table 4.8. Measuring Project Value with Net Income
U.S. dollars

Year	1	2	3	4	5	6
Production units (000)	1,000	1,000	1,000	1,000	1,000	1,000
Selling price, $/unit	270	270	270	270	270	270
Operating cost, $/unit	140	140	140	140	140	140
Revenue	270,000	270,000	270,000	270,000	270,000	270,000
Less operating costs	(140,000)	(140,000)	(140,000)	(140,000)	(140,000)	(140,000)
Less depreciation	(80,000)	(80,000)	(80,000)	(80,000)	(80,000)	(80,000)
Taxable income	50,000	50,000	50,000	50,000	50,000	50,000
Less income tax payable	(20,000)	(20,000)	(20,000)	(20,000)	(20,000)	(20,000)
Net income	30,000	30,000	30,000	30,000	30,000	30,000

Source: Authors John Stermole and Frank Stermole.

on cash operating costs and depreciation), the operation would continue through year six. To illustrate the importance of after-tax cash flow, if the net income were related to an earlier investment of $480,000, then the cash flow from invested capital would be as shown in Table 4.9.

Despite an operating profit (revenue minus operating costs) of 48 percent of gross revenue, and net income–to-revenue of 11 percent, this project is not economically sound when it comes to long-term, overall value as indicated by NPV or other discounted cash-flow criteria. The NPV shown above is 12 percent, and IRR is 9.93 percent (less than 12 percent), both of which are economically unacceptable. For a minimum rate of return of 12 percent, the overall project is therefore unacceptable. Thus, the example shows that management and investors can't rely on net income alone (or cash flow, for that matter) in any one year as a measure of overall project profitability. Instead, a series of calculations are used to measure overall profitability and other variables, such as financial risk.

Capital investment aside, if operating costs were changed to an escalating scenario as described in Table 4.10, at what point would management recommend shutting down operations?

Table 4.9. Measuring Project Value with After-Tax Cash Flow
U.S. dollars

Year	0	1	2	3	4	5	6
Net income		30,000	30,000	30,000	30,000	30,000	30,000
Plus deprec.		80,000	80,000	80,000	80,000	80,000	80,000
Capital	(480,000)						
After tax cash flow	(480,000)	110,000	110,000	110,000	110,000	110,000	110,000

Source: Authors John Stermole and Frank Stermole.
NPV at 12%   (27,745)   IRR = 9.93%

Table 4.10. Economic Cutoff with Net Income
U.S. dollars

Year	1	2	3	4	5	6
Production units (000s)	1,000	1,000	1,000	1,000	1,000	1,000
Selling price, $/unit	270	270	270	270	270	270
Operating cost, $/unit	90	85	95	130	190	215
Revenue	270,000	270,000	270,000	270,000	270,000	270,000
Less operating costs	(80,000)	(85,000)	(95,000)	(130,000)	(190,000)	(215,000)
Less depreciation	(80,000)	(80,000)	(80,000)	(80,000)	(80,000)	(80,000)
Taxable income	110,000	105,000	95,000	60,000	0	(25,000)
Less income tax paid	(44,000)	(42,000)	(38,000)	(24,000)	0	10,000
Net income	66,000	63,000	57,000	36,000	0	(15,000)

Source: Authors John Stermole and Frank Stermole.

From a viewpoint of net income, the breakeven cutoff point could be the end of year four or year five, depending on whether a net income of zero is considered to be financially acceptable. However, if the project after-tax cash flow is considered and the economic measures calculated, the long-run economics appear to add value for shareholders, as shown in Table 4.11.

The cash flow is still positive each year, and the $116,000 in year four and $80,000 in year five would be contributing to an increase in the overall project NPV. In fact, without those years, the project NPV for years zero through four is negative (Table 4.12).

Table 4.11. Economic Cutoff with After-Tax Cash Flow

U.S. dollars

Year	0	1	2	3	4	5	6
Net income		66,000	63,000	57,000	36,000	0	(15,000)
Plus depreciation		80,000	80,000	80,000	80,000	80,000	80,000
Less capital	(480,000)						
After-tax cash flow	(480,000)	146,000	143,000	137,000	116,000	80,000	65,000
NPV at 12%	13,915						

Source: Authors John Stermole and Frank Stermole.

Table 4.12. Cutoff Impact on NPV

U.S. dollars

Year	0	1	2	3	4
Net income		66,000	63,000	57,000	36,000
Plus depreciation		80,000	80,000	80,000	80,000
Less capital	(480,000)				
After-tax cash flow	(480,000)	146,000	143,000	137,000	116,000
NPV at 12%	(64,410)				

Source: Authors John Stermole and Frank Stermole.

With an additional deduction related to the remaining write-off of $160,000 (taken in year four, assuming the investor could use that deduction), the NPV would increase to $23.74, still indicating an unsatisfactory investment opportunity. Assuming all parameters remained the same, the only way this project could ever have been approved is if the years five and six after-tax cash flow were included in the business plan. In addition, if the same business plan were to focus on net income, the result would suggest terminating the project at the end of year four to maximize value.

If a project is generating positive cash flow, in the end it is still adding value; however, criteria based on net income may punish such projects. To reiterate, optimizing the life of a project, or any asset used in a project, is or probably should be one of the first steps in establishing the economic model upon which a decision to accept or reject a project might be based. This decision will be influenced by the taxes, including royalty, imposed by the host government that is depending on the underlying viability of the project.

The mining world does not always provide such straightforward approaches as optimizing the life of a mine. In the case of South Africa, the goal of many jurisdictions is to maximize a mine's life rather than to economically optimize the mine. Mining companies face this issue frequently in both developing and developed countries. In other regions, local communities and indigenous peoples do not want their territory "optimized." Instead, they may want to minimize the environmental impact and maximize the mine life so that the mine will support employment in the region over the longest possible time.

Copper Model and Cutoff Grade

To illustrate the cutoff grade economics, the copper model introduced in the first part of this chapter was adjusted to reflect a declining average annual grade for copper (also see Appendix A2.4). The initial grades were increased to an average of 1.8 percent contained copper, and the recovery parameters previously described were maintained. The price was held constant at $1.05 per pound. Cutoff grade could be a focus of at least three different measures, including the following: marginal revenue and marginal costs, financial net income, and after-tax cash flow (basis for first analysis and Tables 4.13 and 4.14 and Figure 4.1).

Ultimately, in the development of a project, the economic objective is to maximize NPV to the investor. An NSR royalty has been used for a range of royalty rates, from 0 percent up to the breakeven rate (5.445 percent) that caused the project NPV to equal zero at the minimum rate of return of 18 percent for the leveraged model. In addition, a 6.0 percent NSR royalty rate is included to demonstrate the negative economic impact of royalty percentages on NPV at this level and beyond. Table 4.13 demonstrates how value diminishes to the producer (through NPV) as the royalty rate and subsequent revenues to the government increase.

The transfer of wealth in Table 4.13 really tells only part of the story. Examination of several measures, including annual operating profit, net income, and after-tax cash flow, would suggest that, depending on the magnitude of the NSR royalty imposed on the project, the mine is highly unlikely to remain economically viable for its expected life of 22 years. This is demonstrated in Table 4.14, which tracks project economic data for various NSR percentages up to the breakeven at 5.445 percent. The table also measures lost tonnage resulting from a shortened economic life.

Table 4.13. NPV vs. Cumulative Royalties on Copper and Government Take[a]

NSR royalty rate (%)	NPV at 18% (US$)	Cumulative royalty (US$)	Cumulative government take (US$)
0.000	140,265,487	0	343,869,421
1.000	55,068,448	65,648,085	258,461,918
2.000	42,725,646	131,296,170	302,224,251
3.000	30,376,178	196,944,255	346,032,585
4.000	18,013,580	262,592,340	389,987,012
5.000	5,557,749	328,240,425	433,955,824
5.445	0	357,448,811	453,584,932
6.000	(6,933,718)	393,888,510	478,073,748

Source: Authors John Stermole and Frank Stermole.
a. Calculations are based on $1.05/lb copper, assuming production continues over the entire 22-year life of the mine.

Table 4.14. Economic Data for Different NSR Percentages and Estimated Economic Reserve Data[a]

NSR (%)	IRR (%)	NPV at 18% (US$)	ETR (%)	Estimated economic life (years)	Tonnage produced	Tonnage lost
0.000	20.03	140,265,487	42.05	22	364,705,882	0
1.000	18.90	55,068,448	56.78	17	266,234,882	98,471,000
2.000	18.70	42,725,646	66.40	16	247,999,882	116,706,000
3.000	18.51	30,376,178	76.02	16	247,999,882	116,706,000
4.000	18.30	18,013,580	85.68	15	229,761,882	134,944,000
5.000	18.10	5,557,749	95.34	14	211,529,882	153,176,000
6.000	17.88	(6,933,718)	105.03	14	211,529,882	153,176,000
5.455	18.00	0	99.65	14	211,529,882	153,176,000

Source: Authors John Stermole and Frank Stermole.
a. Calculations are based on a uniform copper price of $1.05/lb.

Figure 4.1 shows that the large negative cash flow in year 11 is the result of anticipated replacement costs for mine and processing equipment. As shown by the marginal magnitude of cash flow occurring after this expenditure, a point-forward analysis of the negative cash flows and costs in years 8–11 might lead to termination of the project as early as year 8, which would further increase the production tonnage lost but maximize NPV at the end of the eighth year. Under a year eight closure, the project NPV is maximized at $67 million. The eight-year life and 3 percent NSR would represent an excess of 244 million tonnes of potential ore left in the ground. Looking at Table 4.15, the royalty take would be dimin-

Figure 4.1. Cumulative NPV Using $1.05 per Pound Copper

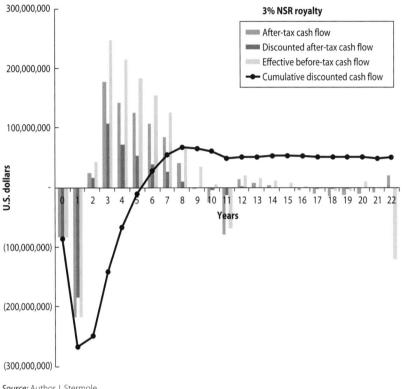

Source: Author J. Stermole.
Note: Graph assumes a 3% NSR.

ished by more than $100 million, and the overall government take would shrink as well.

The overall government take is diminished in the final year by a significant write-off and tax savings that are assumed to occur in the final year along with mine closure costs. This savings reduced the overall government take by some $140 million in the final year. In other words, without the write-off taken in year 22, the cumulative government take would have been closer to $486 million. The actual applicability of such savings to the project would be in question in any country where short-term loss-forward limitations exist, which would eliminate the ability of a producer to capture those savings.

If production were to continue beyond year 8, after year 15 no substantial economic value to the shareholder would result from continued

Table 4.15. NPV vs. Cumulative Royalties and Government Take, Assuming Production Is Continued over the Entire 22-Year Life[a]

NSR rate (%), life	NPV at 18% (US$)	Cumulative royalty (US$)	Cumulative government take (US$)
0.000, 22-year life	140,265,487	0	343,869,421
3.000, 22-year life	30,376,178	196,944,255	346,032,585
3.000, 8-year life	67,077,209	93,730,877	333,043,288

Source: Authors John Stermole and Frank Stermole.
a. Calculations are based on $1.05/lb copper.

operation of the mine at this level of royalty and the stated economic parameters. This is visually demonstrated by the flat NPV line out beyond
year 15. In fact, as mentioned earlier, the project NPV is truly maximized
in year eight and declines beyond that point. It is interesting to note that
although before-tax operating profit is positive in most years, the net
income is negative in many of the years because of a buildup of loss-forward deductions that end up being carried forward to the final year of the
project. However, even though the model assumes an economic benefit
in the final year, the project does not generate sufficient revenue to use
this deduction. Although the 3 percent NSR copper model described in
Figure 4.1 is not a measure of true financial net income, it does indicate
that the project is not going to be financially attractive from a banking or
stock market perspective. Furthermore, after-tax cash flow is approaching zero in the later years but remaining slightly positive. However, considerable financial pressure to close the mine may exist to minimize the
impact on overall net income.

The intent of the above example was to demonstrate as simply as possible the complex issues regarding the economically optimal life of a project. Overall economics were considered in examining the impact of royalties on the possible cash-flow stream from the government perspective.
Further complexity can be introduced by varying the price realized for
the commodity in future years. This has an effect similar to changing the
ore grade or recovery rate, but at perhaps a slightly different magnitude.

Figure 4.2 and Tables 4.16 and 4.17 summarize some of these findings for a forecast of copper prices cycling between a high of $1.30 and a
low of $0.90 per pound. The variation is not statistically rigorous from a
historical perspective but it is similar to the variations that have occurred
over the past 12 years. As shown in Figure 4.2, the NPV represented on
the cumulative discounted cash flow line is increasing up to the final reclamation year of the project. Hence, value is realized in the later years under

Figure 4.2. Cumulative NPV Using Cyclical Copper Pricing

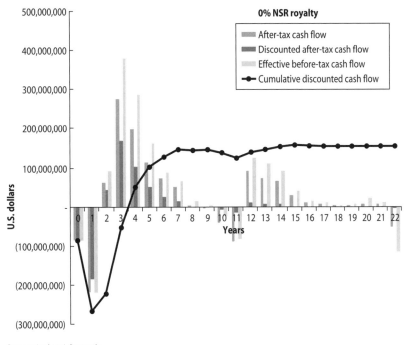

Source: Author J. Stermole.

Note: Graph assumes a 0% NSR.

the 0 percent NSR scenario. The lack of any significant decline in value in the final year is in part due to the time value of money and the significant write-off of loss-forward deductions that are recognized in the final year.

The higher initial price for copper ($1.30 per pound) generates sufficient cash flow in early years to increase the overall project NPV and therefore raise the breakeven NSR royalty rate that could be incurred to 11.67 percent. Once again, higher royalties result in a substantial increase in the overall government take and a transfer of the tax revenue from the income to the NSR side. Higher royalties also increase the possibility of a shutdown before the end of the expected 22-year life cycle. Therefore, although many financial and economic factors affect the management decision to shut down a mine earlier than expected, it is assumed for this study that when after-tax cash flow goes negative and is projected to stay negative, the mine will be closed.

The copper model shows that even with higher initial pricing, higher royalty percentages diminish the project NPV as they increase the ETR

Table 4.16. NPV vs. Cumulative Royalties on Copper and Government Take[a]

NSR royalty rate (%)	NPV at 18% (US$)	Cumulative royalty (US$)	Cumulative government take (US$)
0.000	157,085,997	0	379,753,606
1.000	144,202,695	69,274,939	425,085,777
2.000	131,051,898	138,549,878	470,425,476
3.000	117,854,567	207,824,817	516,098,845
4.000	104,583,953	277,099,756	562,033,672
6.00	50,404,627	554,199,513	749,016,126
9.000	36,743,159	623,474,452	795,752,452
11.670	0	808,423,759	920,510,096

Source: Authors John Stermole and Frank Stermole.
a. Based on cyclical copper prices and assuming project operation over the 22-year life.

Table 4.17. Economic Data for Different NSR Percentages and Estimated Economic Reserve Data, Based on a Cyclical Variation in Copper Prices

NSR (%)	IRR (%)	NPV at 18% (US$)	ETR (%)	Estimated economic life (yrs)	Tonnage produced	Tonnage lost
0.000	20.35	157,085,997	40.31	22	364,705,882	0
1.000	20.18	144,202,695	45.12	22	364,705,882	0
2.000	20.01	131,051,898	49.93	22	364,705,882	0
3.000	19.83	117,854,567	54.78	17	282,670,882	82,035,000
4.000	19.64	104,583,953	59.65	16	266,234,882	98,471,000
5.000	19.44	91,051,168	64.60	15	247,999,882	116,706,000
6.000	17.78	50,404,627	79.50	15	247,999,882	116,706,000
9.000	18.60	36,743,159	84.46	15	247,999,882	116,706,000
11.670	18.00	0	97.70	15	247,999,882	116,706,000

Source: Authors John Stermole and Frank Stermole.

incurred by the producer. Furthermore, tonnage lost as a result of the early shutdown of the mine would mean a smaller overall government take. Under the 3.0 percent NSR, considering that the project is closed by the end of year 15, the cumulative NSR royalty might be expected to reach $174,201,833 rather than $207,824,817. If the mine lasted 22 years, the cumulative government take would have been greater than what is shown in Table 4.16 (approximately $80 million greater for the 3.0 percent NSR).

Economic theory would suggest that an investor's true minimum rate of return reflects the other opportunities that exist for available capital budget dollars. Hence, the opportunity cost of capital represents the opportunity forgone or the internal rate of return passed up by selecting another alternative. Many publicly traded companies determine their minimum rate of return based on the minimum obtainable return for the use of capital, which may not represent investments in projects. Instead, minimum rate of return reflects a weighted average of two components, including (1) the cost of debt, and (2) the cost associated with providing shareholders the return they seek from dollars invested in the common stock shares of a company, which often is referred to as the cost of equity.

The return on equity is derived from dividends that might be paid and from appreciation in the stock price, both of which are a direct function of the after-tax cash flow the company generates. Companies might realize this return on equity by repurchasing existing stock in the marketplace. When debt is paid off early, the cost of servicing the debt is forgone, and the forgone interest to be paid is the return to the company for using its cash to retire the debt. Combining the average cost of existing debt that could be paid off or retired with the cost of equity provides a measure often known as the weighted average cost of capital. Often this is thought to be the minimum rate of return for available capital budget dollars. Companies that use a weighted average cost of capital as their minimum rate of return often set economic "hurdles" or benchmarks that project economics must exceed in order to be economically competitive with other perceived available rate of returns. Therefore, if a company discounts project cash flows at 8 percent, for example, that company might demand that the project exceed a hurdle rate of $250 million in NPV before it is considered to be economically attractive. Such an NPV measure might translate into an equivalent internal rate of return of 20 percent. The point here is that, for each company, depending on the approach to economic modeling, a project NPV of zero may not represent its perceived breakeven point.

Without using more detailed calculations, Table 4.17 shows that, for a company seeking an NPV in excess of $100 million from a project, any royalty rate in excess of 4 percent would cause the project to be economically unacceptable. Furthermore, the perceived risk that the royalty rate might go higher could be sufficient reason to withhold investment, because the project would be perceived to be economically marginal relative to other returns for available capital budget dollars.

The examples provided above show that the imposition of a royalty can influence decisions relating to interrelated production parameters such as cutoff grade, mine life, and reserves. Government policy makers for taxation need to be aware of the impacts that royalties can have on companies' decisions to optimize mines. In particular, it is important to understand that if a royalty method and rate impose too high a burden, overall tax take may be diminished as the cutoff grade is shifted to a higher value or when the mine life is shortened.

Discussion of Quantitative Results

Quantitative analysis is a useful aid when considering royalty policy design and implementation. Models such as those reported in the first sections of this chapter can be used as tools to evaluate the amount of royalty that can be generated using different assessment methods and to understand the impact that they have on a mining company's level of profitability. However, care must be used in the application of generic models. Every mine has unique economics reflecting factors such as its location relative to infrastructure and markets, the physical positioning of the ore body, the mine plan, the metallurgical qualities of the ore, the nature of the workforce, and so forth. A mine model that is used to establish an equitable balance between government and companies may in practice be less than equitable, favoring the government for some mines and companies for others.

To improve the possibility that a system will be mostly equitable, many governments undertaking tax reform will select a number of mine types to model that are representative of the types of mines currently operating or likely to be operating in the future. These models are then amended to study a number of scenarios, varying product prices, costs, and levels of taxation. In the end, the use of quantitative models will not yield an optimally equitable royalty for all mines, but will help policy makers better understand how possible types and levels of royalty will affect company profitability and other tax revenue levels. As discussed in Chapter 3, many other factors besides project economics—such as social objectives—will also influence the selection of royalty policies and methods. Among these factors is the possible goal of providing a taxation system that not only is equitable, but is, for exported mineral types, globally competitive. Calculated measures such as ETR and IRR are particularly useful for this purpose.

Mining companies use models such as those covered in this chapter both to make a decision on the economic feasibility of a project and to optimize mine design in order to maximize its profitability. Such models should always include taxation, including royalty, because taxes, like all other types of costs incurred by a project, can affect basic operating parameters such as cutoff grade (for nonhomogeneous ore bodies), mine life, and reserves. As reflected in the data reported in this study, most nations today impose a low level of royalty on most minerals. Thus, the effects of production decisions at many mines may be fairly minimal over the life of the mine.

A modest royalty will probably not affect a decision to proceed except in the case of economically marginal ore bodies. For the model mines in this chapter, for example, imposing a 3 percent NSR royalty, deductible for income tax purposes, would lower the IRR from 23 to 20 percent for the model gold mine (using the medium price scenario), from 24 to 22 percent for the copper mine, and from 22 to 20 percent for the bauxite mine. Although these impacts are anything but trivial, most investors would find the after-tax IRR still good enough to meet profitability criteria. The impact of royalty on more marginal mines may of course prove critical and lead to a decision not to invest.

In addition to decision factors such as IRR and NPV, some companies may also look at cost competitiveness. For example, a company may decide that if a potential gold mine would not be in the lowest 50th percentile of gold mines based on annual operating costs, the operation will not be built. Royalties are a cost and may move a mine's cost position relative to other mines. Mine models such as those in this chapter can be used to generate operating cost information useful for such comparisons.

The three mine models (copper, gold, and bauxite) compare how much royalty would be generated by nine different royalty methods. The nine methods were selected as generally representative of those used by various jurisdictions around the world, but they were not taken directly from any one nation. These sensitivity analyses emphasized that the breakeven rates might vary dramatically depending on royalty methodology, but also demonstrated the dramatic shift in the source of revenue to a government as well as the transfer of project risk. The models also imply that by allowing companies to recover capital expenditures from the mine profits, host governments that base royalties on profit are willing to assume some of the risk that goes with any mining project. The chapter also demonstrated the possible complexities of such methods, in terms of the auditing process. Audits are performed to verify that the appropriate deductions are considered and to monitor the possible inefficiencies created when companies are, in effect, encouraged to spend more money on projects so as to defer royalties or avoid an incremental change in the royalty rate.

The second section of this chapter used a variation on the copper model to demonstrate the impact of a newly imposed NSR royalty on the economic cutoff point. The discussion presented the theory of optimizing value by maximizing NPV. Other parameters that might affect the decision to shut down a mine were also discussed, including financial criteria such as net income, operating profit, and after-tax cash flow. The model first looked at a more substantial decline in copper grade to maintain a uniform price and then varied the price with the declining grade to demonstrate the impact. The economic life in these simple royalty models varied from the original estimated ore reserve of over 22 years, reducing it to only 8 years. A variation in mine life of more than 50 percent no doubt would drastically affect the desire of any company to undertake such a project, especially in light of tax or other uncertainties. This in turn would obviously affect the fiscal tax receipts of any government in which such a property might exist.

The next chapter moves away from the impacts that royalties have on individual mines to once again address broader issues that are of concern to companies, governments, and society. Informed government policy makers concerned with taxes must accommodate royalty issues at both the microeconomic and macroeconomic levels.

References

Cawood, Fred. 1999. "Determining the Optimal Rent for South African Mineral Resources." PhD diss., University of the Witwatersrand, Johannesburg.

Lown, Christopher J., ed. 2004. *The CRB Commodity Yearbook*. Commodity Research Bureau, Chicago, 112.

Otto, James, John Cordes, Maria L. Batarseh. 2000. *Global Mining Taxation Comparative Study*, 2nd ed., 92. Golden, CO: Colorado School of Mines.

Stermole, Frank, and John Stermole. 2006. *Economic Evaluation and Investment Decision Methods*, 11th ed. Investment Evaluations Corporation, Lakewood, CO.

Note

1. New York Mercantile Exchange, Inc., One North End Avenue, World Financial Center, New York, NY 10282. Data obtained March 23, 2005, http://www.nymex.com.

CHAPTER 5

Implications of Royalties for Investors, Civil Society, the Market, and Governments

This chapter examines the impacts that royalties may have on investors, civil society, markets for mineral commodities, and governments.

The Investment Climate

A mining country that relies on private firms to find and exploit its mineral resources must compete with other countries for investment. Its investment climate, which reflects how attractive the country is to domestic and foreign investors, depends ultimately on two considerations: first, the expected rate of return the country offers investors on their investments in domestic projects, and second, the level of risk associated with those projects. These two critical determinants in turn vary with a host of factors, including the country's geologic potential, political stability, level of corruption, tax regime, and government regulations.

National Ideology and National Reality
National ideology also plays an important role in shaping the investment climate. During the 1960s, 1970s, and 1980s, the Soviet Union, China, and other centrally planned economies made it clear they were not interested in private investment. Instead, these states assumed the responsibil-

ity for finding and developing their mineral resources. The same was true in many developing countries, including Bolivia, Chile, Peru, República Bolivariana de Venezuela, and Zambia, where private mining companies were nationalized and state enterprises were created. These actions were driven in part by the belief that the host country was not receiving a fair share of the wealth created by mining, and in part by the ideology of socialism, that the means of production should be owned by people collectively.

During these decades, four countries—Australia, Canada, South Africa, and the United States—attracted the bulk of the private investment flowing into the mining sector. The favorable investment climate that these countries enjoyed reflected in part their geologic potential, but equally or more importantly the fact that many countries with promising geologic conditions simply withdrew from the competition for political reasons.

In the late 1980s and early 1990s the global investment climate changed dramatically. Poor economic performance ultimately led to the breakup of the Soviet Union and the abandonment of central planning. The resulting shift toward greater reliance on the marketplace and private enterprise promoted changes in investment laws and other policies that enhanced the investment climate. Similarly, in many developing countries the failure of state mining enterprises produced a reversal of policy that favored private investment, particularly from abroad. As a result, by the early 1990s the global competition among mining countries for private investment had increased greatly. No longer could Australia, Canada, South Africa, and the United States count on receiving most of the world's investment largely by default. Chile, and to a lesser extent Indonesia, for example, received the lion's share of private investment in new copper mining capacity during the 1990s.

Now, early in the 21st century, signs are appearing in at least some developing countries of disillusionment with the widespread competition for private investment. Peru has recently imposed a royalty, and Chile, South Africa, and Zimbabwe are actively considering doing the same in the hope of extracting greater social benefits from their mining sectors. At the same time, in many parts of the United States and in other developed countries, there appear to be growing reservations, and in some instances open hostility, toward new mining projects for environmental and other reasons. Whether these developments will ultimately reverse the rising competition among mining countries for private investment funds, and if so by how much, remains to be seen.

Because countries compete with each other for private investment, a country's ultimate success in this endeavor depends less on the absolute attractiveness of its investment climate than on its attractiveness relative to other countries. Though this reality is often overlooked, the revenues and other benefits a country can realize from its mineral sector depend not only on its own geologic potential, political stability, and tax regimes, but also on events elsewhere in the world. For example, when political instability in Indonesia causes the investment climate in that country to deteriorate, investors tend to redirect their attention toward other mining countries.

In the early 1990s, the increase in competition among countries for mineral investment enhanced the options, and hence the bargaining power, of private investors relative to governments, thus allowing firms to retain more of the benefits derived from mining. To the extent that mining companies also compete among themselves, they presumably passed on most of these benefits to the consumers of mineral commodities in the form of lower prices.

Because the producers of mineral commodities are often (though clearly not always) developing countries, consumers are largely developed countries (though not always),[1] one might question the desirability of this redistribution of benefits. However, producing countries' efforts to alter this situation would require collusion to restrain their competition and to artificially raise their returns. History suggests that such endeavors are rarely successful for more than a few years. Moreover, while these practices are in effect, they tend to encourage new supply and reduce demand, which ultimately have a depressing effect on prices and the industry as a whole.[2]

Case Studies of Chile and Australia—Two Countries with Favorable Investment Climates

This section focuses on Chile and Australia, two countries that are widely perceived as having successfully fostered a favorable investment climate for mineral producers. The following section then examines Jamaica, Papua New Guinea, and South Africa, three countries that many believe have been less successful in this regard. The objective of both sections is to assess the role that royalties have played in shaping the investment climate in these countries, and ultimately in promoting the well-being of their citizens. This comparison, it turns out, is far from easy, in part because royalties are just one of a number of taxes that constitute the tax regime of a country. In addition, although the tax regime is a significant factor affecting a country's investment climate, other considerations— geologic potential, political stability, and national ideology, for example— are important as well. As a result, it is easy to misrepresent the role that royalties play in determining a country's investment climate. There are countries with and without royalties that enjoy favorable investment climates, and similarly countries with and without royalties that do not. In the grand scheme of things, the presence or absence of a royalty, though not insignificant, usually is not the overriding determinant of a country's investment attractiveness. Political stability, geologic potential, and the rest of the tax regime are typically more important.

Moreover, the goal of public policy is ultimately to maximize the social benefits a country derives from its mineral sector, which coincides, only up to a point, with increasing the investment climate. As Chapter 2 points out, there is a tax rate that maximizes the net present value of the tax revenues (and also a tax rate, which may be different, that maximizes the net present value of all the social benefits) that a country receives from its mineral producers. This optimal tax rate is not zero—even though a zero tax rate might very well maximize the investment climate from the perspective of private investors.

Given these caveats, what can be said about the use of mineral royalties in Chile and Australia? Have the governments of these countries implemented balanced royalty policies that promote the investment climate and serve their national interests?

Chile   Chile has offered private investors a very favorable investment climate over the past 20 years. The Fraser Institute annually conducts a poll of mining company officials (vice presidents for exploration), asking them to rank states, provinces, and countries according to their investment attractiveness. Chile has almost always been ranked at or very near the top.[3] Cross-country comparisons also indicate that Chile has a very favorable mineral taxation regime (Otto, Cordes, and Batarseh 2000). Perhaps most telling of all is the fact that Chile is home to most of the world's copper mines developed over the past two decades.

Because Chile does not have a royalty on mineral production (at least at the time this is written), one might conclude that the case of Chile indicates that the best royalty is no royalty. Yet within Chile, two quite different points of view can be seen on this issue. One school, reflected by the current government of Ricardo Lagos and its efforts to introduce a royalty, claims that a royalty would have little negative effect on the country's investment climate and would, among other benefits, significantly increase the revenues the country receives from the mineral sector. The opposing school, which not surprisingly includes many of the multinational mining companies operating in the country, contends that a royalty would seriously undermine the investment climate and appreciably reduce the benefits the country receives from its mineral sector, particularly in the long run.

The truth probably lies somewhere between, but which is the more realistic position cannot be known, particularly because of the still considerable uncertainty over the size and nature of the royalty to be imposed, assuming one actually is imposed. However, the ultimate impact of a royalty would depend on two important considerations. The first consideration is the effect of the increased tax burden and the resulting reductions in the expected internal rate of return (IRR) or net present value (NPV) on potential projects. A very modest royalty with little effect on expected tax revenues would presumably have little effect on the expected IRR of projects, but a royalty that doubles expected tax payments would. Similarly, a royalty that can be deducted or credited against a firm's corporate income tax would have less of a negative effect on after-tax revenues and the IRR of projects than a royalty that does not alter a firm's other tax obligations.

The second important consideration is the impact a royalty would have on the risks associated with domestic projects, as perceived by potential investors. Here several possible concerns may play a role:

- Royalties could increase the stability of the existing tax regime by reducing the political pressure to change the regime when mineral commodity prices are low or when mining companies are earning no profits and hence paying no corporate income taxes. Increasing the likelihood of the tax regime's permanence or stability might reduce political risk for many investors.
- Royalties are often based on value, weight, or volume of production and so have to be paid whether the producing firm is profitable or not (see Chapter 3). As a result, the introduction of these types of royalty, even if the expected tax is largely offset by reduction in income taxes, would force mining companies to accept more of the economic or market risk associated with new investment, while reducing the risk previously borne by the government.

- The introduction of a royalty could increase the perceived risks in yet another way. The Chilean government has in the past promised that the tax regime for mining companies would not be changed selectively once new mineral projects were in place. So the introduction of a royalty at this point could undermine the private sector's confidence in the credibility of the government and increase perceptions of political risk.

Another related and important issue that has received little attention concerns the sensitivity of investment flows to changes in investment climate. For example, if Chile introduces a royalty that has modest effects on the expected IRR of domestic projects and on the perceived risks associated with those projects, can it be confidently concluded that the royalty will that have little or no effect on future investment flows? Unfortunately, the answer is no. No prediction can be made as to how seriously private investment would be altered if perceptions of Chile's investment climate slipped slightly, so that the investment community perceived the country to be, for example, among the top five countries rather than the top one or two. Interestingly, more information may be available regarding this issue in the case of Chile in the near future. The Fraser Institute in Canada conducts an annual survey of top officials in mining companies, asking that they assess, from the perspective of private investors, the mineral potential and the policy environment for a large number of mining countries and states. The results are then used to calculate an Investment Attractiveness Index. In the 2003/04 survey, Chile was at the top of the list, indicating that it was considered the most attractive nation for investment by the companies surveyed. In the 2004/05 survey, corporate officials considerably reduced their assessment of the country's policy environment, presumably as a result of concerns over the government's plans to introduce a royalty, and as a result the country fell from first to fifth place on the index. The top four places were filled by Nevada, Western Australia, Quebec, and Ontario, in that order.[4] Of those, Nevada, Quebec, and Ontario impose royalties based on profits. What is not known, at least yet, is how sensitive private investment flows are to a modest drop in a country's investment climate, such as from first to fifth place, in the case of Chile.

In summary, the introduction of a royalty could have little or no effect on a country's investment climate or a dramatic effect, depending on the circumstances and the nature of the royalty. Similarly, it might or might not serve the public interest, depending on how it alters the benefits the country receives from its mineral resources. This uncertainty is troubling but probably unavoidable.

Australia   Australia is another country whose investment climate has been widely considered quite favorable. Moreover, unlike Chile, the country has considerable experience with mineral royalties. Under the Australian constitution, states have the right to collect royalties, and the governments of the six Australian states and the Northern Territory have done so for most minerals for many years. These royalties take a variety of forms—unit-based, ad valorem, and profit-based.

This discussion focuses on the gold royalty imposed recently by the state of Western Australia. Since the early 1890s, Western Australia has accounted for most of the country's gold production. The questions addressed here are: To what extent did the royalty undermine the investment climate in the gold mining industry of Western Australia? And did the royalty ultimately promote or undermine the welfare of the state?

Precise answers to such questions require comparing two scenarios: what happened with the royalty in place and what would have happened had the royalty not been imposed. Because the latter is a hypothetical situation, considerable uncertainty surrounds the answers to these questions. This uncertainty is compounded by the fact that the legislation introducing the royalty was passed only in 1997, and so the long-run situation with the royalty in place is also unknown.

However, if the royalty has seriously undermined the investment climate, manifestations of this would already be seen in the behavior of the industry. One might, for example, look at trends in gold production in Western Australia before and after the imposition of the royalty or, even better, trends in Western Australia's share of total Australian or world gold production.[5] Still, this measure suffers from gold production's lack of sensitivity to changes in the investment climate in the short run. The costs of exploration and development for operating mines are already sunk, so the mines are likely to stay in production for some time even though their profitability is significantly reduced or even eliminated.

A more useful measure might focus on trends in Western Australia's share of Australian or world expenditures on the development of new gold mines and the expansion of existing mines. However, since the exploration costs associated with new mine projects have already been made, an even more sensitive, early indicator of changes in the state's investment climate is Western Australia's share of total Australian or world exploration expenditures for new gold reserves. Annual gold exploration expenditures over the period 1996 to 2004 are reported in Table 5.1 for both Western Australia and all of Australia in millions of current Australian dollars. This table also shows that over this period Western Australia accounted for about 70 percent of the country's total gold exploration expenditures. While this share varied from a low of 67.3 percent in 1999 to a high of 74.5 percent in 2001, there is no clear downward trend following the introduction of a "reasonable" royalty on gold production in Western Australia in 1997. This suggests that the gold royalty in Western Australia has not seriously undermined the industry's investment climate in the state.

Again, it is important to stress the uncertainty surrounding this finding, because Table 5.1 shows only the actual trends in exploration expenditures before and after the royalty. These trends reflect changes in all the factors affecting Western Australia's share of total Australian exploration expenditures for gold between the two periods, of which the imposition of the royalty is but one. For example, the Australian income tax rate dropped from 36 percent to 30 percent around 2000/01, which may have reduced the impact of the royalty. The passage of the Australian Native Title Act in 1993 also is likely to have influenced exploration trends. Still, had the royalty been a major deterrent to investment in Western Australia, a more negative effect on the state's share of Australian gold exploration expenditures would have been apparent following the introduction of the royalty.

Table 5.1. Annual Gold Exploration Expenditures in Australia and Western Australia, 1996–2004

Year	Australia expenditures ($A millions)	Western Australia expenditures ($A millions)	Western Australia share of total Australian expenditures (%)
1996	623	430	69.1
1997	737	512	69.5
1998	562	410	72.9
1999	405	273	67.3
2000	372	260	69.9
2001	351	261	74.5
2002	355	253	71.2
2003	374	260	69.6
2004	414	284	68.5

Source: Australian Bureau of Statistics.

This conclusion still leaves two questions: First, Why did the Western Australian gold royalty not have a greater impact on the state's investment climate? Second, has the royalty served the public interest by promoting the welfare of the people of Western Australia?

Drawing on the previous case study of Chile, the modest effect of the royalty on Western Australia's investment climate can be assumed to reflect the fact that the royalty did not greatly alter the expected returns (IRR or NPV) of gold projects in the state or the perceived risks associated with those projects. One reason for this was likely the manner in which the royalty was applied. At the time the legislation introducing the royalty was passed, in 1997, it was to be a 2.5 percent ad valorem royalty that would take effect in 1998. However, because of depressed market conditions and the low price of gold, the royalty was applied at 1.25 percent from July 1998 and increased to the full rate of 2.5 percent in July 2000. However, from July 2000 to July 2005, the rate of 1.25 percent was applied in each quarter that the average spot price of gold was less than $A450 per ounce. Moreover, the first 2,500 ounces of gold production from each gold royalty project were exempt from the royalty.

Referring to these changes, Rob Fraser, an economist then at the University of Western Australia, in 1999 wrote:

> In doing so, the WA government has responded to the expressed concerns of the industry in relation to the detrimental impact of the royalty on profits, especially in times of relatively low prices. Moreover, at the same time it has created a novel form of resource taxation, where the revenue base of the tax is modified to take account of periods of unusually low profits, and where the price of gold is treated as a simple proxy for the level of profits. (35)

In short, despite the original intent to tax the value of gold output, the royalty as implemented taxes the value of output only when prices are sufficient for most firms to be profitable. This substantially reduces firms' expected costs of the royalty and the risk borne by the private producers arising from the cyclical nature of gold prices.

The final question, then, is, has the royalty served the interests of the citizens of Western Australia? If it is true that the royalty has had little impact on the state's investment climate, as suggested above, then the royalty has given the state and in turn its citizens a larger share of the pie (of rents or profits) created by its gold mining industry without significantly reducing the size of the pie. As stressed earlier, however, the evidence regarding the impact of the royalty on the investment climate, though suggestive, is not conclusive.

Case Studies of Jamaica, Papua New Guinea, and South Africa—Countries Where Taxation May Have Negatively Affected the Investment Climate

This section turns to three countries that have, at times, projected a less favorable investment climate: Jamaica, Papua New Guinea, and South Africa. Again, the objective is to assess the role that royalties have played in these countries, first, in affecting the investment climate, and second, in promoting the welfare of their people. It is worth highlighting, too, that the ultimate goal of public policy is to promote the well-being of society. Up to a point, countries that rely on private investors to find and develop their mineral resources will serve this goal by promoting a positive climate for private investment. Eventually, however, the two objectives will part, because promoting the welfare of society requires some taxation and other measures designed to increase the state's take of the mineral rents and profits, even though this means less for private investors and a somewhat less attractive investment climate.

Jamaica   The potential discrepancy between these two objectives—promoting a favorable investment climate and promoting the welfare of society—often makes it difficult to determine when public policies do and do not serve the public interest. An interesting illustration of this is the increase in taxes that Jamaica, along with most of the other Caribbean producers, imposed on bauxite exports in the 1970s, not long after the Organization for Petroleum Exporting Countries (OPEC) substantially raised the price of oil.

In the 1960s Jamaica imposed a royalty of US$0.26 per tonne on bauxite exports and, in addition, realized income taxes from bauxite production that averaged about US$2.25 per tonne. In 1974, the government raised the royalty to US$0.55 per tonne and imposed an additional tax on production equal to 7.5 percent of the average realized price of aluminum metal on world markets. These changes increased the revenues received by the Jamaican government from its bauxite sector many fold (Nappi 1979).

At the time, many observers argued that Jamaica was making a mistake. Unlike the consumers of oil, they noted, Alcoa, Alcan, and other aluminum producers had access over the longer term to many alternative sources of bauxite. Time proved the critics right, as Jamaica's share of world bauxite production dropped as the years passed. As a result, it is now widely thought that the Jamaican tax policy was based on a misunderstanding of the bauxite market and, regrettably, failed to serve the interest of the Jamaican people.

An alternative explanation was advanced by Carmine Nappi (1992), a Canadian economist at the University of Montreal and more recently chief economist for Alcan. He raised the possibility that Jamaican government officials understood the bauxite industry quite well and knew that, for various reasons, their country's share of the world bauxite market would inevitably decline. Given this situation, it made sense to raise taxes and exploit the country's market power while it still possessed some. If this interpretation of events is valid, the rise in taxes, though it undermined the country's investment climate, may well have served the public interest by promoting the welfare of the country.

Although it will probably never be known whether the conventional view or the view that Nappi suggests is closer to the truth, what the Jamaican experience illustrates is that promoting the investment climate and maximizing social welfare can be conflicting goals. Clearly, the new taxes the country imposed in 1974 seriously undermined the investment climate. Less clear, however, is whether or not the taxes served the welfare of society and the public interest of the country.

Papua New Guinea   In the latest Fraser Institute survey of mining companies, Papua New Guinea ranks 19th of a total of 64 jurisdictions on the survey's Investment Attractiveness Index, and Western Australia and Chile rank second and fifth. Although differences between Papua New Guinea and these two countries arise for many reasons, a reasonable case can be made that differences in their mineral royalties, at least until quite recently, have been in part responsible.

During the period 1996–2000, the government raised the royalty from 1.25 percent to 2 percent and imposed a 4 percent mining levy on assessable mining income (in effect, an additional royalty). These changes were imposed on top of a corporate income tax, a dividend withholding tax, an additional profits tax, and significant restrictions on deductions for off-site exploration expenditures. In addition, the state reserved the right to assume up to a 30 percent equity share in all projects at the time a mining lease is issued at a cost based on the project's exploration costs, not its full market value. This regulatory regime existed within a general environment of depressed metal prices, widespread concerns over sovereign risk, and the general political situation within the country.

By 2000, it was clear that the country had become uncompetitive in attracting new investment into its mineral sector. While exploration declined worldwide over the 1996–2000 period because of depressed metal markets, exploration within Papua New Guinea contracted even more rapidly, and the country's share of global exploration fell significantly. With the assistance of the Asian Development Bank, the country undertook a study of its fiscal regimes for mining and hydrocarbons. That study, known as the Bogan review, proposed a number of changes.

Responding to the recommendations of the Bogan review, the government in 2000 scrapped the mining levy for all new projects and proposed phasing it out for existing operations over a period of time. It also lowered the tax rate for the additional profits tax (APT) but simultaneously lowered the threshold IRR at which the APT comes into effect, from 20 percent to 15 percent. The mining industry and investment community welcomed the elimination of the mining levy but were unhappy with the reduction in the threshold rate of return for the APT, a tax that from its initiation had caused concern. As a result, the country remained uncompetitive, and its share of world exploration expenditures failed to recover.

In the hope of improving this situation, the government in 2002 conducted another study of its mining taxation regime. This review led to the complete elimination of the APT in early 2003, with reductions in the corporate income tax to 30 percent and the dividend withholding tax to 10 percent. The royalty rate was fixed at 2 percent of net smelter returns, and the restrictions on deducting off-site exploration expenditures were relaxed. The government also agreed to reassess its policy regarding the option it retains to acquire up to 30 percent of the equity in new mining projects.

Though it is still too early to assess the long-run effects of these changes, the initial signs are promising. Exploration has rebounded in the country, and its share of world exploration expenditures has begun to recover. Table 5.2 provides further support for this conclusion. The table, which is based on a study conducted for the 2002 government review, shows the IRR earned by foreign investors on a representative copper mine across 24 mining countries and states. The figures for Papua New Guinea are estimated twice—once under the tax regime that prevailed in 1999, and then for the tax regime in 2003. In 1999, Papua New Guinea was ranked

Table 5.2. Foreign Investor Internal Rate of Return and Total Effective Tax Rate for a Model Copper Mine in Selected Countries and States

Country	Foreign investor IRR (%)	Total effective tax rate (%)
Lowest taxing quartile		
Sweden	15.7	28.6
Chile	15.0	36.6
Argentina	13.9	40.0
Papua New Guinea (2003)	**13.8**	**42.7**
Zimbabwe	13.5	39.8
Philippines	13.5	45.3
2nd lowest taxing quartile		
South Africa	13.5	45.0
Greenland	13.0	50.2
Kazakhstan	12.9	46.1
Western Australia	12.7	36.4
China	12.7	41.7
United States (Arizona)	12.6	49.9
2nd highest taxing quartile		
Indonesia (7th, COW)	12.5	46.1
Tanzania	12.4	47.8
Ghana	11.9	54.4
Peru	11.7	46.5
Bolivia	11.4	43.1
Mexico	11.3	49.9
Highest taxing quartile		
Indonesia (non-COW 2002)	11.2	52.2
Poland	11.0	49.6
Papua New Guinea (1999)	10.8	57.8
Ontario, Canada	10.1	63.8
Uzbekistan	9.3	62.9
Côte d'Ivoire	8.9	62.4
Burkina Faso	3.3	83.9

Source: Otto 2002.

20th based on the estimated rate of return for foreign investors in the country; in only four countries was the return lower. In 2003, by contrast, Papua New Guinea enjoyed the fourth highest rate.

Although the above data are encouraging, more significant is the rise in mineral royalty to 6 percent during the 1996–2000 period, on which a number of other negative factors were superimposed, seriously undermining the investment climate in Papua New Guinea. Had the government not made changes in the level of royalties, and in the tax regime more generally in recent years, the adverse effects on mining would soon have reduced the benefits that the country derives from this important economic sector.

South Africa   The climate for mineral investment in South Africa is less favorable than in Chile, Australia, and many other countries for a variety of reasons. This section, like those preceding it, assesses the country's use of royalties. In particular, it considers the extent to which the recently announced royalty changes have contributed to the negative perception toward the country's investment climate and how successful those changes have been in promoting the welfare of South Africans.

Historically, royalties in South Africa have been determined on an individual mine basis by direct negotiations between the private investor and the owner of the mineral rights. In most cases the owner was a private individual or company, but in some instances, primarily at mines on state-owned lands, it was the state, represented by the Department of Minerals and Energy. The result has been a variety of different royalty rates and bases, with a lack of consistency across types of mineral commodities, kinds of ore bodies, and mine profitability.

The government, however, is in the process of changing this situation. With the introduction of its new mining law, the state took custodianship of minerals and, along with its new mining law, released a draft royalty bill in 2003. (Nothing in the act takes away common-law ownership of mineral rights. Instead, by claiming custodianship, the state controls access to mineral properties, rather than ownership, which implies expropriation.) A second draft bill is expected in the near future, and as a result of industry comments and concerns, that bill may be quite different.

The current draft royalty bill would impose an ad valorem royalty with rates that would vary by commodity—2 percent on total revenues for copper and other base metals, 3 percent for gold, and 8 percent for diamonds. Both the Chamber of Mines of South Africa (n.d.), which represents the country's larger mining companies, and the South African Mining Development Association (2003), which represents the country's junior mining companies, have expressed serious reservations about the draft bill. In particular, the organizations are troubled by the adverse effects they believe the proposed legislation would have on low-profit or marginal mines, the country's mineral reserves, the ability of the mineral sector to attract foreign investment, and the entry of historically disadvantaged South Africans into the mineral sector, which is an important goal of current mineral policy.

The Chamber of Mines (2003), for example, on the basis of a gold mine model developed to estimate the impact of a revenue-based royalty, concluded the following:

> Assuming a constant gold price, the 3 per cent gold royalty on turnover would have raised working costs from R318.40 to R330.40 per tonne using real 2002 numbers for the past decade. The cutoff grade would have risen from 4 to 4.2 grams per tonne. This means that the economically recoverable reserve base would have decreased by about 3.7 per cent from 16 250 tonnes to about 15 650 tonnes. In other words some 600 tonnes of gold would have effectively been sterilized by the introduction of a 3 per cent gold royalty on gross turnover. Using 2002 money terms this sterilization of 600 tonnes of gold underground is worth R62.5 billion or R1.6 billion per year over a 40-year period. This compares to the R1 billion in royalties achieved through a 3 per cent royalty . . .
>
> Based on employment numbers in the gold sector of about 207 000 workers on average in 2002 a 3 per cent royalty will sterilize about 4 per cent of the current economically recoverable ore body. Given the 91 per cent correlation between employment numbers and tonnes broken underground, a 4 per cent decline in the ore reserves will in the short-term probably reduce employment numbers by about 2 per cent, since there will be a lagged effect as companies restructure to survive the imposition of a royalty. In the longer-term the smaller ore body due to the royalty will result in a full 4 per cent decline in employment level. A 2 per cent decline in employment numbers constitutes about 4 100 employees whilst a 4 per cent decline covers 8 200 workers . . .
>
> The impact of the gross revenue royalty modeled for gold is equally applicable to all other minerals in South Africa. The imposition of a gross revenue royalty will raise cutoff grades and sterilize ore in the ground that will therefore never play any role in generating economic benefits for South Africa. (13–15, and Annex A)

Of course, mining companies have a strong interest in lower rather than higher taxes, so their desire to modify the proposed legislation is not surprising. Though this needs to be taken into account in assessing their concerns, their submissions to the government contain a number of case studies showing the effect of the proposed legislation on the profitability of specific companies. These studies suggest that the draft royalty bill would significantly alter the investment climate for many existing mines and presumably for a number of undeveloped mineral deposits as well, raising some legitimate questions regarding how well the proposed royalties would serve the public interest for the country as a whole.

Moreover, concerns regarding the impact of the pending legislation on the investment climate in South Africa are not confined to mining companies. They are also found in the trade press. The following, for example, are excerpts from an article in the *Mining Journal* (Swindells 2005):

> Uncertainty, delay and confusion have become the hallmarks of the Minerals and Petroleum Resources Development Act, which will become the bedrock legislation of democratic South Africa's mining industry by transferring exploration and mining mineral rights to the state, effectively abolishing all privately-held rights and paving the way for royalty taxes and 'black economic empowerment' (BEE) . . .
>
> The uneasiness over the workings of the act, which is stifling exploration activity and deterring badly needed foreign investment, comes as the industry tries to tackle a strong rand which has taken the shine off the global commodity price boom.
>
> It is also contributing doubts about the attractiveness of South Africa as a destination for foreign mining investment. (26–28)

Concerns that the proposals for a royalty and other changes in mining regulations are undermining the investment climate in South Africa, and hence not in the country's long-run interests, raise the question: Why does the situation in South Africa differ from that of Western Australia, where the recent introduction of a gold royalty apparently has not greatly altered the investment climate and seems to have served the public interest? Four important differences are readily apparent.

First is the overall investment climate in South Africa, which is adversely affected by a host of considerations not found in Western Australia. These include a much greater incidence of HIV/AIDS and tuberculosis, more crime and violence, greater costs associated with government-mandated social investment projects (including government efforts to promote "historically disadvantaged South Africans" by giving them preferential access to mineral resources), and the greater political uncertainty arising from public efforts to significantly transform the society in many important respects.

Second is the royalty rate, which in Western Australia is lower—only 2.5 percent of revenues on gold production compared with a proposed 3.0 percent in South Africa. Moreover, firms in Western Australia did not have to pay the full royalty when gold prices were depressed and profits were low or negative. This greatly reduced the royalty's impact on the expected returns from investment projects, and in turn on the economic risk associated with such projects.

Third is the historical common-law ownership of mineral rights in South Africa. In the past, mines were allowed to purchase mineral rights as immovable property, which gave mine owners the necessary security of tenure to develop the very deep gold mines. These mineral rights were acquired at huge expense, and with the new changes, mines will effectively pay a second time for essentially the same rights, this time as a royalty to the state. In cases in which mines have entered into long-term mineral royalty agreements (rather than sales agreements) with private owners of mineral rights, they will have to pay a double royalty under the new system—that is, paying a royalty to the state following the introduction of the new law while still honoring their contracts with common-law private owners of mineral rights.

Fourth, and perhaps most important, is the uncertainty created by the many new policies and laws that have been introduced in quick succession since 1994. The long delay with the new royalty regime has also contributed to the difficulty of predicting long-term cash flow. Finally, the new regime is unclear and untested, culminating in a higher risk premium for mineral development in South Africa, particularly compared with Chile and Australia.

Macroeconomic Implications—Government Revenue and Socioeconomic Indicators

Substantial differences in the investment climate of countries also arise as a result of their macroeconomic characteristics. Australia, Canada, Finland, Sweden, the United States, and other countries that have been successful in promoting economic development currently enjoy high per capita incomes. Because of that wealth, they enjoy strong legal systems and other well-developed social and political institutions. They also have a well-educated workforce and good infrastructure. All of these macroeconomic characteristics promote a favorable investment climate (the section "Impact on the Government and Host Country" in this chapter examines how mineral royalties can affect governments and the macroeconomy).

Revenue Distribution—Implications for Communities

A central policy question that must be addressed by any government levying a royalty is, should monies collected go into the central government's general expenditure fund (the fiscus), or should some or all of the royalty be set aside for a selected party, such as an affected community? The concept of collecting a tax with predetermined beneficiaries, other than for the public at large, is tied to the concept of *fiscal decentralization*. Otto (2001) has offered the following observation:

> The issue of fiscal decentralization is not new; it is an issue that every government is faced with. It goes to the heart of governance. Taxation is a means by which private capital is transformed into public capital for the benefit and use of society. Taxes are collected and then through the budgeting process are disbursed for public purpose. This budgeting process is arguably the most politically sensitive part of governance and is a major factor in the distribution of regulatory power. It can be argued that the entities that control the purse control the actions of the state. If one accepts this premise, then it follows that policies that define fiscal decentralization also define the distribution of power within the state (or vice-versa). Thus, in most systems of governance the power to levy taxes is approached with great caution and is inextricably linked to the basic structure of government as defined within the national constitution, organic act and similar primary laws. (1)

The sharing of revenues, as Otto has noted, may be dependent on the relative power of respective levels of governments. Although individual communities have relatively little power compared with the central government, they can exert a large effect on a mine, perhaps to the extent of preventing it or closing it. Thus, local activism can lead, in some instances, to rebalancing the distribution of a unique tax such as royalty.

The extent to which royalty collection and expenditure are decentralized from the general national budget varies widely. In many major mineral-producing nations the royalty is absorbed into the fiscus, but in many others, for example Argentina, Australia, Brazil, Canada, and Peru, to mention a few, royalty distribution is either left to provincial or local government budgets or forwarded to specific entities.

The concept of promoting sustainable development at the level of the affected community has gained interest over the past decade, and a key question that has arisen is how such efforts can and should be funded. Royalty, being a unique tax levied mine by mine, is, along with property value–based taxes, well suited for local distribution. Increasingly, governments are looking at distributing a portion of the fiscal benefits that arise from a mine to affected communities or districts. However, this interest is far from being a trend. Many nations still prefer to see all major taxes that are collected flow to the general fund, allowing central or provincial government to equitably determine where and how monies should be expended for the good of the public as a whole.

The following sections are examples of distribution systems in three regions: Africa, Asia and Pacific, and Latin America.

Africa   The methods of revenue distribution and beneficiaries of mineral royalties vary widely in Africa. Administration is mostly at the national level for the benefit of the general fund. This implies that mineral royalty funds lose their identity upon entry into the fiscus and are added to the government revenue pool. South Africa is an example of having a central fiscus from which funds are distributed to pay for services and for apportioning to lower levels of government. Mozambique does it differently. Its mining law provides for a percentage of royalties to be paid directly to lower levels of government.[6] Some countries, for example, Ghana and Namibia, have created a minerals development fund (MDF) for distribution purposes.

Ghana. Ghana has created an MDF to return part of the royalty income to communities directly affected by mineral development. Of collected mineral royalties, 20 percent are paid into the fund. Proceeds are then shared among the local government authority, landowner, and communities that are adversely affected by mining.

Namibia. Namibia has also created an MDF, but its expenditure is more broadly targeted than in Ghana. The Namibian MDF is aimed at the following:

- Promoting and supporting all aspects of mining.
- Broadening the contribution of the mining sector to the national economy through diversification and by stimulating economic linkages.
- Providing funds for the development of training and education facilities and programs.[7]

South Africa. South Africa has introduced an alternative revenue distribution with its newly promulgated Mineral and Petroleum Resources Development Act (MPRDA).[8] Although there is no provision for lower levels of government to benefit through mineral royalties, local communities have the potential to benefit substantially.

They are given the option to obtain a "preferent right"[9] over land and minerals registered in their name, which effectively gives such a community negotiation powers equal to those of the owners of the mineral rights and fosters community development and social uplift. To receive a preferential right, the community must submit a development plan to the Department of Minerals and Energy, which can be easily renewed for five-year periods. A preferential right permits the holder to either prospect or mine for the benefit of the community or, alternatively, to lease such rights to a mining company for a fixed consideration payable directly to the community.

The charter to the MPRDA gives preferential treatment, in accordance with black economic empowerment (BEE), in mine ownership, procurement, employment, and community inclusion into mine decision-making structures.[10]

Asia and Pacific   Within the Asia and Pacific region, most governments bring all royalty-type taxes directly into the central fiscus, but some allow a more decentralized approach. Examples are provided below from China, Indonesia, Papua New Guinea, and the Philippines.

China. China levies two different royalty taxes, one of which is deposited solely with the national treasury for the fiscus. The second one, called the mineral resources compensation fee,[11] is collected by the appropriate level of county, provincial, or city government, with 50 percent of the amount collected remitted to the central government and 50 percent retained by the provinces and cities. In autonomous regions the split is 40 percent to the central government and 60 percent to the region.

Indonesia. Over the past decade, Indonesia has embarked on a major effort to decentralize tax authority. This effort has also affected fiscal revenues derived from the mineral sector. Under current law, state receipts from natural resources, including mining, are distributed in the ratio of 20 percent to the central government and 80 percent to the region. The latter is split as 64 percent to the regencies and 16 percent to the provincial government.[12]

Papua New Guinea. In Papua New Guinea, the government levies royalty taxes under its mining act.[13] Provisions in the act dictate that owners of private land receive 20 percent of the total royalty paid for mining leases on the land. In practice, the amount payable to landowners can exceed 20 percent, such as the OK Tedi and Lihir mines, which pay 50 percent. Mining companies pay the landowners directly and pay the balance to the state, which expedites and ensures payments to landowners, subject to the state checking and endorsing the landowners' share for correctness.

Philippines. In the Philippines, by statute, local government units receive a 40 percent share of the gross collection from excise taxes on mineral products, that is, royalties, from mines in their territorial jurisdiction.[14] This amount is distributed as follows: 20 percent to the province; 45 percent to the component city and municipality; and 35 percent to the barangay (village or district).

Latin America   In Latin America, some nations collect royalty centrally, with the amounts going to the general revenue fund for expenditure through the regular budgeting process. However, several major mining countries provide for the royalty to be distributed to a variety of entities identified in the law. In Argentina, individual states are empowered to levy and collect royalty and to determine how it is to be expended. In Peru, royalty is collected by the national tax authority, and the amount collected is then distributed to statutorily defined parties according to specified percentages. In Brazil, the royalty law also provides that a variety of parties are to be paid statutorily defined percentages of the royalty, and most of these parties are paid directly by the miner. Inherent in any system in which payments go to the central tax authority for later distribution is the risk of a budget shortfall, so that payment to the other parties, even though set out in law, may be deferred or not made. This has been a recurring problem in some developing nations. Nations that allow entitled parties to be paid directly by the miner avoid this problem.

Argentina. Argentina's constitution vests ownership of minerals to the province in which they occur. It also gives the congress the exclusive power to levy direct taxes but allows delegation of that power. The premise is that royalty is a compensation fee payable to the mineral owner, and thus the ability to levy and collect royalty is given to the provinces. The federal government has an interest in the promotion of national interests, so although the state governments have the power to set royalty rates and to collect and spend the royalty, this power has been limited through the mechanism of a federally imposed upper cap of 3 percent.[15] The result has been that some provinces have opted to levy the maximum rate of 3 percent, but others have decided not to impose a royalty. For example, in the case of Catamarca, a principal mining province, the royalty rate has been set at 3 percent. Of the amount collected by the province, 15 percent is for distribution to the municipalities where the mining project is located to finance public investment projects; the remaining 85 percent is used to finance provincial projects or public investments in other departments or municipalities.

Brazil. In Brazil, taxation authority is set out in the constitution. It also states that, with regard to mineral resources, the states, federal district, and municipalities, as well as the federal government, are assured a "share in the results" of mineral resource exploitation in their respective territory. In accordance with the constitution, statutory law provides that certain proportions of royalty are to be paid to lower levels of government and other parties.[16] The distribution is defined as follows: 23 percent to the states and federal district, 65 percent to the municipalities, 2 percent to the national fund of scientific and technological development, and 10 percent to the mining and energy ministry, which shall give 2 percent of its share to environmental protection of the mining regions.[17]

Peru. In Peru, provincial and local community dissatisfaction with perceived nonparticipation in the benefits of mining led to political pressure that culminated in a royalty tax being imposed in 2004.[18] The royalty is to be paid to the central government and then distributed as follows: 20 percent to the district municipalities where the exploitation takes place (50 percent of that goes to the communities where the mine is located); 20 percent to the provincial municipalities where the exploitation takes place; 40 percent to the district and provincial municipalities; 15 percent to the regional government; and 5 percent to the national universities of the region where the mine is located.

As is illustrated above, in some cases the affected communities share directly in royalty revenues. However, such examples remain the exception. It is more prevalent for communities to share in a property tax, that is, a levy based on the book or market value of a mine's capital assets, than to have access directly to royalty. Many countries have no direct tax link between mines and communities.

Most mining companies probably prefer that some portion of royalties, if payable, be destined to affected communities. Because mining companies are increasingly concerned about maintaining a "social license to operate" and invest in affected communities, a royalty provides a relatively easy mechanism to channel funds. Direct investments in a community—for example, in roads, schools, medical support, and training programs—are not deductible for income tax purposes in many countries. Royalties are tax deductible in almost all nations.

Impact of Royalties on Social Commitments

Although their agendas are different, proponents of no, low, and high mineral royalties argue that a royalty has the potential to affect political risk.[19] Political instability is possible when governments charge little or no royalty, allowing the national patronage to be exported without benefit to the public. Mining companies may argue that mineral royalties that are too high will hamper a mine's potential positive developmental impacts, such as contributions to affected communities in whatever form, the creation of employment opportunities for nationals, and assistance to First Nations, in the North American context, or BEE in the African context.[20]

The impact of mineral development on communities is hard to establish without appropriate legislation and an effective government administration. There is little doubt that a mining company would prefer paying taxes to an efficient government administration that is able to deliver social services at all levels. However, this is rarely the case for developing countries, where the situation requires that the mining industry commit additional funds for social uplift in the areas that they operate. Their reasons differ from country to country and range from government regulation to voluntary contributions to community projects. This leaves the mining industry and its shareholders in uncertain territory and divorced from core business activities. Expectations of improved services escalate when mining companies move into new areas, resulting in the allocation of additional company resources to fulfill government functions. The return on this social commitment is measurable through the degree of political stability it affords. In other words, the company is awarded a social licence to operate. Table 5.3 shows examples of how mineral law can accommodate social contributions.

Governments can do a lot to close the emotive expectation gap that is often present in communities. Mining companies know that direct

Table 5.3. Relationship between Social Commitment and Mineral Royalties

Description	Canada Northwest Territories	Ghana	Namibia	Papua New Guinea	Philippines	Peru	South Africa	Tanzania
Social contributions:								
Social requirement	Yes	No	Yes	Yes	Yes	Yes	Yes	Yes
States willing to sacrifice royalties (set in law)	Yes	Yes	Yes	Yes	No[a]	No	Yes	Yes
Mineral royalties:								
Directly to community	Yes	No	No	No	Yes[b]	No	Yes[c]	No
Payable to state	Yes	Yes	Yes	Yes	Yes	Yes	Yes	Yes
Provision for sharing	Yes	Yes	No	Yes	Yes	Yes	No	No

Source: Author F. Cawood.

a. A higher royalty rate is applicable.

b. Through trust funds, 1 percent minimum contribution.

c. Through the community holding a preferent right.

payments to communities are fraught with trouble and may easily lead to political instability. Governments can assist in this regard by helping the community establish appropriate structures to communicate with mining companies, prove legitimacy, and receive and manage royalty and other social contributions. Typical challenges would be the need to identify the following:

- Which communities need help
- Who will administer contributions to the community
- Who decides how it should be spent
- The extent to which the mining company should be involved
- Whether company involvement in community decisions would result in a patronage mentality and whether that would be good or bad

The application of integrated environmental standards in mineral law has become the norm in most countries. Although the understanding of social commitment is not the same internationally, it has become standard practice to link developmental initiatives with mineral development rights. For example, Ghana requires a detailed program for the recruitment and training of Ghanaians when companies apply for mining rights. A minerals development fund was created to return part of the government income from mining to communities directly affected by such activities. Of the mineral royalties collected, 20 percent are paid into the fund, which is shared between the local government authority, the landowner, and the communities affected by mining. In Namibia, preference for employment is given to nationals, and provision must be made for training programs to ensure the transfer of technology and skills.[21] At the mineral development stage of a mine in South Africa, applications for mining rights must be accompanied by social, labor, and work programs. Monitoring of the programs' success is through annual reports in order to ensure that Scorecard goals are met. In Tanzania, social plans, labor plans, and local procurement plans express social commitments. These initiatives were implemented to address the global concern that benefits seldom accrue to host communities who bear the brunt of mining-related impacts. However, remote communities seldom provide skills suitable for mine employment, and in practice, royalties payable to the central government rarely revert back to the affected region, even when the legislation specifies that this should be the case.

It is expected that legislation requiring social commitment is likely to grow significantly in the future as states implement sustainable development principles in their mining regimes. Compliance with work, environmental, and social plans is measured through regular reporting to public and regulatory authorities. Compliance and reporting appear to have become the major instruments for ensuring and measuring good corporate governance. This situation is all well and good in theory, but it will be of little significance if host governments do not have the capacity to review, interpret the information, and act appropriately when assessing company reports.

Good corporate citizenship has received significant media attention in recent years. According to a report by the King Committee on Corporate Governance (2002) in South Africa, *corporate citizenship* could be defined as "Business decision-making linked to ethical values, compliance and legal requirements, and respect for people, communities and the environment" (p. 96). Corporate governance issues were raised as a consequence of corporations' historical disregard for communities and the environment, exacerbated by their drive to increase shareholder value. In the case of mining, this quest for profits has sometimes left a negative footprint characterized by environmental degradation and social decline over time, to the extent that it has caused political unrest at mine sites and long-term liability of host communities and governments. The public outcry in response to this situation and the sustained pressure on governments to prevent negative impacts have left communities with a bigger say in the future of mineral development in their immediate vicinity. Today, an increasing number of countries protect community rights with legislation, often at the constitutional level. Compliance and good governance issues have been elevated to the extent that the King report used the following motivation for good governance: "If there is a lack of good corporate governance in a market, capital will leave that market with a click of a mouse."

The impact of royalties on social commitment was recently evident in Peru. The Tambo Grande incident illustrated the power of communities to stop mine development if they perceive local benefits to be inadequate. The confrontational tactics against the mine included blockades, demonstrations, and a national march by affected communities. In June 2002, the community voted against the development of the mine, despite the fact that the government of Peru had already authorized Manhattan Minerals (a Canadian mining company) to do so.[22] In addition to objecting to the inadequacy of community benefits, protestors cited the involuntary relocation of community members and adverse impacts on the environment. The response in Peru was to mitigate the political risks associated with mining projects by implementing a new royalty law and distribution scheme (see Appendix A1).

Mine environmental issues are frequently used as a front in order to motivate companies to improve community benefits. A well-publicized[23] international example is Newmont's Minahasa Raya project in Indonesia. The project has a history of allegations, such as forced resettlement of villagers, inadequate compensation to villagers, and pollution of Buyat Bay by mine tailings. The pollution charges remain unproven, and one could conclude that the real issue is the perceived inadequacy of community benefits, mainly as a result of unfulfilled expectations. Newmont is also affected by a similar situation at Yanacocha (a gold mine in Peru), where claims against the company range from water pollution and subsequent fish kills, to social degradation caused by prostitution and crime as a result of mining near communities. At the heart of this problem is inadequate infrastructure and social services. Normally, governments will provide these functions but because of the belief that Newmont initially obtained the rights at a bargain price without allowing for sufficient follow-up royalties to pay for improved government services to the affected community, the project was resisted. According to Newmont (2004), the new royalty regime will take care of these issues.

Some states have a provision that when mineral royalties threaten the existence of the firm, such royalties could be reduced or even waived. This could be interpreted as mine survival—corresponding social commitments are more important than the receipt of mineral royalties to some governments. The sacrifice of mineral royalties in times of economic hardship helps to avoid political instability caused by retrenched mine workers and their dependents. An alternative view on this issue is that the shortfall in government revenue as a result of nonpayment of royalties may further exacerbate the government's inability to deliver services, which could also lead to political unrest.

Royalties affect the cost of production, and when mines are expected to contribute to social development (also a production cost), socioeconomic contributions may be at risk when the price mines receive for production is not sufficient to pay for these costs. This poses the question, what can states do to balance the need to charge royalties with the development needs of communities? What is required is a more flexible system that allows some trade-offs to be made between the allocation of benefits to local communities and the collection of royalties, thus benefiting broad-based public empowerment.

To answer the question posed above, a reevaluation of the following issues might be necessary:

- The traditional hierarchy of claims to mineral revenues, which currently favors recipients of royalties
- The allowable deductions for calculating the royalty base, which may allow community contributions as a deduction before calculating the royalty payment
- An increase in the royalty rate in order to include the community contribution, which will be collected by states and paid over into dedicated community funds
- Waiving of royalties in favor of community contributions in times of economic hardship

Fear of Losing Brownfields Competitiveness

Exploration efforts are often classified as being either greenfields or brownfields. The term *greenfields* refers to exploration efforts to locate new economical deposits apart from known deposits. Most explorers consider brownfields exploration to be devoted to extending reserves within a known ore body, searching for extensions to it, or looking for associated ore bodies in the immediate vicinity of the mining rights area.

Aside from the different technologies and methodologies employed in greenfields and brownfields exploration, they may also differ in terms of internal funding. Large firms often segregate the funding of greenfields exploration from that of mining and establish separate budgets and companies for the two purposes. The funding for brownfields exploration often will flow from the mining company and its budget rather than from the exploration company and its budget. This distinction can be important. Subsidiary exploration companies are not expected to generate profits—they explore, not produce. In contrast, subsidiary mining units are expected to generate profits. Royalties are a direct cost of a mining operation and thus affect profits. When a mine manager is pressed to show a profit—particularly when profits are low or nonexistent, such as when mineral commodity prices dip—he may be reluctant to invest in brownfields exploration. This can lead to fewer new reserves being identified, at least in the short run. However, when budget allocations are made at the "parent" level in the company (above the level of an individual mine manager), greenfields budgets will almost always be sacrificed in favor of brownfields budgets during hard times, because such exploration is cheaper and the risks are much lower.

Natural competitiveness is shaped by natural economic forces and is traditionally measured by the impact of working costs. Upward changes to mineral royalties, which cause the costs of existing mines to increase, are feared by industry, whose cash flow forecasts are done at the mine development stage. If the upward adjustment is significant, greenfields competitiveness will be affected almost immediately, because the investment decision (potential projects are in different royalty jurisdictions) will favor the location with the lowest cost. However, operating mines have fewer options and will have to either increase efficiency (resulting in lower costs) or relinquish expansion plans and further investment in exploration. At that stage, brownfields competitiveness is lost, because new opportunities will not be considered unless the quantity and quality of the ore body can make up for the loss of competitiveness. In summary, the less profit that can be earned, the less money spent on exploration. The imposition of a new or increased royalty is less likely to curtail brownfields exploration than greenfields because the major investment has already been made.

Royalties in any form will reduce brownfields' competitiveness. Unit-based royalties may have the greatest impact during periods of low prices because they are insensitive to both profit and price changes. Ad valorem–based royalties may have a lesser effect because, although they are insensitive to profits, they do move up and down relative to price. Profit-based royalties will have the least budgetary impact. Almost all nations allow brownfields exploration to be expensed as costs are incurred, if it occurs within the tax-paying mine's mining rights area.

Perception of Tax Regime Stability and Country Risk
Mines represent captive capital; once built they are not amenable to being moved. This implies that they are more vulnerable to changes in national tax policy than other forms of investment that are portable and suitable to relocation to a friendlier tax jurisdiction. Many mines are long-lived, and companies are reassured by systems that reduce their fiscal vulnerability, particularly during the loan and project payback periods. Mining investors will be concerned about the stability of the fiscal system, including royalties, and will view frequent changes to the fiscal system as a risk to their portfolio.

However, though fiscal stabilization options are attractive to investors, many governments are hesitant to use them. A basic tenet of state sovereignty is that one generation of lawmakers should not "bind the hands" of future lawmakers. In addition, tax stabilization is sought by all sectors because it reduces fiscal uncertainty. If stabilization is offered to one sector, such as mining, other sectors will also seek it.

If taxes are stabilized for various mines, an administrative challenge can arise over time. As the underlying tax laws change, each stabilized mine will have a tax regime dating to the time the stabilization arrangement was entered into. This means that at any one point in time, different mines will be subjected to different tax regimes, and the government agency charged with tax administration will face an increasingly complicated situation of monitoring and enforcing each regime.

The government has a dilemma. On one hand, stabilization arrangements enhance the potential for mineral sector investment, and on the other hand, they complicate the tax system and present administrative challenges. Stability is important to investors and to their lenders, and many nations that have been successful in maintaining substantial foreign investment in their mining sector, such as Argentina, Chile, Indonesia, Papua New Guinea, and Peru, offer stabilization options.

There are a number of ways that governments can reduce investors' perceptions of risk regarding fiscal instability. The most obvious way is to provide a means whereby the entire fiscal system, or a portion of it, is stabilized for a given period of time. Such stabilization can take the form of a stabilization agreement[24] or be provided through statutory law provisions. The following extract from Mongolia illustrates a method whereby the general tax law and the mining law empower the appropriate minister to enter into a fiscal stabilization agreement with a mineral title holder.

Example of power being granted to a government official under the mining act to enter into a fiscal stabilization agreement:

4.   A stability agreement on behalf of the Government of Mongolia shall be concluded by the member of the Government in charge of finance issues within the framework of the law.[25]

Article 20. (Stability Agreement)
1.   If a mining license holder undertakes to invest in its mining project in Mongolia no less than 2 million US Dollars for [the] first five (5) years of the project, and if the mining license holder sub-

mits an application to enter into a stability agreement, then the Government, acting through the Minister of Finance, shall enter into such a stability agreement to provide a guarantee for a long term environment for such mining license holder.

2. The form of the stability agreement shall be approved by the Government and shall contain provisions regarding the stability of the tax rates for a definite time period, the right of the license holder to export and sell its products at international market prices, a guarantee that the license holder may receive and dispose of hard currency income derived from such sales, and provisions with respect to the purpose, amount, and term of the license holder's investment.

3. Within twenty (20) business days following receipt by the Minister of Finance of the application and draft of the stability agreement, the Minister shall determine whether or not further clarification is required. If the Minister determines that no further clarification is required, the Minister shall enter into the stability agreement with the applicant.

4. If the amount of the initial investment in the Mongolian mining project is no less than 2 million US Dollars, the term of the stability agreement may be ten (10) years. If such investment is no less than 20 million US Dollars, the term of the stability agreement may be fifteen (15) years.[26]

Example of mining act that gives precedence to royalty terms specified in an agreement over royalty terms set out in the present or a future mining act

(4) The Minister may, by notice in the Gazette, vary, amend or modify any or all of the provisions of the Second Schedule including the manner in which royalties may be computed whether in relation to market value of any mineral, the profitability of any mining operations or otherwise . . .

(5) Nothing is this section shall render unenforceable any agreement for payment of royalties (being royalties which accrue to the state) which was entered into prior to the date of the coming into operation of this Act and stipulating for the payment of royalties at a rate, or calculated in a manner, other than that prescribed in the Second Schedule, and such royalties shall, in such event, be payable in lieu of the payment of royalties at the rate so prescribed.[27]

Although some nations offer a formal means, such as the agreement approach illustrated above, to stabilize some or all taxes, most do not. However, other means can be used to reduce the risk of frequent or discriminatory changes to royalty rates and methods.

Key among these approaches is the means taken to define the royalty rates and the methods of determining the royalty basis. Generally speaking, most nations have a two-level approach to making law. First, *statutory law* is made through a process involving elected officials (parliament or congress), and second, *administrative law* is made by appointed officials. For example, in many common-law nations, the mining law, which addresses broad topics, is created by an act of parliament, and the mining regulations, which contain details to implement actions, are promulgated by the minister responsible for mining. Statutory law tends to be more permanent and less prone to amendment than administrative law.

Most investors would view royalty rates set out in statutory law as more stable than rates set out in regulations or in an administrative decree. Likewise, the greater the level of detail provided in statutory law to define the basis on which the royalty is to be calculated, the lower the chance that the method of calculation will change in the short run. The following Nigerian example, based on an administrative law approach, would be viewed as risk prone by most investors.

> 15.-(1) Any mineral obtained in the course of prospecting or mining operations shall be liable to such royalty as may be prescribed by the Minister and published in the Gazette.[28]

Where to Invest

Governments can influence companies' decision to invest in two ways. The first uses a positive approach, namely, by designing policies that focus on fostering competitiveness, attracting investment, and perhaps creating apparent competitiveness where mineral deposits are inadequate (Peck, Landsberg, and Tilton 1992). This approach does not necessarily mean no taxation or low levels of taxation; rather, it involves appropriate policies that have incentives for desirable behavior and penalties that discourage undesirable behavior. The second way government can influence decisions to invest may be negative from an investment perspective, because the fiscal regime renders an otherwise economic ore body uneconomic; that is, the policy prevents natural competitiveness.

Mining companies have many countries to choose from when deciding where to allocate their investment budgets. The decision criteria they apply in this allocation process will vary from company to company, but most will consider taxation along with other factors. All other things being equal, companies will prefer to invest in low-tax jurisdictions (of course, all other things are never equal). The importance of taxation is demonstrated by a number of surveys and polls, which indicate that taxation is important and that investors do take it into consideration.

In a 1980 survey of international mining companies, conducted by Charles Johnson of the East-West Center (1980), over 50 percent of the respondents considered tax stability as one of six crucial investment factors, along with geology, security of tenure, the right to repatriate profits, management control, and equity control. In a subsequent survey published by the United Nations, over 40 major and junior mining companies were asked to rank 60 possible investment factors as to their importance in investment decision making (see Table 5.4). Four criteria related to taxation made the top 20 ranking of most important: measure of profitability, ability to predetermine tax liability, stability of fiscal regime, and method and level of tax levies. Neither of these surveys considered royalty as a separate criterion.

The Otto-Bakkar Ranking model of 1992 (Otto and Bakkar 1992), which targeted multinational mining investors, included royalty-related issues among the top 10 criteria at both the exploration and mining stages. At the mining stage, three of the top five criteria are influenced by mineral royalties: project profitability, stability of mining terms, and the ability to predetermine the tax liability.

In recent years, the Fraser Institute, a Canadian nonprofit entity, has conducted an annual survey (2005). One part of that survey asks companies whether the tax environment is an incentive or disincentive to investment. In the 2004/05 survey, 259 major and junior mining companies responded. Table 5.5 contains a partial list of countries and some of their responses. The Fraser survey, like the two surveys mentioned above, did not break out royalty as a separate taxation factor, but it is interesting to note that those with mainly profit-based royalties are considered most favorable by investors. Table 5.6 lists the top 10 in order of tax system attractiveness, and of those, 7 had either no royalty or a system that was based in some way on profits.

In its definition of what makes a "good investment climate," the *World Development Report of 2005* suggested that a good climate focuses on, among other things, minimizing costs caused by taxation and policy uncertainty. This conclusion is supported by the *African Development Report*

Table 5.4. Mining Company Ranking of Investment Decision Criteria
(out of 60 possible criteria)

Importance Ranking		
Exploration stage	*Mining stage*	*Investment decision criteria*
1	n.a.	Geological potential for target mineral
n.a.	**3**	**Measure of profitability**
2	1	Security of tenure
3	2	Ability to repatriate profits
4	9	Consistency and constancy of mineral policies
5	7	Company has management control
6	11	Mineral ownership
7	6	Realistic foreign exchange regulations
8	4	Stability of exploration and mining terms
9	**5**	**Ability to predetermine tax liability**
10	8	Ability to predetermine environmental obligations
11	**10**	**Stability of fiscal regime**
12	12	Ability to raise external financing
13	16	Long-term national stability
14	17	Established mineral titles system
15	n.a.	Ability to apply geologic assessment techniques
16	**13**	**Method and level of tax levies**
17	15	Import-export policies
18	18	Majority equity ownership held by company
19	21	Right to transfer ownership
20	20	Internal (armed) conflicts
21	14	Permitted external accounts
22	19	Modern mineral legislation

Source: Otto 1992a.
Note: n.a. = not applicable.

of 2003, which proposed a strategy for Africa that includes managing the three critical "C"s—conflict, competitiveness, and corruption. An appropriate mineral royalty regime will affect one of these, namely, the competitiveness of the host state.

Royalty has a role to play in balancing potential risks and rewards. If royalties are too high they will diminish rewards, and if they are not based on profitability, they pose a risk that taxes will need to be paid irrespective of profitability. When devising fiscal systems for their mineral sectors, governments need to be aware that investors take taxation into consideration when deciding where to invest.

Table 5.5. Fraser Institute Survey of Companies' Perceptions of Tax Systems in Selected Nations

Country	Attractiveness score based on geology and policy factors (out of 100)[a]	Taxation system survey response (% of respondents)				
		Encourages investment	Not a deterrent to investment	Mild deterrent	Strong deterrent	Would not pursue investment because of tax system
Africa						
Botswana	27	11	44	22	11	11
Ghana	61	14	57	7	14	7
South Africa	53	5	16	53	16	11
Tanzania	41	9	55	9	18	9
Zambia	55	17	42	17	17	8
Zimbabwe	13	7	29	21	21	21
Asia and Pacific						
China	66	4	52	39	0	4
India	46	20	50	30	0	0
Indonesia	58	6	44	19	19	13
Mongolia	42	7	43	36	0	14
Papua New Guinea	56	13	47	20	7	13
Philippines	46	13	44	44	0	0
Australia						
New South Wales	52	17	61	17	0	6
Northern Territories	53	12	71	12	0	6
Queensland	67	10	65	20	0	5
Western Australia	82	19	57	19	0	5

(continued)

Table 5.5. (continued)

Country	Attractiveness score based on geology and policy factors (out of 100)[a]	Taxation system survey response (% of respondents)				
		Encourages investment	Not a deterrent to investment	Mild deterrent	Strong deterrent	Would not pursue investment because of tax system
Europe						
Finland	45	8	38	46	8	0
Russian Federation	56	7	29	21	29	14
Latin America						
Argentina	65	14	54	21	11	0
Bolivia	26	14	43	19	19	5
Brazil	66	10	57	27	7	0
Chile	77	25	53	19	3	0
Mexico	71	7	54	33	7	0
Peru	74	8	39	26	17	4
Venezuela, R. B. de	32	13	39	26	17	4
North America						
Arizona	63	3	71	23	0	3
British Columbia	67	26	33	29	10	3
Nevada	98	29	56	13	2	0
Northwest Territories	53	9	35	46	9	2
Ontario	81	22	45	30	3	0
Saskatchewan	51	16	44	35	5	0

Source: Fraser Institute "Annual Survey of Mining Companies 2004/05," derived from Table A6, pp. 64–65 and Figure 17, p. 49.

Note: Appendix A1 contains detailed royalty information on the survey countries reported in the table.

a. Approximate composite attractiveness score based on geology and policy factors (out of 100).

Table 5.6. Top 10 Selected Jurisdictions, Ranked by Tax System Attractiveness

Jurisdiction	Percentage of companies that rate tax system as attractive	Royalty system (for most nonbulk minerals)
Nevada	29	Profit based
British Columbia	26	Profit based
Chile	25	No royalty
Ontario	22	Profit based
India	20	Ad valorem
Western Australia	19	Ad valorem
New South Wales	17	Ad valorem and profit-based
Zambia	17	Ad valorem
Saskatchewan	16	Profit based and ad valorem
Ghana	14	Profit linked ad valorem

Source: Fraser Institute "Annual Survey of Mining Companies 2004/05."

Impact on Civil Society

Pressure from civil society shapes government's attitude toward foreign investment and, consequently, its view on mineral royalties. Politicians are increasingly compelled to deliver evidence to the electorate ensuring them that mineral resources are developed in a sustainable manner that benefits the current as well as future generations. This requires the balancing of two conflicting issues: reducing government's take to foster competitiveness and ensuring adequate compensation for the loss of a national asset. The need for mineral investment demands a political and economic climate that enables mineral developers to operate. Otto (1992b) investigated this need to attract foreign investment and came to the conclusion that developing countries are in competition with each other, mostly because of domestic capital shortages. In this pursuit for foreign capital, states are obliged to offer favorable terms and conditions to the relatively small fraternity of international mining investors. Otto found that, in an attempt to attract mineral investment, some developing countries lowered their royalty rates while others charged no royalties at all. Examples of countries that had no royalties were Chile, Peru, South Africa, and Zimbabwe. This situation may not be acceptable to the public in the long run. Adjustment may become inevitable as political pressure builds, because civil societies will witness the depletion of a national asset without direct fiscal benefit.

An easy way for politicians to change this public perception is to raise turnover royalties. This explains why Peru recently introduced royalties, and Chile, South Africa, and Zimbabwe have commenced legislative processes to potentially do so. Depending on government's attitude toward foreign investors, the rates could be competitive (1 to 3 percent, as in Peru) or, alternatively, extremely high (10 percent, as proposed in Zimbabwe). Such actions have caused investors to brand countries like Zimbabwe as more risky, because they view tampering with royalties as "changing the rules of the game while the game is on." Although the theory of mineral royalties dates back to ancient times, governments seem to still find it difficult to design appropriate models because of the ever-changing political will of civil society.

The impact of mineral royalties on mine profitability makes the royalty a powerful fiscal instrument to either attract or discourage investment in the mineral sector. Royalties that are too low or too high will necessitate changes to royalty rates whenever there is an adjustment in the economics of the mining firm. At first the public welcomes investment into the sector in the hope that society will benefit. However, the expectation gap is seldom filled, which results in a change of public opinion in the long run. The response by government is then to move from low or no royalties at all to a level that threatens the economics of the firm. Marginal mines are particularly vulnerable when this happens. Shareholders will not commit capital when there are no assurances of getting a return on their investment. Therefore, in return for investing in high-risk marginal mines, shareholders demand a bigger reward when prices suddenly rise. To balance this risk-reward relationship, shareholders need to predict the expected return after discounting for risk. The integrity of such forecasts depends on how accurately economic parameters and fiscal instruments can be quantified over the life of the project. It also explains why investors are willing to pay a premium in those countries that traditionally have stable taxes and reasonable mineral royalties.

Impact on Marginal Mines

In the absence of a universal definition for the concept of a marginal mine, one may look at special provisions in mineral law for guidance. Such a provision appears in section 52 of the South African MPRDA,[29] which allows the holder of a mining right to notify the Minerals and Mining Development Board when mine profitability could affect employment. This interpretation of *marginal* reads:

52(1)(a)   where economic conditions cause the profit to revenue ratio of the relevant mine to be less than six per cent on the average for a continuous period of 12 months; or

52(1)(b)   if any mining operation is to be scaled down or to cease with the possible effect that 10 per cent or more of the labour force or more than 500 employees, whichever is the lesser, are likely to be retrenched in any 12-month period.

The above section should be read with the structure of the sliding-scale tax formula for gold mines, which effectively exempts mines from paying corporate tax when profitability falls below 5 percent over the year of assessment. South African gold mines are taxed according to a sliding-scale formula that determines the rate of taxation by the degree of profitability. Although not designed as such, the formula has some features of a mineral resource rent tax because it attempts to capture excess profits in times of high gold prices. The formula takes the following form.

$$Y = a - (ab/X)$$

where: Y = tax rate expressed as a percentage of taxable income
a = marginal tax rate (constant)
b = tax-free revenue portion (constant which is currently 5)
X = profit-to-revenue ratio

The understanding of marginal in Tanzania is also linked to profitability. The Mining Act makes provision for reduction, remission, or deferment of mineral royalties when the cash operating margin (revenue from gross sales value minus operating costs) falls below zero.[30] Whatever the correct meaning of a marginal mine, many governments prefer to avoid the risk and impact of mine closure and to provide for royalty relief in certain circumstances (see Chapter 3 for specific examples). Countries with mineral-led economies will ensure that the definition gives early warning of a sudden rise in unemployment, whereas mine closure in an industrial economy may be an insignificant event.

Some forms of royalty affect marginal mines less than others. For example, the Northern Territory of Australia made provision for the impact of a royalty on marginal mines by charging royalties on net value. By allowing operating, capital, and exploration costs to be deducted before calculating the royalty amount, the system automatically reduces the impact on marginal mines. On top of having a profit-based royalty, the system allows for an additional deduction for extraordinary circumstances and events.[31]

The main reasons mineral royalties are so important to investors in marginal mines are the impact of the royalty on the cutoff grade and on fixed and operating costs, the royalties' prominent position in the hierarchy of claims in the benefits chain,[32] and the positive relationship between turnover royalties and the effective tax rate. All these issues have the potential to move a mine from being marginal to being loss-making. Figure 5.1 demonstrates the positive relationship between turnover royalties and the effective tax rate using South African case studies. Considering that the large gold mines employ more than 10,000 workers per mine, the potential local impact of mine closure is severe. Thus, developing these deep ore bodies necessitates a considerate royalty regime. The South African government's intention to charge the gold mining sector a 3 percent additional royalty sparked a debate that provides an excellent example of evaluating the impact of a royalty on marginal mines. The lessons currently coming from South Africa are therefore useful to consider in the international quest to design balanced royalty regimes.

In a study considering the impact of mineral royalties on marginal mines, the views of the mining industry are fairly predictable and are focused on the following issues:

- The industry has a clear preference for a profit-based royalty because of the "ability to pay" principle.
- They fear losing brownfield competitiveness when revenue-based royalties raise the mining pay limit. An investigation using actual 2002

Figure 5.1. Correlation between Mineral Royalties and Effective Tax Rates in South Africa

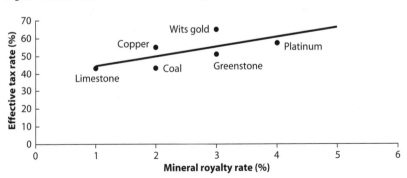

Source: Cawood and Macfarlane 2003.

reported information indicated that the proposed South African 3 percent royalty on gold will increase working costs by an average of 3.7 percent; increase the cutoff grade from 4.0 to 4.2 g/tonne; reduce the reserve base from 16,250 to 15,650 tonnes; and reduce the value of production by R1.6 billion over the next 40 years (Chamber of Mines of South Africa 2003).
• They fear that job losses would lead to sensitive negotiations with labor unions.

Impact on Unemployment

The number of workers per mine varies significantly from project to project. Labor-intensive mines can provide more than 10,000 jobs per mine, whereas large-scale but capital-intensive mines may employ less than 100 workers. The first impression is that capital-intensive projects have an insignificant impact on unemployment. This may be true in terms of the national unemployment rate, but capital-intensive industries rely heavily on secondary industries for efficient operation, so the multiplier effect on indirect job losses can be significant for individual communities. In addition to job losses in secondary industries, mine closure also affects employment of head office staff. If this head office is in another country, the impact of local closure will be international.

The impact of large-scale mine closures on the national economy are well illustrated by the coal mining sector in the United Kingdom. In 1981, the coal industry employed 229,000 workers. The closures that followed the 1984/85 dispute resulted in large-scale dismissals. It is now 20 years later and still 90,000 of these coal mining jobs have not been replaced by other sectors of the economy (BBC 2005b). Today the situation in the United Kingdom is so sensitive that the closure of one mine employing a relatively small workforce causes significant bad publicity. For example, when Ellington Colliery (340 jobs) announced its intention to close in January 2005, the response by the National Union of Mineworkers was, "It is absolutely ridiculous to play the safety card on an issue such as this." (BBC 2005a). In Australia, mining job losses must be considered in the context of job losses across all other industries. According to the World Socialist Web site (Cook 1999), the Australian mining sector lost more than 3,000 jobs in the 18 months leading to March 1999. It is estimated that for every job lost on an Australian coal mine, another three are lost in the community as a direct result (Maher 1999). The impact of mining job losses on layoffs in other sectors was recently investigated at

New Mexico's Phelps Dodge Mining Company. The study found that the decision to lay off 400 workers at the mining operation will result in 250 job losses at the smelter, the loss of 300 local jobs in Grant County, and the loss of an additional 950 jobs nationwide (Moffett and Hall 2001).

Royalties have the potential to cause job losses not only at large mines, therefore a royalty regime should also consider the small-scale mining sector. Many states appreciate the importance of the small-scale mining sector for generating employment opportunities. The Philippines declared its policy by stating the importance of balancing the need for employment with the need for an equitable royalty regime for the subsector.[33]

> It is hereby declared . . . to promote, develop, protect . . . viable small-scale mining . . . to generate more employment opportunities and provide an equitable sharing of the nation's wealth.

This balance is often achieved through relaxed terms of conditions and reduced royalties for the small-scale mining sector.

Political Instability

Mineral royalties appear to have the potential to affect political stability when high rates lead to unemployment, resulting in economic hardship for affected communities and, ultimately, a rise in poverty levels for mineral-dependent economies. Impoverished nations are more likely to question the motives of politicians who are entrusted with managing the country's mineral wealth. If governments are unable to introduce mechanisms to change the situation at a grassroots level, community unrest may escalate to political instability.

Disadvantages of unit-based, ad valorem, or revenue-based royalties include a negative impact on the required return on the investment, an increase in the cost of mining, and in the long run, the potential withdrawal of investments, causing reduced economic activity and retrenched employees. The impact on the cost of mining has an immediate effect on mine profitability and, for marginal mines, possible job losses. An increase in royalties raises the pay limit, renders marginal reserves uneconomical, and shortens the lives of existing operations. This situation may lead to production decisions that do not optimize the reserve as mines attempt to weather bad times. An example of such a suboptimal strategy is to mine less volume at a higher grade over long periods in order to meet metal content targets. The Chamber of Mines of South Africa (2003) has assessed this situation. Figure 5.2 clearly illustrates that unemployment

Figure 5.2. Employee Numbers, Tonnes Milled, and Average Grade Milled in South African Gold Mines (base indexed to 1961)

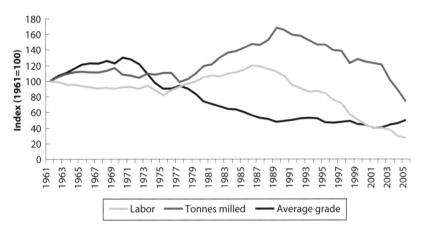

Source: Chamber of Mines of South Africa, data provided in 2005.

rises with volume cuts. Retrenchment of employees becomes inevitable, and the resulting increase in unemployment may be a catalyst for political instability.

The potential for experiencing political instability as a consequence of mine closure has prompted the South African government to legislate investigation of such closures through section 52 of the MPRDA, which reads:

> 52(2) The Board must, after consultation with the relevant holder, investigate-
> (a) the circumstances...; and
> (b) the socio-economic and labour implications thereof and make recommendations to the Minister.
> 52(3) (a) The Minister may ... direct in writing that the holder of the mining right in question take such corrective measures subject to such terms and conditions as the Minister may determine.

In conclusion, when designing the royalty regime for a country, it is important to delicately balance the expectations of the many diverse stakeholders of mining. These stakeholders are citizens, who expect to benefit from the depletion of their national mineral heritage; their representatives in public office, who must engineer a balanced approach; the mining industry, which requires an enabling investment environment;

labor organizations, which represent those who depend on the industry for their daily livelihoods; and potential investors, who must ensure that the investment returns justify the risks taken.

Impact on the Market

This section examines the impact of royalties on the markets for mineral commodities, including the effects on commodity prices, producing countries, other materials, secondary production, and consuming firms.

Mineral Commodity Prices

For producing firms, a royalty is part of the cost of production. As a result, introducing or increasing a royalty normally is associated with an increase in production costs and, hence, a leftward or upward shift in the market supply curve. This shift, in turn, tends to increase the equilibrium market price and reduce the market equilibrium output. However, there may be exceptions.

In commodity markets where firms exercise market power and set the market price at its optimal level using producer prices or other mechanisms, the introduction of a royalty may not change the perceptions of those firms. Firms may maintain the same price even though they are now required to pay the government a royalty.

Even in competitive markets, where firms have no power to determine prices, the introduction of a royalty may not alter the market price. In such markets, the industry marginal cost curve determines the market supply curve, and the intersection of the latter with the market demand curve determines equilibrium output and price. As a result, a royalty imposed by a country that has no marginal mines will alter the costs of only intramarginal mines. This changes the shape of the industry supply curve, but not in the region of the curve that intersects with the market demand curve. Figure 2.4 shows the intramarginal mines (A through F) and the marginal mine (G). If a royalty raises the costs of mines A through F but not of mine G, perhaps because mine G is in a different country, the market price may remain unchanged.

Despite such caveats, however, royalties generally do raise the market prices for mineral commodities. This is true both in the short and long runs, because for producing firms a royalty is a charge on output.

Competitiveness among Producing Countries

Royalties can alter the competitiveness among producing countries in two important ways. First, they influence the attractiveness of the investment climate in producing countries, as discussed at the beginning of this chapter. However, royalties are just one of a number of variables affecting the ability of mining countries to attract new investment, and it is important not to exaggerate their overall significance. A country's geologic potential, political stability, and overall taxation regime are likely to be of equal or greater importance.

Second, royalties affect the competitiveness of producers in the short run by altering the costs of production of operating mines. As Figure 2.2 shows, royalties may change the rankings or positions of mines on the comparative cost curve. If mines A and C are in Chile, the imposition of a royalty by the Chilean government will raise the average variable costs of these mines. If the increase is substantial, mines B, D, and E may subsequently have lower average variable costs and move to the left of mines A and C. Should the market price fall, mines A and C would be less able to compete in the short run and would be more vulnerable to closure.

Competitiveness with Other Materials

In many end uses, metals compete with other materials. The beverage container market perhaps provides the most dramatic example of this competition. Glass, steel, tin, chrome, aluminum, and plastic have historically fought for the privilege of being the container of choice for soft drinks and beer. Other examples are found in communication wire, piping, and automobile radiators.

Royalties affect the competitiveness among materials only to the extent that they alter their relative prices. The introduction of a royalty that has little or no effect on the market price for a mineral commodity should have little or no effect on its ability to compete with other materials. When that is not the case, when royalties have a significant impact on the market price, there are both short-run and long-run impacts on competitiveness with other materials. In a few end uses, producers can quickly and easily substitute an alternative material in response to changes in relative prices. For example, in response to a jump in the price of aluminum siding, construction firms building residential homes can use wood or composite siding instead. Similarly, it is sometimes possible to substitute a little more of one ferroalloy for another in the production of specialty steels and still maintain the important attributes of the alloy. The available empirical literature, however, suggests that such short-run responses are likely to be modest, at least compared with the longer-run effects (Tilton 1983, 1991).

Material substitution often requires new production equipment and the retraining of personnel. Such changes take time and can be expensive, so they are undertaken only once it is clear that the new price levels are likely to continue. Higher prices also provide strong incentives to search for new technologies that create opportunities to substitute less expensive materials and reduce the demand for the higher-cost materials in other ways.

So although royalties can significantly affect the ability of a metal to compete with other metals and materials, whether this actually occurs depends on the extent to which royalties raise their market prices.

Competitiveness with Secondary Production

Mineral commodities are supplied by both primary and secondary producers. Primary producers engage in mining and the processing of the extracted ores. Secondary producers supply the market by recycling metal scrap and other secondary materials that arise in the process of producing new goods and by reclaiming materials when consumer and producer goods reach the end of their economic lives. Just as the primary producers of mineral commodities compete among themselves and with the producers of alternative materials, they also compete with secondary producers (see Tilton 1999).

Many believe that over the long run secondary producers will become more competitive as mineral depletion drives up the costs of primary production, but there is little evidence of this to date (Tilton 2002). Although depletion has forced primary producers to exploit lower-grade and poorer-quality deposits over time, any tendency for the real costs of primary production to rise as a result has, for nearly all mineral commodities, been offset by the cost-reducing effects of new technology. As a result, the share of total production accounted for by primary production has not displayed a systematic tendency to decline over time. Moreover, where declines have occurred, they can for the most part be explained by other considerations. The rise of secondary production in the lead industry in recent years, for example, is largely the result of government regulations driven by health and environmental concerns.

Because royalties increase the costs of primary but not secondary producers, one would expect a similar increase in the competitiveness of secondary producers at the expense of primary producers. However, this will happen only if royalties raise the market price, which may not be the case. If royalties do increase the market price, the adverse effects on the competitiveness of primary producers depend on the magnitude of the increase. A small or modest price increase will have only a small or modest effect on the competitiveness between primary and secondary producers.

Impact on Consuming Firms

Royalties can also have an impact on firms that consume the affected mineral commodity, though once again, this depends on whether royalties cause an increase in the market price of the materials they use. If royalties do push market prices up, the consequences for consumers in most instances are modest for several reasons. First, in many cases the rise in prices caused by royalties is modest. Second, consuming firms can at times mitigate the adverse effects by substituting less expensive alternative materials. Third, where the demand for the consuming firms' product is highly insensitive to changes in price (*inelastic*), consuming firms can pass on the rise in costs to their customers in the form of higher prices. Of course, there are exceptions, and at times the impact on consuming firms is more significant.

Impact on the Government and the Host Country

This section examines the impact of royalties on the government and the host country as a whole. It begins by examining two major macroeconomic issues and then turns to other concerns.

Impacts on Economic Growth and Stability

The field of macroeconomics is largely dedicated to two aspects of economic performance at the national level: long-run growth and development, and short-run cyclical fluctuations in the economy.

Growth and development   Australia, Canada, Finland, and a few other developed countries are among the world's major producers and exporters of mineral commodities. For these countries there is widespread if not universal agreement that, over the years, mining and mineral processing have contributed positively to economic growth and development.

Much more controversial, however, is the role of minerals in the growth and development of developing countries. A number of cross-country comparisons have found that mineral exporting countries have generally performed poorly over the past several decades.[34] In some cases, real per capita income has actually fallen. Even where real per capita income has risen, the increases generally have been less than in other countries at similar stages of development whose economies do not depend on mineral production and exports. These findings have led some to conclude that resources are a curse. Within this group, a few even advocate that developing countries eschew mineral production and keep any mineral resources they might have in the ground.

Of course, such suggestions have not gone unchallenged. Scholars on the other side of the debate question the extent to which the empirical evidence has established a cause and effect relationship between mineral dependence and economic growth. They also challenge the extent to which the empirical findings can be generalized to other time periods and, in particular, to the future. Disagreement also exists over the possible reasons for suspecting that mineral dependence might cause slow economic growth.

Though the debate on the resource curse is far from over, there is growing agreement on several points. First, mineral production and exports have fostered economic growth in some developing countries. Chile and Botswana are often cited as examples. Second, mineral production and exports have impeded economic growth in some developing countries. Just why this is the case is not fully understood, but among the possible explanations is that the wealth created by mineral production promotes civil strife, corruption, and other antigrowth activities. The Democratic Republic of Congo is often cited as an example of a country that falls within this group. Third, rich mineral deposits provide developing countries with opportunities, which some countries have used wisely and others poorly. The consensus on this third point is important, as Davis and Tilton (2005) point out:

> It means that one uniform policy toward all mining in the developing world is not desirable. The appropriate public policy question is not should we or should we not promote mining in the developing countries, but rather where should we encourage it and how can we ensure that it contributes as much as possible to economic development and poverty alleviation.

The above suggests that mineral royalties may have a positive or negative effect on economic growth and development. Where royalties push the level of overall taxation beyond the optimum level (see Figure 2.1), the resulting reduction in investment in a country's mineral sector reduces the rents and other opportunities flowing from the mineral sector to the government. Where the level of overall taxation is below the optimum or, alternatively, where the country does not have the ability to use the opportunities generated by its mineral sector wisely, just the opposite is the case.

Cyclical fluctuations in the economy   The short-run cyclical volatility of the economy associated with the business cycle is the second major aspect of national economic performance that is addressed by the field of macroeconomics. In mineral-exporting developing countries, cyclical fluctuations in their economies are driven largely by fluctuations in the demand for their exports. These, in turn, are largely produced by the business cycles in the developed countries and, in recent years, in a few developing countries, such as China. When the economies of the developed countries are booming, the demand for mineral commodities rises sharply. This relationship exists because most mineral commodities are largely consumed in economic sectors—consumer durables, capital goods, transportation, and construction—whose output varies over the business cycle with gross domestic product (GDP) but in a far more pronounced manner. When GDP is up by 3 percent, the output of the construction sector or the capital equipment sector may increase by 10 percent.

Because external forces are largely responsible for short-run fluctuations in the economies of most mineral-producing countries, one might assume that royalties have little or no effect, either in accentuating or mitigating this volatility. Although this is largely true, it is important to note that unit-based and ad valorem royalties are a relatively stable source of government income over the business cycle. As long as mines continue to produce, the government usually collects revenues from royalties. That is not the case for the corporate income tax. When the domestic and world economies are in recession, mineral prices tend to fall. Therefore corporate profits and, in turn, government revenues from corporate income taxes decline, because both output and prices are depressed. Indeed, during such periods, corporate profits often evaporate.

Consequently, mineral-exporting developing countries that receive a significant share of their mineral revenues from unit-based and ad valorem royalties enjoy a more stable flow of income over the business cycle. In particular, they enjoy more income during a downturn in the business cycle than would be the case if royalties provided a modest or zero share of mineral revenues. Thus, these countries can spend more domestically, particularly in the areas hit hardest by the economic downturn. Such spending helps mitigate the impact of the global recession on the domestic economy.

Microeconomic Impacts

Royalties can have a number of microeconomic impacts on the government and host country, including on the climate for private investment and the distribution of risk.

Climate for private investment   The impact that royalties can have on the domestic environment for private investment is treated in some detail at the beginning of this chapter. It is thus sufficient to simply note here that the domestic investment climate, particularly in the case of mineral-producing developing countries, can greatly affect the ability of those countries to attract capital and technology from abroad. This, in turn, has important implications for long-run growth and development.

Distribution of risk   Tax regimes that depend heavily on unit-based and ad valorem royalties tend to produce a more stable and certain flow of revenues than those that rely heavily on corporate income taxes, even though the expected revenues may be the same. So a royalty, in addition to the impact it may have on the expected share of the rents that the government receives, will also shift more of the economic risk associated with mining and mineral production to the private investors and producers. Although this may reduce the investment risk from the perspective of private investors, this need not be the case if the government is willing to accept a smaller share of the expected rents associated with mineral projects (thereby compensating private investors for the increase in risks).

This raises the interesting question of who should bear the bulk of the risks associated with mineral investments and production—the government, the private investors, or third parties. For risks that cannot be controlled, which is the case with fluctuations in profits due to price instability, plus other types of economic risks, the answer depends on which of the three has the lowest level of risk aversion. Thus, one would normally assume, the answer would be the private investors or perhaps third parties, such as speculators who invest in futures or other financial derivatives. Where the risk can be controlled, completely or partially, those who can influence the risk are usually in the best position to assume the risk. For example, the government is likely to have a much lower rate of risk discount than the private companies with respect to the probability of a change in tax regime, since it controls this risk. As a result, mechanisms for shifting this risk to the government may be appropriate.

References

African Development Bank. 2003. *African Development Report 2003: Globalization and Africa's Development.* Oxford: African Development Bank and Oxford University Press.

Amazon Financial Information System. Red List Risk Profile. http://www .redlist.org (accessed March 8, 2005).

Australian Bureau of Statistics. 2005. "Mineral and Petroleum Exploration, Australia." Table 5. Mineral Exploration (Other than for petroleum)—Expenditure by Mineral Sought. http://www.abs.gov.au (accessed March 25, 2005).

BBC News (UK). 2005a. "Mining Job Losses Not Replaced." BBC. http://news .bbc.co.uk/2/hi/uk_news/england/tyne/4208195.stm, January 26, 2005 (accessed March 21, 2005).

———. 2005b. "Jobs Lost After Flood Wrecks Mine." BBC. http://news.bbc .co.uk/1/hi/wales/4317517.stm, March 4, 2005 (accessed March 21, 2005).

Cawood, F. T. 1999. "Determining the Optimal Rent for South African Mineral Resources." PhD diss., University of the Witwatersrand, Johannesburg, South Africa.

Cawood, F. T., and A. S. Macfarlane. 2003. "The Mineral and Petroleum Royalty Bill." *Journal of the South African Institute of Mining and Metallurgy* 103 (4): 213–32.

Chamber of Mines of South Africa. 2003. "Memorandum to the National Treasury on the Draft Mineral and Petroleum Royalty Bill." Submission by the Chamber of Mines of South Africa, Johannesburg.

Cook, T. 1999. "Job Losses Mount in Australia as Company Profits Rise." World Socialist Web site. http://www.wsws.org/articles/1999/mar1999/jobs-m03 .shtml, March 3, 1999 (accessed March 21, 2005).

Davis, Graham A., and John E. Tilton. 2005. "The Resource Curse." *Natural Resources Forum* 29(3): 233–42.

Fraser Institute, The. 2005. "Annual Survey of Mining Companies 2004/2005." Fraser Institute, Vancouver, Canada, 64–65.

Fraser, Rob. 1999. "An Analysis of the Western Australian Gold Royalty." *Australian Journal of Agricultural and Resource Economics* 43 (1): 35.

Johnson, Charles. 1980. "Ranking Countries for Minerals Exploration." *Natural Resources Forum* 14 (3): 175–185.

King Committee on Corporate Governance. 2002. "King Report on Corporate Governance for South Africa." Institute of Directors, Johannesburg, South Africa.

Kosich, D. 2005. "Buyat Bay Doctor Recants Toxic Claims." http://www.mineweb.com (accessed February 15, 2005).

Maher, T. 1999. "Encouraging Response to Our Public Campaign to Save Jobs" Common Cause. http://www.cfmea.asn.au/, April 1999 (accessed March 21, 2005).

Moffett, M., and D. W. Hall. 2001. "Losing More Than Copper: An Analysis of the Impact of Recent Layoff Announcements on New Mexico's Economy." New Mexico Department of Labor. http://www.dol.state.nm.us/, November 29, 2001 (accessed March 21, 2005).

Nappi, Carmine. 1979. *Commodity Market Controls: A Historical Review*, 123. Lexington, MA: Lexington Books.

———. 1992. "Aluminum." In *Competitiveness in Metals: The Impact of Public Policy*, eds. Merton J. Peck, Hans H. Landsberg, and John E. Tilton, 212–41. London: Mining Journal Books.

Newmont. 2004. Response to articles in the Denver Post of December 12–13, 2004. http://www.newmont.com (accessed March 8, 2005).

Otto, James. 1992a. "Criteria and Methodology for Assessing Mineral Investment Conditions." In *Mineral Investment Conditions in Selected Countries of the Asia-Pacific Region*. United Nations ESCAP.

———. 1992b. "International Competition for Mineral Investment: Implications for the Asia-Pacific Region." In *Asia Pacific Resource Development: Mining Policy Directions*, ed. Peter Crowley. Vancouver: Pacific Economic Cooperation Council, Minerals and Energy Forum.

———. 1995. "The International Competition for Mineral Investment—Implications for Africa." Institute of Mining and Metallurgy Namibian Section, Windhoek.

———. 2001. "Fiscal Decentralization and Mining Taxation." World Bank Group Mining Department, Washington, DC.

———. 2002. "Materials for a Workshop on the Position of the Papua New Guinea Tax System as Compared to Mining Taxation Systems in Other Nations." Prepared for the PNG Department of Mining and the World Bank.

Otto, James, and P. Bakkar. 1992. *Mineral Investment in Asian Regions—A Checklist for Success.* CPMLP Professional Paper Series. SP1 ISBN 0 906343 51 8, 8 pp.

Otto, James, and John Cordes. 2002. "Chapter 4 Mineral Agreements." *The Regulation of Mineral Enterprises: A Global Perspective on Economics Law and Policy.* Westminster, CO: Rocky Mountain Mineral Law Foundation.

Otto, James, John Cordes, and Maria L. Batarseh. 2000. *Global Mining Taxation Comparative Study*, 2nd ed. Golden, CO: Institute for Global Resources Policy and Management, Colorado School of Mines.

Peck, Merton J., Hans H. Landsberg, and John E. Tilton, eds. 1992. *Competitiveness in Metals: The Impact of Public Policy*, 212–41. London: Mining Journal Books.

Riley, M., and G. Griffin. 2004. Denver Post Newmont Series—"Shadowy Figures, Deals Marked Mine Battle," pt. 1, and "Fighting Back," pt. 2, December 3, 2004. Circulated on glomin@jiscmail.ac.za, CEPMLP, University of Dundee, Scotland (accessed December 14, 2004).

Roger, Christopher D. 1992. "Tin." In *Competitiveness in Metals: The Impact of Public Policy*, eds. Merton J. Peck, Hans H. Landsberg, and John E. Tilton, 242–65. London: Mining Journal Books.

Sachs, Jeffrey D., and Andrew Warner. 1997. "Sources of Slow Growth in African Economies." *Journal of African Economies* 6 (3): 335–76.

———. 1999a. "The Big Push, Natural Resource Booms and Growth." *Journal of Development Economics* 59: 43–76.

———. 1999b. "Natural Resource Intensity and Economic Growth." In *Development Policies in Natural Resource Economies*, eds. Jörg Mayer, Brian Chambers, and Ayisha Farooq, 13–38.Cheltenham, UK: Edward Elgar.

———. 2000. "Globalization and International Competitiveness: Some Broad Lessons of the Past Decade." In *The Global Competitiveness Report 2000*, ed. Michael E. Porter. New York: Oxford University Press.

———. 2001. "Natural Resources and Economic Development: The Curse of Natural Resources." *European Economic Review* 45 827–38.

South African Mining Development Association. 2003. "Submission to the Department of Finance Regarding the Proposed Mining Royalty Bill," unpublished report, Johannesburg, April 30.

Swindells, Steve. 2005. "South African Fight Over Rights." *Mining Journal* (February 25), ed. John E. Tilton, 26–28. 1983. *Material Substitution.* Washington, DC: Resources for the Future.

Tilton, John E. 1983. *Material Substitution: Lessons from Tin-Using Industries.* Washington, DC: Resources for the Future.

———. 1991. "Material Substitution: The Role of New Technology." In *Diffusion of Technologies and Social Behavior,* eds. Nebojsa Nakicenovic and Arnulf Grubler, 383–406. Berlin: Springer-Verlag for the International Institute for Applied Systems Analysis.

———. 1999. "The Future of Recycling." *Resources Policy* 25 (3): 197–204.

———. 2002. *On Borrowed Time? Assessing the Threat of Mineral Depletion.* Washington, DC: Resources for the Future.

World Bank. 2004. "World Development Report 2005: A Better Investment Climate for Everyone." Oxford: World Bank, Washington, DC, and Oxford University Press.

Notes

1. In recent years, China has become the largest, or one of the largest, consumers of many mineral commodities. A significant though unknown portion of this consumption, however, is used in the production of goods that are ultimately exported to consumers in the United States and other developed countries.

2. For an interesting description of the efforts by tin producing countries to raise the tin price through the International Tin Agreement, and the ultimate collapse of that effort, see Roger (1992).

3. The results for the Fraser poll are available from http://www.fraserinstitute. ca/shared/readmore.asp?sNav=nr&id=648, accessed on March 25, 2005.

4. The Fraser Institute surveys are available from its Web site at www.fraserinstitute.ca, accessed on March 25, 2005.

5. Trends in production of gold in Australia and elsewhere are influenced by a variety of factors, including changes in the market price and new production technologies that reduce costs. As a result, Western Australia's share of total Australian or world gold production is likely to reflect changes in the state's investment climate more closely than trends in the state's mine output of gold.

6. Mozambique, Mining Code, Law No.14/2002 of June 26, 2002.

7. Namibia, Act No. 19 of 1996.

8. South Africa, Mineral and Petroleum Resources Development Act 28 of 2002, 3 October 2002, Government Gazette Vol. 448, No. 23922 (date of commencement 1 April 2004).

9. Section 104 of MPRDA 28 of 2002.

10. Broad Based Socio-Economic Empowerment Charter for the South African Mining Industry, 2003. Available from http://www.dme.gov.za, accessed July 2, 2005.

11. China, Regulations for the Collection and Administration of the Mineral Resources Compensation Fee, N.150. 1994.

12. Indonesia, Law No. 25/1999.

13. Papua New Guinea, Mining Act 1992.

14. Philippines, Section 287, The National Internal Revenue Code of the Philippines [Tax Reform Act of 1997] Republic Act No. 8424.

15. Argentina, Mining Investment Law (Federal Law No. 24.196).

16. Brazil, Law 7990, of 12/28/1989.

17. Brazil, Law 8001, of 03/13/1990.

18. Peru, Law of Mining Royalty N° 28258.

19. The reader should refer to the section in Chapter 2 called "Rationale for Imposing a Royalty" for a discussion on the public perception of mines enriching themselves at society's expense.

20. An example of regulating social commitment and BEE is the SA Mining Charter and Scorecard. "Scorecard for the Broad Based Socio-Economic Empowerment Charter for the South African Mining Industry," *Government Gazette* Vol. 470 No. 26661, Republic of South Africa, Pretoria, 13 August 2004.

21. Labor issues are regulated through the Labour Act of 1992, the Social Security Act of 1994, and the Affirmative Action (Employment) Act of 1998, in addition to the requirements for mineral development rights stipulated in the Minerals Act No. 33 of 1992.

22. See Amazon Financial Information System (2005).

23. Riley and Griffin 2004, and Kosich 2005.

24. A long-term tax stabilization agreement may not be enforceable in at least some jurisdictions. For a more complete discussion see Otto and Cordes (2002).

25. Mongolia, Article 2, Part 4, General Law on Taxation of Mongolia, November 23,1992, unofficial translation.

26. Mongolia, Article 20, Part 4 Mineral Law of Mongolia, July 1, 1997, unofficial translation.

27. Botswana, Article 53, Mines and Minerals Act, 1967.

28. Nigeria, Mineral and Mining Decree, 1999, No.34.

29. Mineral and Petroleum Resources Development Act 28 of 2002, 3 October 2002, *Government Gazette*, Vol. 448, No. 23922 (date of commencement 1 April 2004).

30. Section 87 of Mining Act 15 of 1998, assented to July 1, 1998.
31. In terms of Section 10(2) the Mineral Royalty Act of 1982—see Appendix A1 for details.
32. See Otto and Cordes (2002) for a detailed explanation.
33. Section 2 of Act No. 7076 of 1991—see Appendix A1 for details.
34. See, in particular, studies by Jeffrey D. Sachs and Andrew Warner (1997, 1999a, 1999b, 2000, 2001).

CHAPTER 6

Transparency, Governance, and Management of Revenue Streams

Other chapters of this study examine the policy and administrative foundations of fiscal regimes for the mining industry, with a principal focus on royalties. Taxing the mining sector in an equitable and internationally competitive manner, while at the same time attracting investment away from competing destinations, requires a delicate balance between government and company expectations. However, international attention is also increasingly focused on how governments and companies account for and disclose the taxes and payments the mining sector generates. Accordingly, this chapter discusses the transparency, governance, and management of the revenue streams of the extractive industries.

The Case for Transparency

The issue of transparency is important and is gaining international momentum. The final communiqué of the Gleneagles G-8 Summit in July 2005 included a call for improved governance in general. In terms of extractive industries, major initiatives have been launched within the past five years, such as Publish What You Pay, the Extractive Industries Transparency Initiative, and the Global Reporting Initiative. This effort has been spearheaded by developed countries and nongovernmental organizations (NGOs), but an increasing number of developing countries are emphasizing the issue. Many major resource companies in petroleum and mining have voiced their support for improved transparency and governance of revenues. In addition, the Organisation for Economic Co-operation and Development (OECD) countries, as well as their securities exchanges, have adopted more stringent disclosure rules in the wake of various corporate governance scandals. Certain governments, such as the United States and some European countries, have legislated requirements for disclosure of payments and taxes made nationally and internationally. Finally, international financial organizations and major banks have tightened corporate principles governing the funding of resource development projects. For instance, the International Finance Corporation, an affiliate of the World Bank, now requires assurances on good governance of revenue streams in order to provide funding to extractive industry projects.

The movement to enhance transparency and governance of the extractive industries is the result of serious questioning by reputable observers. Critics have cited many problems regarding the economic contributions of extractive industries and their impacts on human well-being in many developing countries, notably those discussed in the following sections.

The Resources Curse, or the Paradox of Plenty

The so-called resource curse, or paradox of plenty, holds that countries that are heavily dependent on the extractive industries perform less well economically than countries not as heavily dependent on them.[1] The works of Thorvaldur Gylfason, Jeffrey Sachs, and others purport, through regression analysis, to show the negative relationship between economic growth and resource dependency.[2] Notably, some reservations about the veracity and pertinence of the data used in the analyses have been raised (Davis and Tilton 2002). Exceptions to the resource curse include, for example, Botswana, Chile, Malaysia, and Norway, which are frequently cited as countries that have managed the revenues generated by extractive industries well. However, most observers find the curse/paradox label worthy of closer reflection, because many countries (e.g., Angola, Nigeria, Papua New Guinea, Peru) have had, or currently have, difficulties managing the revenues produced by their extractive sectors.

Civil Strife

In some cases, a relationship appears to exist between the presence of resource wealth from extractive industry and civil war. In many developing countries, particularly in Africa, there is considerable rivalry among various factions and ethnic groups for control of natural resources and the revenues they generate. In the most extreme cases (Angola, the Democratic

Republic of Congo, Sierra Leone, and Sudan), attempts to control such resources have led to prolonged and bloody civil wars. Works by Collier and Hoeffler (2000) and others show that the pertinent variables that explain the presence of civil strife in many countries are extreme poverty, low growth, a large diaspora, and the presence of mineral resources that are easily looted. Clearly, numerous factors explain civil war, but competition to control revenue streams of extractive industries seems to be a key factor in some countries.

Corruption

In some countries, revenues from the extractive industries are said to heighten corruption. For instance, Transparency International's corruption index for many countries is positively correlated to the dependency of their economies on mineral or petroleum resources. The nature of the industries' revenue streams—very large in relation to the local economy, quickly generated, and subject to contracts between the government and private companies that are mostly confidential—are factors that can help explain the proclivity toward corruption. However, it should be pointed out that many countries that are not dependent on extractive industries also score poorly on the corruption index.

Because of the above drawbacks, some argue that countries should defer development and exploitation of their resources. However, it is not realistic to expect countries and companies to abandon exploitation of mineral (and petroleum) resources as a viable economic activity. A more balanced approach is to make development of the resources and continued exploitation of them subject to better governance. Thus, emphasis needs to be placed on ensuring that the revenues are properly accounted for and that they are directed toward programs that improve the quality and delivery of public services. One of the keys to doing so is disclosure of the revenues, including royalties, paid by the companies and received by governments. In this fashion, citizens of the country concerned can make their own informed judgments about the amounts and sources of revenues from the sector and require their political leaders, through their own political process, to provide a proper accounting of the funds and the uses to which the funds are allocated.

General Principles of Disclosure and Reporting

It is generally agreed that the fundamental requirement for good governance is, first, compliance with law, and second, transparent and full disclosure of revenue streams. However, disclosure raises a number of questions that need to be carefully taken into consideration. For instance, how relevant is the information disclosed? Who discloses the information: individual companies or the sector as a whole? If disclosure is made on a regular basis, what are the reporting periods? What standards are to be used and are they consistent? To what extent are various types of taxes paid reported in a disaggregated form for public access? Are sanctions to be applied if disclosure is not made or if it is deemed erroneous and, if so, what should those sanctions be? Who certifies and validates the information as disclosed? These and some additional issues are discussed below.

Relevancy

The data or information disclosed must answer the questions being asked. For instance, government officials, political leaders, and other members of the public may not find the numerical value of taxes paid and received relevant. It is more relevant to report taxes paid as a percentage of total taxes or as a percentage of revenues paid or received. Similarly, information and data on production, payroll, social expenditure, and other indicators of the benefit streams produced by a mining operation are more relevant if they are put into context. For instance, the value of production has more relevance if reported as a percentage of total GDP; the relevance of employment is enhanced if reported in relation to local employment overall. This is often just a matter of presentation, and in most instances making such adjustments is simple. In other instances, however, compilation and analysis of additional data may be required. Disclosing information in a relevant way allows for those outside of the industry to better understand the importance of the revenues and benefit streams.

Materiality

Accounting and reporting of data on taxes and revenues paid by companies and received by governments are bound to have misstatements, errors, and omissions. These would be considered material if they are of a magnitude and nature to influence the decisions of a user of the information. For instance, there could be discrepancies in the amounts of royalties declared paid by companies and the amounts declared received by government. Similarly, reporting of value-added taxes and reimbursements sometimes show variances between company- and government-supplied data. In most cases, the mismatch can be explained in slight variations of reporting periods, or cash versus accrual methods of accounting. Current best practice for disclosure of revenue streams is that these should be made on a cash basis. Companies and governments will therefore need to reconcile the various financial statements to delete accrued tax assets and liabilities (e.g., amounts of value-added taxes payable and reimbursable). Reasons for any discrepancies in numbers reported should be fully explained. More importantly, definitional issues as to timing, reporting period, and accounting methods need to be agreed upon.

Tiers of Reporting

Mining is a competitive business, and the disclosure to the public of detailed information pertaining to an individual operation, such as costs to operate and prices paid by smelters, refineries, and customers, may harm that mine's ability to compete. On the other hand, the ability of the public to access detailed information on individual operations can act as a check that may not be present when monitoring is conducted solely by regulatory agencies. This dilemma often results in two tiers of reporting: reporting by companies and reporting by government. Detailed information is provided to government by mines; that information is then made available to the public in a form that preserves confidentiality (see below) but still serves the needs of the public. Government reporting can, for example, aggregate revenue information for like mines or aggregate all taxes and fees paid by any one mine in order to preserve a workable business environment. Although complete disclosure may be useful for allowing a full understanding of benefit streams, a very detailed disclosure, particularly with regard to costs and prices, may provide valuable and otherwise unobtainable information to competitors.

Confidentiality

Companies have legitimate concerns regarding confidential information (e.g., specific payroll data) or information that, if disclosed, could result in commercial disadvantage (e.g., production cost data). Companies also often enter into one or more confidentiality agreements with third parties (suppliers, customers, or joint venture partners). In such instances, the government and the company will need to determine which data to disclose or withhold and how this may or may not affect existing confidentiality agreements. That said, the presumption should be in favor of full disclosure; withholding of data on confidentiality grounds needs to be fully explained and justified.

Understandability

There is a growing recognition that information and reported data are of interest to a wider audience than traditional financial, industry, or government specialists. The purpose of disclosure is to inform a diverse set of local stakeholders (communities, employees, civic groups, and businesses) who may not have the in-depth knowledge of the mining sector, finance, or taxation. Furthermore, in many developing countries, disclosure must recognize differences in language, education levels, and culture. In addition, it is quite common for the general public to have inflated expectations regarding the revenue streams produced by an operation and the length of time it takes before tangible benefits appear. Sensitization and training workshops for key stakeholders in civil society can be useful to explain the fundamentals of the mining operations (production cost, value added, investments required, and market fluctuations) and realistic expectations regarding revenues and benefit streams (taxes, jobs, supplier contracts, and social contributions). Also, data and information must be made public in a form that is easily accessible and understood by all audiences. Publication on the Internet may not be the best way to inform villagers in proximity to the operation (a key stakeholder group), who may not have access to electricity or computers. Publication of complicated numerical tables in company reports, legal filings, or government statistical annexes are neither accessible nor comprehensible to general audiences. Outreach to these stakeholder groups is required to explain the nature, scope, and importance of the information disclosed. Finally, much can be gained if the government and company engage stakeholder groups to get their suggestions on how to ensure that the information provided is understandable and disseminated effectively.

Reliability

Several elements need to be taken into account to ensure that the disclosed data and information are reliable. Data can be deemed reliable only if transparency has been respected. In addition, all relevant issues should be noted and explained in a factual and coherent manner, and information reported should be documented in a way that is traceable to source documents. All important or critical assumptions should be documented. Precision in the collection and analysis of the information by both the companies and governments is key to establishing integrity and credibility. Although the financial management systems of most international companies are capable of such precision, financial management systems and the capacity of personnel in many developing countries' companies and governments may not be of the same caliber. The information must be complete, that is, without material omissions in relation to the reporting periods and the definitions established for the data point in question. For instance, discrepancies in taxes that are reported paid and received are sometimes due to different reporting periods used by the companies and the governments, which are also sometimes compounded by confusion about cash- and accrual-based accounting systems. Precise definitions of the nature and calculation methods of the tax, payment, or royalty are also sometimes problems. Not only are these definitions often complicated, but frequently mining development agreements reflect definitions used in the company's home country, which may be at variance with those used in the host country.

Timeliness

Information and data not supplied in a timely fashion after the close of the reporting period may lose relevance. Though considerable progress has been made in recent years with the introduction of automated financial processing systems in many developing countries, it still sometimes takes many months before governments can amalgamate and disclose information on revenues and benefit streams. International companies generally report shortly after the close of their financial reporting period, but sometimes the government and company reporting periods are not the same and need to be synchronized. Also, many smaller local mining companies do not prepare timely financial statements or prepare no statement at all. This is a problem particularly when a company is not publicly listed and thus not subject to securities exchange regulations, which establish strict audit standards. Often statements used by smaller companies are simply geared to reporting requirements for tax declaration purposes, which have deadlines many months removed from the reporting period in question.

Therefore, to disclose data in a timely fashion, allowances can be made to disclose preliminary data, with the proviso that such a preliminary declaration is fully explained and documented. Many regulatory schemes for the mineral sector require that royalties be reported and paid on a monthly or quarterly basis. In markets where the producer is the price setter, this information can be quite sensitive, because it will, for some ad valorem–based types of taxes, provide competitors with information that they may use to their competitive advantage. In markets where the producer must accept the market price, immediate disclosure of royalty payments is usually not an issue. For that reason, it is common for governments to aggregate royalty payments from a single producer over a year before public disclosure or to aggregate royalties from like producers.

Auditability

Data and information disclosed should be recorded, compiled, and analyzed in a way that would enable internal or external auditors to attest to their reliability. The audit function and profession are well established in most developed countries. In countries with large natural resource or mining industries, firms specialize in resource accounting and audit practices. However, this is not the case for most developing countries, where the profession is not as well established or, in some cases, is lacking altogether. This "capacity gap" can have serious ramifications for the collection and reporting of data in a way that would allow proper auditing, especially among local firms and government agencies. To cite one example, an audit of the quality and quantity of gold shipments to establish ad valorem royalty payments can be problematic if the government does not have the independent capability of assaying sample shipments or access to original documentation concerning sales and refining contracts. In most cases, these governments simply rely on information supplied by the companies, and the information may not be of a quality to permit adequate audit.

Comparability and Consistency

To ensure comparability of revenue information reported by companies and governments, clear definitions need to be established for the types of data to be reported consistently over time by both the companies and the governments. For instance, information on a benefit stream, such as employment in a mining operation, should be easy to report. In reality, because each company has different employment practices (part time, full time, staff employees, contractors, etc.), information on jobs should be normalized to a "full-time equivalent basis" using consistent calculation coefficients applied to all companies operating in the country. This should match the definitions established by the government's employment commission or labor department. Another criterion is the data's ability to distinguish trends; data need to be comparable over various time periods. This can be a problem if reporting procedures or definitions have changed over time. Furthermore, royalties and other tax payments can go up or down, depending on production levels and international market prices. Full explanations of fluctuations over time can help to put community and government expectations into perspective.

Key Challenges in Disclosure

Extractive industries' experience with fuller disclosure of revenues and benefit streams is rapidly evolving. This section summarizes the significant challenges to be met and how best to meet them.

Individual Company- or Sectorwide Disclosure

Should data disclosed by companies be on an individual basis or aggregated on a sectorwide basis? This question is one of the most difficult in the current movement toward greater disclosure and transparency. There are valid concerns on both sides of the issue.

On one hand, companies argue, reasonably, that very few, if any, governments in developed countries with significant mining industries disclose individual taxpayer information. Some information is commercially sensitive, and disclosure would be prejudicial to the company's competitive position. Disclosure of taxes and other payments on an individual basis could single out a company for possible recriminations or discriminatory treatment. As a matter of best practice, it is argued that governments should continue to hold individual taxpayer data on a confidential basis. In addition, companies lawfully optimize their taxation obligations on a worldwide basis, because most large mining companies are active in more than one country. Taxes paid in one country may be offset by credits and allowances in another. This results in significant variations in effective tax burdens, though the complex and complicated rules that govern the management of allowances, offsets, and credits are rarely understood by nontax professionals. The potential for misunderstanding on the part of the general public is high and could give rise to demands to renegotiate valid mining agreements or tax regulations.

On the other hand, some responsible NGOs argue that companies routinely disclose on an individual basis the main elements of taxes paid and revenues generated in their home countries. This disclosure is principally through required filings under rules of the securities exchanges where they are publicly listed. The NGOs maintain that there is little justification to withhold information on the main elements of tax payments from the public of the country where the operations take place. Truly commercially sensitive data can be withheld on a case-by-case basis. The experience of companies that have disclosed tax and other payments on an individual basis has not necessarily validated the kinds of fears the companies express.

Disclosure of Mining Development Agreements

As a matter of international best practice, the fundamentals of the tax package should be codified and set in the mining or tax legislation. This has been done in developed countries or those with large mining industries, such as Australia, Canada, Chile, and South Africa. In reality, when companies invest in developing countries, most will require, and governments are prepared to grant, tax stabilization or special mining development agreements. Tax stabilization agreements usually freeze, for a defined period of time, the types of taxes payable, the company's tax rates, and their method of calculation, as set out in the statutory law at a particular point in time. Such agreements are typically disclosed and, for any one nation, may take a standard form for like types of mines. In contrast, a mining development agreement typically addresses a broad range of issues, supersedes statutory law, and is negotiated with only one project in mind. The disclosure of mining development agreements and, in the case of the oil and gas industries, production sharing agreements, is currently a matter of debate. Many NGOs argue that these agreements should be fully disclosed. A few governments (e.g., Timor-Leste) are moving in this direction. However, companies and the government ministries in charge of the extractive industries sector are generally hesitant about disclosing such agreements.

Multiple reasons exist for disclosing special mining development agreements. Risks inherent in exploration and technical specifics of the ore body sometimes require special conditions. In some instances, the government (either at public expense, or sometimes funded by international donors) has invested substantial sums in exploration to delineate a deposit. In those circumstances, a special agreement may be warranted to compensate the government for previous expenditures, eventual discovery premiums, and work-expenditure commitments by the company to bring the deposit into production. For countries that may lack an established mining industry and track record in dealing with large multinational companies, special agreements are necessary to address the concerns of shareholders and financial institutions. Finally, even though many countries in the past 10 years have passed new and internationally competitive mining laws, the mining regulations and ancillary legislation have not yet been promulgated. Special agreements can be used to fill these gaps and to define whatever special conditions could be required by the country with respect to its home country taxation liabilities.

Mining development agreements vary in scope, with some sticking quite closely to the tax package as defined in the general legislation and supplementing it as necessary with accounting and other interpretations. In other instances, the agreements can diverge significantly from existing legislation, especially if the ore body is particularly large or if it has been the subject of considerable previous exploration. Generally, to the extent not already defined in the laws, the agreements may include accounting definitions, depreciation and amortization rules, provisions for state ownership participation, royalty structures and calculation methods, land taxes payable nationally or subnationally, fuel taxes, contributions to various social funds, depletion allowances, rates and possible exemptions from customs duties, payment and reimbursement of value-added taxes, bonus and discovery premium payments, reimbursement of previous exploration expenses, work commitments, foreign exchange and repatriation obligations, use of offshore escrow accounts, and other dispositions. The master agreement or subsidiary agreements may define the mining operation's contribution and management of other benefit streams going to the provincial and municipal communities.

The concern about disclosure of such agreements is that the inherent trade-offs of fiscal dispositions are complicated and complex and are unlikely to be fully understood by members of the public. For instance, granting one company a reduced royalty in return for an increased government equity stake in a mining venture may or may not compare favorably in the court of public opinion with an increased up-front payment to reimburse previous exploration expenditures with a reduced government equity position. Similarly, the difficulties in bringing a deposit into production or international market conditions may require special tax considerations for one company, whereas these same conditions may not apply to another. Companies' fear arising from disclosure of these complicated agreements is that they could be singled out for discriminatory treatment and recriminations.

Accounting and Auditing Standards

A fundamental prerequisite for transparency in the mining sector is the choice of accounting and auditing standards. This is important not only to accurately reflect the revenue streams in an individual country, but also to permit comparison across international boundaries. Even though much progress is being made to adopt international financial reporting standards, in reality, accounting standards and practices still vary greatly from country to country and from company to company. Several challenges need to be addressed.

International companies naturally opt for the accounting principles and standards of their home country or the country where they are publicly listed. However, accounting and auditing standards for companies from China and Russia are not the same as for companies from Australia or Canada. In addition, the home country standards may be at significant variance with the standards of the host country, which requires that considerable time and effort be devoted to harmonizing the accounts. Not only is this a burden, but it can lead to serious difficulties, because fundamental accounting definitions to match expenditures to revenue may not be the same. Finally, in many developing countries the accounting profession is not well developed, and local capacity for accounting and auditing does not exist, including within the government. There is much work to be done to build such capacity and to train government officials to account for and monitor revenue streams adequately on a consistent basis.

Another challenge is the audit of state-owned mining companies and other parastatals operating in the sector. Many of these have been operating for years under opaque supervision and regulatory requirements. Experience has shown that state-owned enterprises sometimes resist opening themselves to internationally accredited audits. Where audits have been conducted, significant deficiencies have been noted in the financial reports and internal management controls. In many cases, accounts are incomplete or bear little resemblance to commonly accepted accounting principles, even in the country concerned. Because of the lack of transparency in state-owned enterprises' accounts, a key first step to introduce good governance to the mining sector is to conduct an independent audit of these companies, applying international auditing standards. Independent audits of privately held companies in the sector should be undertaken as well, or if they already exist, they should be made publicly available.

Certification and Validation

In an ideal world, disclosure of revenue streams by the government would be certified or validated by an independent agency. Without such certification mere disclosure may lack credibility. The continuing evolution of the Extractive Industries Transparency Initiative (EITI, more on this later in the chapter) is addressing this issue. The EITI coins the term "the administrator" and assigns a role similar, but not identical, to that of the international auditor. Whereas the typical role of the auditor for an individual company is to certify the truthfulness of the company's financial statements, the role of the administrator is to reconcile the revenue streams reported as being paid by the companies with those same revenue streams reported as having been received by the government. This is most often done on an aggregated sector basis (i.e., individual companies are not identified) rather than on a company-specific basis, though disclosure on an individual company or sectorwide basis is still being discussed in some countries. The administrator would apply international auditing standards to reconcile the accounts and identify any gaps or discrepancies. Finally, the administrator would publish an opinion attesting to the truthfulness of the revenue streams reported.

As of this writing, no country has actually had the disclosed revenue streams produced by the mining sector certified by an independent agency or administrator. Traditional auditing firms are cautious in entering this uncharted territory. It has been suggested that the World Bank or another international body could undertake the role of administrator and certify disclosures. Another possibility would be modelled on the "competent" person concept for certification of ore reserves, or perhaps use independent verification companies. The latter, for example, are used by governments to monitor conformance with technical specifications and to control the quality of imports and exports. In any event, there is a role for some entity to certify mining sector revenue disclosures, though currently no fixed standards or obvious candidates exist.

Inclusion of Civil Society

To what extent should civil society and NGOs be involved in determining methods for reporting revenue streams and managing their use? Over the past 15 years these groups have become more vocal in articulating demands for greater involvement in the mining industry, at the national and, in particular, the local level. At the national level, debate is often focused on total revenues of large companies or the sector as a whole. Civil society and local NGOs are often supported by larger internationally recognized NGOs, for example Global Witness, Publish What You Pay, and the Soros Foundation, which have been particularly active on various transparency and governance initiatives. At the local level, NGOs and civil society are concerned principally with the distribution of revenues and benefit streams. The local communities in and around the mining operation complain that they bear the cost of negative environmental and social disturbances caused by the mining operations and yet receive little, or nothing, in terms of taxes and revenues. Companies generally maintain, quite correctly, that the decision about what portion, if any, of the taxes and fees to be paid or retained at the local level is not theirs to make. Nonetheless, companies often bear the brunt of the recriminations and have difficulty in explaining their true contribution to the local community. Involvement of civil society and NGOs brings a level of sophistication to the debate that requires more substance than the traditional company or government public relations information.

Increasingly, civil society does not want to be spoon-fed information on the benefit and revenue streams, but it does want to participate with the company and government in the design of the methods to collect and monitor the benefits and revenue streams on a continual basis. Moreover, once the monitoring and evaluation system is designed and operational, certain members of civil society would like it to identify benchmarks against which a company's or government's performance can be evaluated. This can substantially raise the stakes for companies and governments because it could imply a set of targets that may or may not be within the company's or the government's sole competence to achieve. This watchdog function can be useful, although it is sometimes not recognized as such by companies and governments. NGOs can also help by training local communities in understanding benefit and revenue streams and the fundamentals of the industry, and these groups often have more credibility than company or government representatives.

Costs and Challenges Associated with Compliance

Since the late 1980s, some governments have introduced national mineral policies and resources rent strategies that, in many cases, were fundamentally different from what those states had before. Because the policies were so significantly different from the past, it became necessary to replace old legislation with new legal frameworks for mineral development, taxation, and the collection of royalties. In addition, new stakeholders, for instance, NGOs and local communities, have become more interested in the reporting of the sector. The result of the new legislation and interest group pressure is an increase in the cost of compliance. Companies' and governments' costs of compliance are increased as well by changes to accountancy rules—for example, the move from generally accepted accounting principles (GAAP) to International Accounting Standards. This is especially important for companies that are listed in more than one jurisdiction. Finally, a key challenge will be to integrate other aspects of good governance of companies, civil society groups, and the government itself into the overall framework of sustainable development. These are relatively new concepts in the extractive industries, and it will take some time before a consensus emerges on a common set of principles. In the meantime, confusion in understanding the issues will increase costs of compliance and could lead to misunderstandings among the interested parties.

Reporting of Other Benefit Streams

Most of the international attention on the transparency and governance issue is focused on the revenue streams generated by the extractive industries. However, any mining or oil and gas project has other important benefit streams. Many of these touch people's lives and well-being directly and hence are of greater relevance to them than the taxes paid by the companies. In fact, community leaders, government decision makers, and NGO representatives frequently question the benefits that the extractive industries bring to the national and local economies. Surprisingly, empirical data on these nonfinancial benefit streams are hard to come by. There does not appear to be a consistently applied methodology that allows for measurement and comparison of such streams from project to project or across national borders. To be sure, companies routinely measure certain benefits (e.g., payroll, charitable contributions, value of infrastructure investment), but companies measure these differently. This lack of a common measure makes comparisons difficult.

A number of initiatives are currently under way to measure these types of benefit streams on a consistent and comparable basis. One in particular is the Resource Endowment Study undertaken under the auspices of the International Council for Metals and Mining (ICMM), an association of major mining companies based mainly in London. The study will produce a template that will allow individual mining operations to measure and report the nonfinancial benefit streams. Some of the most important benefits to be reported by the template follow:

- *Employment and dependents.* Reports on a full-time-employment basis for direct, indirect, and induced employment; on local versus national composition of the workforce; and on social distribution (gender, age, ethnicity, and other dimensions).
- *Value of procurement.* Profiles the supply chain, value of domestic and international procurement, capital versus operational expenditures, and characteristics of the groups that benefit from procurement.
- *Human capital for employees.* Covers internal training programs, number of beneficiaries, financial and time cost, and outcomes in terms of improved performance.
- *Value added to the host economy.* Includes local value added, retained value analysis, and opportunity cost of economic resources.
- *Social and infrastructure provision.* Describes and measures the financial and staff contributions to physical, educational, health, local enterprise, and community development.

A stakeholders working group, supported by expert consultancy services, has been formed to help prepare the reporting template. This is currently being pilot tested at selected mining operations in Africa and South America. Once the pilot tests are concluded and the reporting template has been validated, the ICMM intends to suggest to its member companies that they begin compiling the relevant information on a consistent basis. The World Bank is participating in the preparation of the template and is encouraging countries active in the mining sector to consider implementing the reporting mechanism.

Finally, as noted earlier, simply reporting the amounts spent on various community support projects may not be especially meaningful or relevant to many stakeholders. What these stakeholders and their political leaders want to know are the outcomes of the programs and projects funded. For instance, the company may have built a dispensary and hospital, but has there been an increase in the health of the population as measured, for instance, by longevity statistics? A school vaccination program has been financed, but has there been a corresponding drop in the transmission of infectious diseases such as measles or meningitis? Schoolhouses have been built, teachers recruited, and books purchased, but has there been an improvement in students' test scores? One reason it is difficult to know the value of this approach is that these types of outcomes are not solely related to the company funding but rather are heavily influenced by other factors and externalities. The government or company cannot be held responsible for outcomes that are influenced by factors outside its control. Another difficulty is measurement. Many governments lack the capability of measuring some indicators on education, health, and human well-being. If they do have the capability and methodology, it is often not site specific, so no direct relationships between company programs and outcomes may be inferred from the data. Nonetheless, some progress is being made as the United Nations, the World Bank, and individual governments gather the appropriate statistics. Good starting points for companies interested in assisting in this effort are the Millennium Development Goals (MDGs) and various publications on human development, such as the United Nations Development Program's Human Development Reports (http://hdr.undp.org/reports/global/2004/).[3]

Model Reporting Template for Mining Sector Revenues

The model reporting template in Table 6.1 has been developed for use by all reporting entities, public agencies, state-owned mining companies, and private companies to record various types of revenue streams, source, and value. This basic template can be modified to take into account country-specific conditions.

The Extractive Industries Transparency Initiative

This section is excerpted from the EITI Sourcebook and other documents describing the initiative. Full information is available on the EITI Web site (http://www.eitransparency.org).

Background of the EITI

The United Kingdom's Prime Minister Tony Blair announced the EITI at the World Summit on Sustainable Development in Johannesburg, South Africa, in September 2002. Since then, several governments, companies, civil society groups, and international donor organizations have subscribed to the principles of the EITI and are supporting the initiative. Simply put, the EITI aims to increase transparency in transactions between governments and companies in extractive industries.

Revenues from oil, gas, and mining companies, in the form of taxes, royalties, signature bonuses, and other payments, should be an important engine for economic growth and social development in the developing

Table 6.1. Model Reporting Template

Nature of revenue stream	State from which the revenue stream was received	Value (US$ millions)
Mineral production received in kind		
Taxes on profit and income		
Mineral resources taxes and royalties		
Other taxes, to be reported as separate line items if material, such as:		
• Value-added taxes (net)		
• Withholding taxes		
• Environmental taxes		
• Property taxes		
• Road taxes		
• Employee social payments		
• Customs duties		
• Fuel and excise taxes		
• Emergency taxes		
Fees, to be reported as separate line items if material, such as:		
• License and permit fees		
• Surface rental fees		
• Entry fees		
• Other considerations for licenses and concessions		
Signing bonuses and production bonuses		
Dividends received		
Interest and loans paid by mining company on behalf of government (or government agency)		
Other payments, to be reported as separate line items if material, made by mining company on behalf of government (or government agency)		
Proceeds from sale of mining assets		
Proceeds from long-term borrowings from mining companies and other financial operations		
Proceeds from lease activities		
Contributions to government social funds		
Other significant payments (to be specified)		

Source: EITI.

and transition countries. However, the lack of accountability and transparency in these revenues can exacerbate poor governance and lead to corruption, conflict, and poverty. Extractive industries are important in over 50 developing countries, which are home to some 3.5 billion people. Although a greater degree of transparency of payments is desirable in many sectors, there is a close correlation between the countries rich in natural resources and the countries with high levels of poverty. There is nothing intrinsically wrong with these sectors, but the high risk, high cost, and uncertain nature of exploration—coupled with a long gestation before profits are realized and with the finite nature of the resources—make financial management of this sector difficult. Some countries rich in oil, gas, and minerals have underperformed relative to other countries without natural wealth.

The fundamental rationale behind the EITI is that increased transparency and knowledge of revenues from the extractive industries will empower citizens and institutions to hold governments accountable. Mismanagement or diversion of funds away from sustainable development purposes will become more difficult. It should also benefit developing and transition economies by improving the business environment, thus helping them attract foreign direct investment. Responsible companies stand to benefit from a more level playing field, a more predictable business environment, and better prospects for natural resources and energy security.

The EITI is a consultative process involving the multiple stakeholders in the countries that subscribe to the basic principles (see Table 6.2). These principles were devised at the initial Lancaster House conference in London in 2003, which launched the implementation of the initiative. To launch the EITI in a country, the highest political levels in the country generally must endorse and subscribe to the principles. Experience to date is that subsequent steps involve establishing an implementation committee composed of various stakeholders: key government ministries, private companies, and representatives of NGOs and civil society. The aim of the committee is to achieve an agreement that sets out provisions for annual disclosure of company payments and government revenues. The disclosures, by all parties in each country to a trusted third party, use standardized templates. The data disclosed may then be collated, aggregated where necessary, and summarized into a country output report.

As of July 2005, some 20 countries had endorsed the EITI principles and are in varying stages of implementation of the initiative.

Table 6.2. EITI Lancaster House Principles

1. We share a belief that the prudent use of natural resource wealth should be an important engine for sustainable economic growth that contributes to sustainable development and poverty reduction, but if not managed properly, can create negative economic and social impacts.

2. We affirm that management of natural resource wealth for the benefit of a country's citizens is in the domain of sovereign governments to be exercised in the interests of their national development.

3. We recognize that the benefits of resource extraction occur as revenue streams over many years and can be highly price dependent.

4. We recognize that a public understanding of government revenues and expenditure over time could help public debate and inform choice of appropriate and realistic options for sustainable development.

5. We underline the importance of transparency by governments and companies in the extractive industries and the need to enhance public financial management and accountability.

6. We recognize that achievement of greater transparency must be set in the context of respect for contracts and laws.

7. We recognize the enhanced environment for domestic and foreign direct investment that financial transparency may bring.

8. We believe in the principle and practice of accountability by government to all citizens for the stewardship of revenue streams and public expenditure.

9. We are committed to encouraging high standards of transparency and accountability in public life, government operations, and business.

10. We believe that a broadly consistent and workable approach to the disclosure of payments and revenues is required, which is simple to undertake and to use.

11. We believe that payments' disclosure in a given country should involve all extractive industry companies operating in that country.

12. In seeking solutions, we believe that all stakeholders have important and relevant contributions to make, including governments and their agencies, extractive industry companies, service companies, multilateral organizations, financial organizations, investors, and nongovernmental organizations.

Source: EITI.

Experience with EITI Implementation:
The Case of the Kyrgyz Republic

The Kyrgyz Republic, located in the heart of central Asia, is a nation of some 5.1 million people. At independence in 1992, the country inherited the Soviet economic management philosophy and infrastructure. Since the early 1990s the country has struggled to develop its resources, principally agriculture, hydropower, and minerals. Although the first two offer an existing platform for some growth, gold mining has been developed most rapidly, becoming a significant factor in the economy.

The Kumtor gold deposit in the Tien Shen mountains was discovered by Soviet geologists in the 1960s and thoroughly explored during the 1970s and 1980s. It was not yet developed at independence, when the Canadian uranium company, Cameco, learned of the potential development opportunity. The government of the Kyrgyz Republic and Cameco Gold Company entered into a joint agreement to provide for the development of the deposit. The initial agreement provided that Cameco would have 33.3 percent of the operating company and the Kyrgyz government, through a wholly owned state enterprise (Kyrgyzaltin), would own 66.7 percent. In addition, a number of fiscal and financial provisions were required in order to bring the deposit into production. Development of the Kumtor mine eventually cost US$430 million. The mine opened in 1997 and produces 650,000 ounces of gold annually. At current production rates and prices, the mine accounts for approximately 10 percent of the country's GDP and 40 percent of its export earnings.

In 2003, the government and Cameco began discussing a restructuring of the original master agreement. A number of variants were discussed, and it was decided to create a new freestanding company, Centerra Gold, which would be listed on the Toronto stock exchange. Kyrgyzaltin would contribute its shareholdings in Kumtor Operating Company to the new company, as would Cameco. In addition, Cameco would contribute additional mineral holdings in Mongolia and Nevada. It was anticipated that the market valuation of the shares in Centerra would be significantly higher than could be achieved through the Kumtor Operating Company vehicle, thus maximizing the value of the mineral deposit to both the government and Cameco. Depending on the final market valuation at the time of the initial public offering (IPO), it was anticipated that Kyrgyzaltin would hold approximately 30 percent of Centerra stock.

In December 2003, the government approached the World Bank and the International Monetary Fund (IMF) to solicit views on the proposed restructuring. These institutions highlighted several issues, including the benefit of minimizing the government's risk in contributing valuable state assets to a new, publicly listed company and the need to ensure the transparency of the transaction and the revenue flows associated with it. The Bank and the IMF made three recommendations to address these issues. First, the government would immediately, at the time of IPO, issue a secondary offering of a portion of its shares to generate cash and reduce the risk. Second, the government would endorse and implement the EITI. Third, the government would conduct a "risk control and assurance audit" of Kyrgyzaltin through an internationally recognized accounting firm.

The IPO for Centerra was concluded on June 30, 2004. The government, as arranged, sold approximately 30 percent of its Centerra shares on secondary offering to generate a gain of about US$80 million. These funds were transferred through Kyrgyzaltin to the central treasury. Although the management of Kyrgyzaltin wanted the company to retain possession of the funds, because it was the legal custodian of the Centerra shares, the government, as sole shareholder of Kyrgyzaltin, mandated that the funds be transferred to the central government treasury. By agreement with the international donor community, the government has committed to using these funds for overall poverty reduction activities.

The government moved forward to implement the EITI by issuing a decree endorsing the principles, establishing an implementing committee, and preparing to publish an accounting of the revenue streams generated by the mining sector. The representatives on the committee were drawn from government agencies, private sector companies, and civil society. The committee met regularly and developed a template to record revenue flows. Donor funds (the World Bank and the United Kingdom's Department for International Development) were accessed to provide accounting expertise to the committee and government agencies. Funds were also used to support training and sensitization campaigns conducted by NGOs for civil society. The first report on revenue streams from the mining sector was published in August 2004, both in the national newspapers and on the Ministry of Finance Web page. The vast majority of the funds reported are from the Kumtor mine and the proceeds from the sale of Centerra shares. However, the implementation committee is working to integrate other sectoral data with further iterations of the reporting template. It is anticipated that reports will be issued every six months, and the government is on schedule to achieve this objective.

An audit of the accounts of Kyrgyzaltin was conducted by Deloitte and Touche. The audit report was designed to identify weaknesses in management and control mechanisms within the company with respect to financial and fiscal matters and to recommend remedial actions. The report has been issued by Deloitte and Touche and has, in fact, identified numerous deficiencies and made recommendations for follow-up. The management of Kyrgyzaltin and the government are reviewing the Deloitte and Touche report with a view to implementing its recommendations.

Emerging Lessons

The example of the EITI process in the Kyrgyz Republic illustrates the way in which one country is approaching the transparency issue. In the Kyrgyz Republic, as in all other countries, making the revenue streams the mining sector generates more transparent is very much a work-in-progress. The experience of one country can provide inspiration to another, but it cannot necessarily be replicated exactly. Clearly, one important lesson that is emerging is that one size does not fit all; each country needs to develop its own methods, systems, and legal structures to ensure disclosure and reporting of revenue streams.

Nonetheless, countries that decide to implement the initiative will have to address some fundamental questions within the general guidelines noted in this chapter as well as the specific suggestions of the EITI. Some of the points of current debate follow.

1. The issue of what is material and what is immaterial in terms of reporting on revenue streams is significant in many countries. Though each country will have different views on what is or is not material, all need to define clear criteria or thresholds to distinguish materiality of revenue streams.
2. Although one of the initial concepts of the EITI is to make it voluntary, it is increasingly evident that some companies will participate and others will not, resulting in problems with consistency and equality. Companies that elect to participate also have concerns that they will be singled out for unwarranted scrutiny, whereas competitors that elect not to participate avoid such scrutiny. There is a tendency, therefore, to make disclosure of revenue streams mandatory, as directed by national laws. However, this is not as easy as it may seem, because consensus must be achieved among the various

stakeholders on the nature and extent of reporting requirements. The tendency would be to reduce these requirements to the lowest common denominator, that is, to the levels acceptable to the most reluctant participant.

3. The responsibility of civil society and, in particular, NGOs to declare their revenue streams and sources of finance has also been raised in some countries. More broadly, the definition of civil society and the important selection of who will represent civil society in the dialogue relating to transparency are significant. Self-proclaimed advocates of transparency may or may not truly represent the constituencies they claim; thus, checks and balances need to be put into place to avoid grandstanding on the transparency issue for short-term political gain.

4. There are degrees of transparency and disclosure. Clearly, some jurisdictions will go further and report more completely and professionally on their revenue streams. Are there incentive mechanisms that can be devised to encourage countries to advance the transparency agenda?

5. Several models exist for audits of company and government accounts. Variations depend on the country in question and the nature of the resource base and revenue streams. Is it possible to have internationally recognized models of audits that would provide options that are based on the complexity of the revenue streams and the extent of the national industry?

6. In countries with federal structures, considerable responsibility for the extractive industries devolves to subnational jurisdictions (e.g., Argentina, Australia, Canada, Malaysia, and the United States). To what extent is transparency and governance an overarching responsibility of the national government, or to what extent is it more relevant to the subnational jurisdiction?

7. Do the international development institutions such as the International Monetary Fund and World Bank have a more aggressive role to play in enforcing transparency? Clearly, political pronouncements of both national leaders and leaders of the institutions emphasize transparency, but should bilateral or multilateral aid and lending programs be conditioned on transparency and disclosure?

8. How does the current work on transparency and disclosure fit into the broader agenda of governance, democracy, empowerment of local communities, accountability, respect for human rights, and other issues that now affect operations in the extractive industries? In

the Niger River delta, for instance, the debate on disclosure is often bound together with discussion of these broader issues.

This chapter has focused essentially on how revenue streams are accounted for and disclosed. In the views of many informed persons, that is not enough. Governments should also disclose how they spend the revenues collected from the extractive industries. In theory, full transparency with regard to how revenues are spent would increase government accountability. However, in practice, the public expenditure management systems of many developing countries are as yet too weak to accommodate this level of transparency. International financial institutions such as the World Bank and International Monetary Fund work with developing countries to improve transparency in government budgeting and expenditure processes; however, this is a long-term agenda in most countries and much remains to be done. Thus, the question is whether new mechanisms could be put into place through these institutions or others to ensure greater transparency in public expenditures.

As would be expected with a work in progress, there are as yet no answers to these questions or to the others posed in this chapter. Perhaps in 10 years an accepted body of practice will have evolved—together with guidelines and directives similar to those for environmental assessment and management—that will pertain to disclosure of revenue streams and, possibly, the spending of them. Over the next several years, it is expected that governments, companies, and civil society in all countries will advance the debate on these issues.

References

Collier, P., and A. Hoeffler. 2000. "Greed and Grievance in Civil War." Policy Research Working Paper 2355, Development Research Group, World Bank, Washington, DC.

Davis, G., and J. Tilton. 2002. "Should Developing Countries Renounce Mining? A Perspective on the Debate." Working Paper, Colorado School of Mines, Division of Economics and Business.

Gelb, Alan. 1988. *Oil Windfalls: Blessing or Curse*. New York: Oxford University Press.

Gylfason, T., T. T. Herbertsson, and G. Zoega. 1999. *A Mixed Blessing: Natural Resources and Economic Growth*. Vol. 3 of *Macroeconomic Dynamics*, 204–25. Cambridge, MA: Cambridge University Press.

Sachs, J. D., and A. M. Warner. 1995. "Natural Resource Abundance and Economic Growth." Development Discussion Paper No. 517a. Cambridge, MA: Harvard Institute for International Development.

———. 2001. "The Curse of Natural Resources." *European Economic Review* 45: 847–59.

Notes

1. The phenomenon is generally measured as the percentage of GDP or export earnings that extractive industries represent. The percentage of taxes produced by the sectors to total taxes generated by the economy is also sometimes used.

2. See Gelb (1988); Gylfason, Herbertsson, and Zoega (1999); and Sachs and Warner (1995, 2001).

3. Information on the MDGs is available at: http://www.un.org/millennium goals/. For the Human Development Index, a useful starting point is: http://hdr.undp.org/reports/global/2004/.

Summary and Conclusions

Summary of Findings

The majority of the world's nations have initiated regulatory reform of their mineral sector over the past two decades. An important part of these initiatives has been an examination of the fiscal system imposed on mining activities. In designing mineral sector taxation systems, policy makers must carefully seek to balance tax types, rates, and incentives that satisfy the needs of both the nation and the mining investor. Such systems must be both equitable and globally competitive. The purpose of this study has been to provide a comprehensive, objective, and neutral analysis that can be used by governments and industry in deliberations concerning the merits and demerits of royalties and their various forms.

Most governments impose a royalty tax on producers of minerals. Those nations that do not impose royalty may be reluctant to do so because of the desire to apply nondiscriminatory taxation principles across economic sectors or to present favorable investment conditions to attract investment in a globally competitive marketplace. In those nations that do impose royalty, the methods and rates vary widely, and the justification for such a tax may be to either obtain compensation for the permanent loss of a nonrenewable national resource (that is, an ownership transfer tax), or generate revenue in return for the government's permission to mine (a use tax).

In Chapter 2, mining taxation was discussed in general terms. A core concept was the "optimal level" of taxation. From a macroeconomic government perspective, the optimal level is one that maximizes the net present value of the social benefits flowing from the mineral sector, including government tax receipts, over the long term. This implies a balance, because if taxation is too high, investment and the tax base will decrease as investors shift their focus to other alternatives, and if taxation is too low, the nation will lose revenue useful to serve the public welfare. Determining what the optimal level is poses a challenge for governments, which may need to look to empirical evidence of investor perceptions and behavior for guidance.

The challenge for governments does not stop at determining the optimal level of mineral sector taxation but extends also to the issue of sector discrimination. A key question that should be addressed is whether the mining sector is to be taxed the same or differently in comparison to other sectors. Sector tax discrimination is thought by many economists to lead to problematic distortions in the national economy, but many others would argue that the mineral sector is different from other sectors and requires special tax considerations. Most nations today do provide special tax treatment for the sector, including handling of exploration, development, and capital costs for income tax purposes; reduced liabilities for input and output taxes (import and export duties, value-added taxes on goods and services, withholding taxes, sales taxes, excise tax, etc.); and the imposition of a royalty tax.

The discrimination issue occurs at both the macroeconomic level (how should all mines be treated?) and at the microeconomic level (how should an individual mine be taxed?). At the microeconomic (project) level an extensive body of research has been developed over many decades to look at concepts relating to the idea of economic rent. Here, the theoretical challenge for governments has been to determine how much tax can be extracted from a project to leave enough return for the investor so that the investor will be minimally satisfied. Every mine's economic parameters are different, and this implies that governments seeking to base their taxation system on economic rent principles will need a taxation system that adjusts for every mine. Today, no government has implemented a mining sector taxation system based solely on the concept of economic rent, although some tax methods, such as profit-based taxes, are more in tune with capturing economic rent than other methods. The point was argued that the ultimate objective of mineral taxation is not the capture of economic rents but the promotion of the social welfare, as defined by the prevailing political process. Moreover, in the long run, the existence of economic rents in the mineral sector is called into question by the fact that the wealth created by the discovery of new deposits provides the incentive for exploration.

Governments can choose from many options when they are designing fiscal systems, and the mix and level of taxes selected can negatively or positively affect investors' willingness to invest. A distinction can be made between tax types that are based on units or value (such as unit-based and ad valorem royalties, sales and excise taxes, property and capital taxes, import and export duty, withholding on goods and services, value-added tax, registration fees, land area–based fees, and stamp tax) and those that are based on a measure of profitability (such as income tax, capital gains tax, additional and excess profits tax, profit- or income-based royalty, and withholding tax on dividends). In general, investors prefer to pay taxes that are tied in some way to their ability to pay, that is, based on profitability. In selecting which taxes to apply, government policy makers must balance their own objectives with investor objectives. Governments generally like to collect at least some tax revenue from all mines regardless of their profitability. Although investors will be concerned about tax types, of primary importance will be the cumulative effects of all taxes on their operations. If the net effect of the overall tax system is too great (too high an effective tax rate), an investor may shift its focus to a lower taxing jurisdiction.

Today, nations impose a wide variety of taxes on the mineral sector. The general trend over the past several decades has been a decline in the overall tax burden placed on mines. This same trend has occurred for most other sectors as well, perhaps reflecting revised government perceptions about the optimal level of taxation.

Chapter 3 built on the general tax discussion in Chapter 2 by examining royalty taxes specifically. Here the emphasis was placed on the purpose of a royalty tax, royalty methods and levels that vary by mineral type, examples of the types and levels of royalty taxes, and the application of royalty concepts to private party arrangements. The analysis revealed a wide variety of approaches with no clear trend for global convergence. Most nations impose some form of royalty on their mineral sector, but some nations, such as Chile, Greenland, Mexico, Sweden, and Zimbabwe, do not. (Chile, South Africa, and Zimbabwe are currently considering the introduction of royalty.)

A key policy decision when designing a royalty tax system is to determine the extent to which the system will discriminate between different mineral types. The usefulness of using a unique assessment method for each mineral type is that it can be tailored to the marketing, physical properties, and relative profitability of that mineral. Many nations with extensive and historically well-developed mining industries differentiate between types of minerals, by either royalty tax method or rate or by both method and rate. Other nations use a more uniform approach, and all minerals, or at least all minerals of a like class, are taxed identically. Most systems that discriminate between mineral types are considered "transparent," because the valuation basis is stated in a manner best suited for each mineral product instead of relying on administrative interpretation. However, systems that do not differentiate also have advantages, particularly when applied to mixed-mineral products, such as concentrates from many massive sulfide deposits. One of the clear advantages of royalty systems that are based on profitability or income is that they can be applied to any type or scale of mineral operation without the need to differentiate between the types of mineral being produced.

An examination of the royalty tax systems in over 35 nations revealed that most royalty methods can be classified as one of three types: unit based, value based (ad valorem), or profit based. Some nations, but only a few, apply hybrid systems that combine two of the three methods. The most prevalently used methods are the unit-based and value-based systems, but profit-based systems are increasingly being applied, particularly in diversified economies.

Unit-based methods are often applied to high-volume, low-value homogeneous "bulk" commodities such as construction minerals, bauxite, iron ore, phosphate, and potash. Unit-based royalties are well suited to discriminate between scales of operation, and it is common to see a sliding-scale approach. Unit-based royalties provide a certain and continuous revenue flow and are relatively easy to administer.

Like unit-based royalties, value-based royalties are payable irrespective of whether the mine has profits or losses. However, unlike unit-based royalties they fluctuate following commodity prices. Value-based royalties can be easy or complicated to administer, depending on how value is defined, and when comparing value-based royalty rates in different jurisdictions, care must be taken to not compare rates in isolation unless the royalty base is identical. Value-based royalty rates may be uniform for all sales of that mineral or may vary according to a sliding scale based on the volume or cumulative value of material sold. A common value is net smelter return (NSR), in which the taxable amount takes into account the return to the producer after smelting and refining charges. For the purpose of calculating NSR, costs associated with further downstream processing are deducted before calculating the base value for the NSR royalty.

Profit-based systems are used mainly in developed nations that have both a large mining industry and a strong tax administration. They provide an uncertain revenue flow to government and are administratively complex, but they can yield high-level, long-term tax revenues and satisfy most investor criteria.

Although unit-based royalties are simple to determine, value-based royalties are less so. In the case of unit-based royalties, all that is required is knowledge of the amount of product produced, whereas with value-based royalties, knowledge of mineral value is necessary. Simpler value-based systems use a measure of "realized value" that is based, for instance, on customer invoices. More complex methods impute a mineral value using methods such as applying a reported international reference price to some measure of mineral content, seeking the opinion of an independent appraiser (diamonds), or using imputed value less defined costs such as transportation, insurance, and freight. Profit-based royalty assessment methods tend to be detailed, reflecting the need to carefully consider how all revenues and costs, usually including capital and recurring operating costs, will be handled.

Governments and investors have different objectives and preferences regarding royalty methods, with governments usually preferring unit- and value-based methods and investors favoring profit-based methods. Governments tend to like systems that are stable, equitable, able to generate continual revenue, easy to administer, and amenable to targeted distribution. Companies prefer methods that are based on the ability to pay, allow for early recovery of capital, respond to downturns in market prices, do not distort production decisions such as cutoff grade or mine life, do not add significantly to operating costs, and are amenable to distribution directly to affected stakeholders. Both governments and investors usually favor tax systems with a high level of transparency.

When considering any approach to royalty, governments need to take care that the approach selected can be administered efficiently and effectively. Most governments tend to understaff their tax collection and monitoring offices, and where administrative resources are limited, simpler royalty methods may be preferable to more complex methods. In this study's examination of national and provincial royalty schemes, complex profit-based royalties were a feature mainly in developed nations with relatively well-funded and trained tax collectors and auditors.

The responsibility for royalty collection and monitoring may lie with the department responsible for implementation of the general mining law or maybe the general tax office. If the responsibility is the mining department's, there is likely to be a higher level of understanding of the product being sold and thus an enhanced ability to effectively make sound decisions on matters such as value, but that knowledge also may result in less neutrality in the way the royalty is applied to operations in times of low prices or industry duress. Good royalty systems clearly specify the obligations of the taxpayer, including details such as the final mining product subject to royalty (raw or processed); the valuation method; the manner in which special forms of sales such as futures, forward, hedging, and long-term contracts are to be handled; the form in which the royalty obligation is reported and its frequency (the return); the mode and place of payments; the currency that may be used for payment; measures for adjusting provisional and actual sales; means to correct non-arm's-length sales; how penalties for noncompliance are applied and collected; and the procedures to appeal an assessment or to apply for an exemption or deferral.

Another key issue for government policy makers is the apportionment of royalty. The imposition of a special sector tax like royalty may be politically easier to direct to defined stakeholders (rather than being destined for the general fund) than generally applied taxes. Many nations designate royalty collection and disbursement at the provincial level, and some have joined the debate on whether some part of royalty should be apportioned to affected communities (a few governments now require this).

On a regional basis, in Africa most royalties are collected by the central government and are apportioned through the annual budgeting process. Most governments have opted for value-based royalties with rates generally around 3 percent. Diamonds, which are a key part of mining in many African nations, usually are taxed at a higher rate than other minerals. Most mining codes provide for royalty deferment or exemption in exceptional cases.

In the Asia and Pacific region, some nations impose a royalty to be paid to the central government but others prefer this to be handled at the provincial or local level. Most governments impose unit-based royalties on bulk minerals and valued-based royalties on other minerals. A few nations allow for deferment or reduction of royalty payments during hard times, but most do not. Ad valorem rates are typically in the 2 percent to 4 percent range.

In Australia, royalties are set and collected at the provincial (state) level. The royalty system regulations tend to be highly detailed and vary from one mineral type to another. Most Australian states impose unit-based royalties on industrial minerals and value-based royalties on other types. One state uses a profit-based system for all minerals, but in two other states, profit-based royalties apply to only a limited number of specific minerals. Some states allow for royalty deferment or reductions during hard times, but others do not. Ad valorem rates are generally in the 2 percent to 4 percent range.

Royalties in Latin America are usually based on value, with most rates in the 2 percent to 3 percent range. Some large producer nations, such as Mexico, and some Argentine provinces, do not impose royalty. Nations that impose royalty are apt to distribute them to mandated parties rather than designate them for the central treasury. Most nations do not allow deferment to firms during times of financial distress.

North America, Canada, and the United States do not impose royalties at the central government level. In Canada, royalty jurisdiction lies primarily with the provinces, whereas in the United States, royalty systems are highly complex and usually related to the nature of mineral ownership. In Canada, almost all mineral royalties are profit based, with rates generally greater than 5 percent (with some exceeding 10 percent). In the United States, minerals belonging or occurring in state-owned land are usually subject to value-based royalty, although one important mining state (Nevada) uses a profit-based system.

The ways in which value-based and profit-based royalties are defined in national laws vary considerably from nation to nation, and care must be taken when comparing royalty rates to make sure that the royalty basis is clearly understood. Extracts from royalty legislation are reported in Appendix A1 for a global cross-section of nations. In an examination of these laws, there did not appear to be a strong connection between royalties and the lack of or presence of mineral diversity. Likewise, countries with world-class mines did not tend to impose a higher or lower level of royalty than other nations. The examination of the statutes did find a relationship between national wealth and royalty type; examples of profit-based royalty systems were restricted to developed economies. There did not appear to be a relationship between broad economic indicators such as GDP (and mining's contribution to GDP) and the effective tax rate. The lack of royalty similarities between nations is attributed to the fact that every nation is unique, with its own legal system, history, political institutions, and interest groups.

Although royalty systems differ widely among nations, the variety and range of royalty types among private parties with negotiated agreements is perhaps even greater. The types of royalties arising under private party arrangements are diverse but generally can be categorized in the same way as royalties imposed by governments, namely, unit based, value based, or profit or income based. Although theory suggests that the special qualities of the mineral resource should be the deciding factor when selecting the royalty instrument and corresponding rate, the identity of the owner and his or her risk profile are often the most important factors. An outright selling of the mineral rights for a fixed (sales) amount works well when mineral rights are privately owned and there is an established market for active trading of mineral rights (such as in Australia, Canada, and the United States). Owners who prefer this approach are normally risk averse and have less bargaining power to contract favorable terms and conditions than the minerals companies do. Periodic royalties, on the other hand, are favored by nations because these allow, first, systematic compensation as depletion occurs over time, second, a degree of risk sharing in exchange for a bigger reward when the mineral deposit yields extraordinary returns, and third, demonstration by government that its natural resources are developed for the public good. In nations with state mineral ownership, private party royalties are often tied to a succession of mining rights holders (such as between a major mining company and a junior exploration company). In contrast, where mineral ownership resides with a party other than the state, the private party royalty arrangement is often between the mineral owner and the mining company (such as in South Africa until recently). Occasionally, royalties are also negotiated between a company and a community, tribe, or indigenous group (such as in some lands in Australia, Canada, the Philippines, and the United States). Private party arrangements usually do not negate liability to also pay government-imposed royalties.

Given the wide variety of royalty methods to choose from, how can a tax policy analyst compare one method to another? In Chapter 4, nine royalty calculation schemes were applied to three types of mines (gold, copper, and bauxite) to determine their impact on the mines' economics. The royalty methods modeled were selected because they illustrate the methods that are currently in use and that are often the subject of debate between companies and government tax policy makers. The nine schemes used the three principal royalty types: unit based (one model), value based (six models), and profit based (two models). The exercise clearly demonstrated that the use of such models can be a valuable tool in tax policy analysis. An analyst can quickly determine the impact of a proposed scheme, both on the government take and on the investor's internal rate of return and net present value, under a variety of cost and price scenarios.

It is often argued that the imposition of a royalty can affect production decisions. Mine design is based on fundamental parameters, including cutoff grade, reserves, and mine life, all of which are influenced by costs. The imposition of a royalty in any form, in particular unit- and value-based royalties, is a cost and thus will influence production parameters that are set to optimize mine profitability. These impacts should be of concern to government tax policy makers. If royalties are set at too high a rate, imposing a large cost, net tax revenues may be less than if no royalty was assessed. The royalty is but one tax among several, and all taxes may be affected. If, for example, a royalty causes the mine life to be shortened, then income tax, royalty, dividend withholding, and so forth will be lost for those years that mining would have proceeded given a lower royalty. A copper model was used to demonstrate, for a given set of assumptions, the possible impact of a royalty on investor and government returns.

In the selection of a royalty method and rate, if any, tax policy makers need to consider not only how the tax will affect individual mines but also how it will influence investors. In today's global economy, investors have many nations to choose from when deciding where to invest in exploration and development. When comparing possible places to invest, companies will examine the overall investment environment as well as discrete criteria. In addition to geologic potential, factors of key importance will be those that threaten stability, such as political, ideological, and social risk, and those that threaten profitability, such as costs, environmental obligations, social obligation, and taxes. To illustrate investors' sensitivity to royalty, Chapter 5 presented five brief case studies that described the royalty and investment situation in five jurisdictions: Chile, Jamaica, Papua New Guinea, South Africa, and Western Australia. The studies demonstrated that too high a royalty can have an impact on levels of investment and that quantifying that impact is probably not possible. In Chile and South Africa, the possibility of new royalties has dampened investor perceptions about the relative attractiveness of their investment environment. In Jamaica and Papua New Guinea, large increases in royalty led to, or contributed to, lowered levels of exploration and investment, and in Western Australia, a reasonable and well-reasoned new ad valorem royalty on gold did not appear to have much impact relative to historical investment levels.

Companies also are concerned about how royalty revenues will be distributed. Historically, royalties have been largely retained by the central or provincial government, with little going to the regions or communities where mining occurs. The result is that host communities seldom benefit and instead bear the brunt of mining-related impacts. Although most nations still place royalty receipts into the general fund for distribution through the budgeting process, a growing number, particularly in Latin America, target distribution more narrowly. Distribution schemes were briefly described in Chapter 5 for Argentina, Brazil, China, Ghana, Indonesia, Namibia, Papua New Guinea, Peru, the Philippines, and South Africa. In today's operating environment, companies are increasingly concerned about issues relating to sustainable development, community involvement, and how to pay for these. Most mining companies would prefer that a royalty, if imposed, go at least in part to either affected communities or identifiable public infrastructure. Royalty payments are more amenable to simple and targeted distribution to lower levels of government or affected stakeholders than are general revenues that are collected under income tax provisions. In nations that do not distribute royalty at the local level, the question was raised as to whether royalty, being a cost, reduces the ability and willingness of companies to invest in affected communities.

Royalty can affect exploration investment at two levels: greenfields and brownfields exploration. The impact may depend on the entity within the company that makes decisions on exploration expenditures. If the exploration investment decision is made by the exploration subsidiary, it can be argued that less attention is paid to factors affecting mine profitability than if the decision is made by a mining unit that must achieve profit goals. Greenfields exploration is often within the control of the exploration subsidiary, and brownfields exploration is under the control of the mining unit. Thus, the imposition of a royalty may have a greater impact, at least in the short run, on brownfields exploration than on greenfields exploration.

Another factor that companies will look at when assessing the investment environment is tax stability. Unstable tax systems raise the risk that company economic projections and decisions may be based on faulty assumptions. Royalty methods and rates can be stabilized in a number of ways, including by special agreements and through the use of statutory rates rather than rates set by administrative law.

How important is taxation, and royalty in particular, in a nation's bid to be competitive? An indication of the importance of royalty taxes may be gathered through the use of polls. Results from a United Nations survey of mining companies revealed that, out of a list of 60 possible investment criteria, 4 tax-related criteria were among the top 15 factors. An annual poll by the Fraser Institute compares the relative attractiveness of mining sector fiscal systems for a wide number of countries to determine the percentage of respondents that find that the overall mining tax system either encourages investment, is not a deterrent to investment, is a mild deterrent to investment, is a strong deterrent to investment, or is so onerous as to preclude investment. Unfortunately, no polls look at investor views of royalty apart from the overall mining sector taxation system. In a ranking of the 10 nations with the most attractive tax systems (based on the Fraser Institute survey), 1 imposed no royalty, 3 used a profit-based royalty, 2 others used a combination of profit-based and value-based royalties, 3 used value-based methods, and 1 used a value-based system with a sliding scale based on a profit measure. Clearly, in this poll, companies favored profit-based royalties over other types.

Nations that do not impose royalty will, from time to time, come under pressure from civil society to do so. In the cross-section of nations covered in this study, some Argentine provinces, Chile, Mexico, South Africa, Sweden, and Zimbabwe do not impose royalty. However, at the time that this study is going to press, Chile, South Africa, and Zimbabwe are all considering introducing royalties. Pressure to do so can be particularly acute when mineral prices are depressed and thus the mine is extracting and selling minerals without paying income tax, or when prices are very high and society feels that it is not sharing sufficiently in high profits. Because many mines are owned, at least in part, by foreign interests, they are especially vulnerable to claims of foreign exploitation by those in the political system who use such claims to gain popular support. Countering this vulnerability is the reality that unit- and value-based royalties are a cost that, if imposed, may cause marginal mines to close. Though mines employ only a small percentage of the national labor force, even in the mineral-led economies, they may be very important at the local and community economy level. The multiplier effect on indirect job losses can have significant impacts on individual communities, and constituencies that would be affected by closure can be strong advocates against royalty. Where large numbers of workers are affected by potential closure, such as in Poland (coal miners) and South Africa (gold miners), the threat of major retrenchment can in extreme cases pose challenges to national stability. Sometimes mine survival and corresponding social commitments are more important to governments than the receipt of mineral royalties. For these reasons, many nations allow royalty obligations to be reduced, deferred, or waived during hard times.

Many types of minerals are commodities that compete in global markets. To what extent can royalties affect those markets? The most obvious way royalty affects the market is by simply being a cost. If a producer from one nation must pay royalty and a producer from another nation does not pay, the first producer is less able to compete. If many producers must pay, the consumer will pay more as the royalty cost is passed through to the global market. If the market price of a mineral commodity goes up, that commodity is more vulnerable to being substituted for by a less expensive alternative or by secondary (recycled) production.

In summary, this study has attempted to address the many topics and issues related to royalty taxes. The purpose of this study has been to provide a comprehensive, objective, and neutral analysis of royalty taxation that can be used by governments and industry in deliberations concerning the merits and demerits of royalties and their various forms.

Recommendations and Best Practices

Countries' geological, economic, social, and political circumstances make each nation unique, and an approach to royalty taxes that is optimal for one nation may be impractical for another. It is also not advisable to universally say that royalties are good or bad, because those judgments depend on the circumstances of the parties involved, a project's economics, and the observer's point of view. Even with those constraints, however, it is possible to offer recommendations that can be applied in most situations.

1. When designing a tax system, policy makers should be aware of the cumulative impact that taxes can have on mine economics and potential levels of future investment. When determining which taxes and levels of taxes to apply to the mining sector, policy makers should not only consider ways to achieve individual tax objectives but also take into account the cumulative impact of all taxes. Such awareness must include recognizing the importance of each tax type for achieving specific objectives. The overall tax system should be equitable to both the nation and the investor and should be globally competitive.
2. Care should be taken to weigh the immediate fiscal rewards to be gained from high levels of tax, including royalty, against the long-term benefits to be gained from a sustainable mining industry that will contribute to long-term development, infrastructure, and economic diversification.

3. Mining companies have a role to play in influencing the decisions of governments with regard to royalty. They can provide governments with quantitative assessments of royalty impacts on issues such as potential overall investment, closure of marginal mines and the implications of those closures, changes to the national mineral reserve base, and similar issues. Governments that are informed will be able to arrive at better-reasoned decisions.

4. Where a nation has a strong desire to attract investors, consideration should be given to either forgoing a royalty and relying on the general tax system, or recognizing the investors' strong preference for being taxed on their ability to pay. A nation seeking to differentiate itself from other nations that it competes with for mineral sector investment may find a royalty based on income or profits to be an investment incentive. Although profit-based royalty schemes are inherently more difficult to implement than other royalty schemes, governments that are capable of effectively administering an income tax are positioned to manage a profit or income based royalty.

5. Governments that impose royalty should take the following steps:
   - Consult with industry in order to assess the impacts that changes to the royalty system will have on the mineral sector.
   - Implement a system or systems that are transparent and provide a sufficient level of detail in the relevant law and regulations that make it clear as to how the tax basis is to be determined for all minerals.
   - Select a royalty method or methods that are suitable for efficient and effective administration within the capacity of the tax-collecting authority.
   - Give a high priority to strengthening both financial reporting and the institutional capacity of administrative agencies that are responsible for levying and collecting mineral sector taxes. The government can then consider the complete range of royalty options rather than being limited to the simplest methods.
   - Carefully consider all royalty options based on ability to pay (profit-based systems).
   - Avoid excessively high unit-based or value-based royalty rates that will significantly affect production parameters such as cutoff grade and mine life.
   - Provide a means whereby mines experiencing financial duress may apply for a deferral or waiver of royalty, provided that clearly predefined criteria are met.

- Allow royalty payments to be deducted from income that is subject to income tax or allow royalty to be credited against income tax.
- Impose alternative measures on artisanal and small-scale operators where the general royalty scheme would not be enforceable.

6. Policy makers and companies should consider means whereby affected communities can share directly in the benefits of the mines, including the following:

- Recognition that such benefits may be made available through a variety of means that may or may not include taxation.
- Balancing of the overall mineral taxation system, including royalty, to provide an incentive for companies to invest in sustainable development initiatives at the community and regional level.
- Statutory requirements that allow a share of royalty (or other mining taxes) to be paid directly to communities by the company without the funds moving through the central tax authority, or alternatively a system in which the designated community share is paid centrally but is distributed in a transparent and timely manner.

7. Policy makers and companies should bear joint responsibility to treat royalty payments in a transparent manner that promotes public accountability. Overall, the aim should be for revenues generated by the mining sector to contribute to economic growth and social development. Particularly in developing countries, a lack of accountability and transparency in such revenues often exacerbates poor governance and contributes to corruption, conflict, and poverty. A number of principles for reporting revenues are internationally accepted, but for several issues, consensus on best practices is still in the making. One important development is the Extractive Industries Transparency Initiative (EITI), which is a process by which countries and companies voluntarily agree to systematically record and disclose the revenues received by government and paid by extractive industry companies.

8. From a macroeconomic perspective, the optimization goal of government should be to maximize the net present value of the social benefits flowing from the mineral sector over the long term, including but not limited to government tax receipts. This implies a balance, because if taxation is too high, investment and the tax base will decrease as investors shift their focus to other alternatives, and if taxation is too low, the nation will lose revenue useful to serve the public welfare.

This study is dedicated to the many individuals
and organizations who strive to balance the
fiscal interests of nations with those of
the private sector so that both may benefit.

About the Authors

James Otto, JD, the study's team leader, is Director of Graduate Studies and Research Professor, University of Denver College of Law (United States). Otto is a natural resources lawyer, mineral economist, and engineer with 30 years of experience working with the mining sector. He has worked in more than 40 nations for governments, the private sector, multilateral agencies, and educational institutions on assignments mainly related to mining policy, law, and taxation. He has worked with others to organize and fund regional United Nations mining tax workshops for governments, which have been attended by more than 160 government officers from 45 nations. For governments and the private sector Otto has prepared in-depth fiscal reform analysis for national mining sectors, including work in Australia, Burkina Faso, Canada, Democratic Republic of Congo, Dominican Republic, Indonesia, Papua New Guinea, Peru, Philippines, Madagascar, Malaysia, Mali, Mauritania, Mongolia, Mozambique, Namibia, Nigeria, Peru, Poland, Saudi Arabia, South Africa, and others. He has edited and coauthored four books on mining taxation, including as team leader for the well-known first and second editions of the *Global Mining Taxation Comparative Study*. He brings to the team a wealth of legal and economic knowledge about mining royalty systems worldwide, as well as managerial experience in the implementation of team-implemented taxation studies.

Craig Andrews is a Principal Mining Specialist with the World Bank, Washington, DC. Andrews is responsible for Bank mining projects in countries in Africa, Latin America, Asia, and Central Asia. These projects involve support to governments for mining regulation and taxation reform, revenue management, institutional strengthening and capacity building, earth science and environmental management systems, measurement of benefits and impacts of natural resources projects, and small-scale mining. In addition to his work on World Bank projects, Andrews is a frequent speaker at international conferences, a contributor to industry publications, and an active participant in professional societies and study groups. Before joining the World Bank in 1992, Andrews was manager of international business development for the Broken Hill Proprietary Company Ltd., based in San Francisco, California. Andrews is a graduate of Claremont McKenna College and Georgetown University.

Fred Cawood, PhD, is Senior Lecturer and Associate Professor at the School of Mining Engineering, University of the Witwatersrand (South Africa). Cawood completed his doctorate on the determination of optimal rent for South African mineral resources and now teaches postgraduate courses on mineral policy, mining sector investment, and mineral property valuation. His research is focused on mine valuation, mineral rents and their distribution, mineral taxation, and compliance in the minerals industry. Cawood has lectured before professional and public audiences about the future implementation of royalties in South Africa and has published articles and academic analyses about royalty taxes. He was invited by the South African treasury to discuss royalty taxes and has done analysis for several governments in the South African Development Community region. He brings to the team knowledge about mine taxation policies in African nations, the issues pertaining to distribution of royalty revenues, insight into private party royalty arrangements, and skills in mine valuation.

Michael Doggett, PhD, is Director and Associate Professor, Mineral Exploration Master's Program, Queen's University (Canada). Winner of the 2002 Canadian Institute of Mining, Metallurgy and Petroleum's Robert Elver Mineral Economics Award for his significant contribution in the mineral economics field in Canada, Doggett brings to the team in-depth knowledge of Canadian mineral taxation, exploration economics, deposit characteristics, and mine parameterization. His current research interests include discovery costs for economic mineral deposits, cost-benefit analysis of exploration and acquisition, financing of exploration and mine development, profitability in the mining industry, international competitive positioning for investment in mineral projects, and mineral policy and mining taxation legislation. Doggett has worked extensively for private sector and government clients, mainly on subjects relating to exploration and mine taxation.

Pietro Guj, PhD, is Associate Professor, Mineral Economics, Western Australia School of Mines, Curtin University of Technology, and has a special interest in mineral policy, the financial evaluation of exploration and mining projects, and risk and decision analyses. Guj was the Deputy Director-General of the Western Australian Department of Minerals and Energy (DME) from 1995 to 2002. That service followed five years as Director of the Geological Survey of Western Australia, seven years as a finance executive for the Water Authority of Western Australia, and about 20 years in geology and mineral exploration in Afghanistan, Australia, Namibia, South Africa, and then–West Pakistan. While at DME he played a key role in supporting and regulating the exploration, mining, and petroleum industry in Western Australia, including administering mineral royalty policy and collection at the time that new gold and vanadium royalties were introduced. The vanadium royalties were the first application of a hybrid royalty system in Australia. Guj also led the industry consultation process and reform of the copper and cobalt royalties. He brings to the team practical experience in matching the rigor of economic theory with the imperfect reality of having to efficiently administer equitable royalty systems in a way that does not impose excessive compliance costs on both industry and government and that does not lead to frequent and disruptive litigation.

Frank Stermole, PhD, Professor Emeritus at the Division of Economics and Business, Colorado School of Mines (United States), and
John Stermole, Lecturer at the Division of Economics and Business, Colorado School of Mines, and Adjunct Professor, University of Denver College of Law (United States) are a father-and-son team. They bring to the study their skills in mine financial analysis and computer model development for mining. They are the coauthors of *Economic Evaluation and Investment Decision Methods* and teach courses on this subject both within the university setting and to governments and the private sector.

Their book is now in its 11th edition and is a mining industry standard, with more than 30,000 copies sold. John Stermole is coauthor of the *Global Mining Taxation Comparative Study*, first edition. In addition to their university courses, they have taught over 700 short courses on this subject to more than 17,000 members of government and industry. Both Stermoles have extensive international experience and provide a wide range of analytical work to a broad client base, including many of the world's largest mining and petroleum companies and governments.

John Tilton, PhD, holds the Mineral Economics Chair at the Mining Centre, Pontificia Universidad Católica de Chile, Santiago, Chile, and is Research Professor at the Division of Economics and Business, Colorado School of Mines (United States), where for many years he held the William J. Coulter Chair in Mineral Economics. Tilton brings to the team a keen knowledge about microeconomic impacts of royalties on the production decision, as well as an understanding of public policy. His interests over the past 30 years have focused on economic and policy issues associated with the metal industries and markets, and he has authored numerous books and articles relating to the mineral industry. His recent research includes mineral taxation from the perspective of host governments (he is a frequent speaker and commentator on the subject of royalty taxes in Chile), mining and economic development, long-term trends in metal demand, sources of productivity growth in mining, and changes in comparative advantage in the metal trade. He has held various appointments around the world with universities, multilateral agencies, and advisory bodies. In recognition of his contributions in the field of mineral economics, he has received the Mineral Economics Award from the Society for Mining Metallurgy and Exploration, the Distinguished Service Award from the Mineral Economics and Management Society, and an Honorary Doctorate from the Lulea University of Technology in Sweden.

Index